# THE
# TIBETAN BOOK
# OF THE DEAD

*Bantam Wisdom Editions*

TAO TE CHING:
The Classical Book of Integrity and the Way
*Lao Tzu*
TRANSLATED BY VICTOR H. MAIR

THE BHAGAVAD-GITA:
Krishna's Counsel in Time of War
TRANSLATED BY BARBARA STOLER MILLER

I CHING:
A New Interpretation for Modern Times
SAM REIFLER

THE BOOK OF FIVE RINGS
MIYAMOTO MUSASHI

A GARDEN BEYOND PARADISE:
The Mystical Poetry of Rumi
TRANSLATED BY JONATHAN STAR AND SHAHRAM SHIVA

NO BARRIER:
Unlocking the Zen Koan
TRANSLATION AND COMMENTARY BY THOMAS CLEARY

THE TIBETAN BOOK OF THE DEAD
TRANSLATED BY ROBERT A. F. THURMAN

# THE
# TIBETAN BOOK
# OF THE DEAD

*as popularly known in the West*

*Known in Tibet as*
*THE GREAT BOOK*
*OF NATURAL LIBERATION THROUGH*
*UNDERSTANDING IN THE BETWEEN*

*Composed by*
PADMA SAMBHAVA

*Discovered by*
KARMA LINGPA

*Translated by*
ROBERT A. F. THURMAN

BANTAM BOOKS
New York   Toronto   London   Sydney   Auckland

THE TIBETAN BOOK OF THE DEAD
A Bantam Book / January 1994

Book design by Maria Carella
Color section design by Michael Mendelsohn/MM Design 2000

*Library of Congress Cataloging-in-Publication Data*
Karma Lingpa, 14th cent.
[Bar do thos grol. English]
The Tibetan book of the dead : the great book of natural
liberation through understanding in the between / composed by Padma
Sambhava ; discovered by Karma Lingpa ; translated by Robert A. F.
Thurman.
p. cm.
Includes bibliographical references·
ISBN 0-553-37090-1
1. Intermediate state—Buddhism—Early works to 1800. 2. Death—
Religious aspects—Buddhism—Early works to 1800. 3. Funeral rites
and ceremonies, Buddhist—Early works to 1800. 4. Karma Lingpa,
14th cent. Bar do thos grol. I. Padma Sambhava, ca. 717–ca. 762.
II. Thurman, Robert A. F. III. Title.
BQ4490.K3713 1993
294.3'423–dc20        93–2891
CIP
*Published simultaneously in the United States and Canada*

Bantam Books are published by Bantam Books, a division of Bantam Doubleday Dell
Publishing Group, Inc. Its trademark, consisting of the words "Bantam Books" and the
portrayal of a rooster, is Registered in U.S. Patent and Trademark Office and in other
countries. Marca Registrada. Bantam Books, 1540 Broadway, New York, New York 10036.

PRINTED IN THE UNITED STATES OF AMERICA

FFG      0   9   8   7   6   5   4   3   2   1

*This book is dedicated to the brave and gentle people of Tibet, who have suffered and are suffering one of the great tragedies of our time. The entire world is turning its back, due to fear and greed, while the Chinese government pursues its systematic campaign of genocide. May the conscience of all people cry out in one voice! May the Chinese people inform themselves at long last, find out they have been lied to by several of their own governments, and realize they are in extreme contravention of the laws of humanity and of nature! May their hearts then soften and may they take concrete action to repair the great harm they have inflicted on this innocent people. May the Tibetan people soon regain the sovereign freedom they have enjoyed since the dawn of history! And may the sunlight of Tibetan Spiritual Science once again shine brightly upon a freshened world!*

# CONTENTS

## PART ONE
## PREPARATIONS FOR THE JOURNEY

### CHAPTER 1 · BACKGROUND · 5

### CHAPTER 2 · THE TIBETAN SCIENCE OF DEATH · 23

PART TWO
THE GUIDEBOOK FOR THE JOURNEY
*The Great Book of Natural Liberation
Through Understanding in the Between*


CHAPTER 5  ·  THE BETWEEN PRAYERS  ·  97

CHAPTER 6 • THE GUIDEBOOK TO
THE BETWEENS • 117

PART THREE
SUPPLEMENTARY TRANSLATIONS

CHAPTER 7 • THE DHARMA PRACTICE,
NATURAL LIBERATION OF THE INSTINCTS • 205

# LIST
# OF FIGURES

# LIST OF
# COLOR PLATES

**THE DALAI LAMA**

# FOREWORD

The Bardo Thodol, which has become known in the West as The
Tibetan Book of the Dead, is one of the most important books our
civilization has produced. We Tibetans have a reputation of being very
spiritual, though we usually consider ourselves quite down-to-earth and
practical. So we think of our systematic study and analysis of the human
death process as a cautious and practical preparation for the inevitable.
After all, there is not a single one of us who is not going to die, sooner
or later. So how to prepare for death, how to undergo the death process
with the least trauma, and what comes after death—these are matters
of vital importance to every one of us. It would be impractical of us not
to study these issues with the greatest of care and not to develop methods of dealing with death and the dying in a skillful, compassionate,
and humane way.

*The Book of Liberation Through Understanding in the Between* has
been quite popular for many centuries in Tibet. It is a manual of useful
instructions for people who are facing their death, as well as for their
relatives and friends. It is connected with a large literature in Tibetan
that thoroughly investigates the phenomena of dying. Indeed, the reality
of death has always been a major spur to virtuous and intelligent action
in all Buddhist societies. It is not considered morbid to contemplate it,
but rather liberating from fear, and even beneficial to the health of the
living.

I am delighted that my old friend, Professor Robert Thurman, has
made a new translation of this important work. I am sure he brings to

bear on this text a unique combination of reliable scholarship and personal dedication to produce an accurate, expressive, and lucid translation for Western readers. I hope they will find the book as essentially useful and illuminating as have Tibetans down through the centuries.

January 29, 1993

# PREFACE

Years ago my original teacher, the Venerable Geshe Ngawang Wangyal of the Labsum Shedrub Monastery, gave me a copy of a Tibetan volume printed in India, entitled *The Tibetan Book of the Dead.* He had a way of saying certain things so that you remembered them long afterward, giving them a special impact, as if the words stood outside of time. "Here, you are going to need this!" At the time, working on this book was not a priority for me. But I kept it carefully, knowing my teacher's insight, and thinking that some day I probably would need it.

I had long known the old translation of this same text by Kazi Dawa Samdup and W. H. Y. Evans-Wentz, which had started the misnomer, *The Tibetan Book of the Dead.* I had read it and used it when relatives and friends died. It described a very real process through which we all have to go after death and before the next life that we will most probably have to face. I had also read the Francesca Fremantle and Chogyam Trungpa Rinpoche version, writing a review of it for a scholarly journal some time ago. In spite of its psychologized metaphysic and terminology, it was an improvement on the earlier translation.

The *Tibetan Book of the Dead* was written by the great master Padma Sambhava in the eighth or ninth century for Indian and Tibetan Buddhists. It was hidden by him for a later era, and was discovered by the renowned treasure-finder Karma Lingpa in the fourteenth century. It organizes the experiences of the between—(Tibetan, *bar-do*) usually referring to the state between death and rebirth—according to the expectations of initiates in a particular esoteric mandala (a sacred universe), the mandala of the hundred mild and fierce Buddha deities.

In recent years, I have studied the Unexcelled Yoga Tantras, especially the *Guhyasamaja*, or *Esoteric Communion*, tradition, so lucidly explicated by Lama Jey Tsong Khapa (1357–1419). Unexcelled Yoga Tantra is a highly technical approach to inner experiences, an ancient tradition of spiritual techniques every bit as sophisticated as modern material technologies. It uses special yogically induced states to explore the nature of the self and the mind, of death, life, and the between states. It describes death in great detail: its physiology, its psychology, its normal experience, and its simulated experience in experimental yogas of trance states. I have found it lucid and useful, not only for thinking about death, but also for thinking about life, health, and even breath. When I encountered death, thinking about my own or losing friends, this spiritual science gave me a framework within which I could understand the process.

After these Unexcelled Yoga studies, when I looked back at the *Tibetan Book of the Dead,* it seemed less relevant to me, and to modern experiences of death and dying. After all, it was intended to be a popular manual designed for the ordinary Tibetan layperson and not for the yogic adept. I noted that Stephen Levine and other developers of yogas for dying for contemporary Americans had found its imagery too cumbersome and unfamiliar for the ordinary person confronting his or her death. How many people in Toledo or Topeka can cope with a Heruka (a heroic male archetype deity) or a Dakini (a dynamic female angel)? A peaceful deity? A wrathful deity? Wouldn't it be better for them to use manuals for dying developed within their native Jewish or Christian faith? The technical descriptions of death in the *Esoteric Communion* literature seemed more clear and systematic, though not written for use by ordinary people when confronting the death process.

Thus when Bantam Books first approached me to do a new translation of the basic text with a popular commentary, I was uncertain about taking on the project. I might have declined altogether, had not my teacher's words arisen in my memory. I went home and looked through the Evans-Wentz and the Fremantle and Trungpa versions. I skimmed passages of the Tibetan edition my teacher had given me. I realized that people who are dying need something more clear, usable, and accessible than those translations.

To begin with, we all need to escape from the misleading title, or at least reduce it to a subtitle. No Tibetan expression is translatable as "Book of the Dead." In the actual Tibetan title, *Bardo thos grol, bardo* simply means the "between-state." In common parlance, "the between" refers to the whole process between death and rebirth. More technically,

Tibetans discern six betweens, the intervals between birth and death ("life between"), sleep and waking ("dream between"), waking and trance ("trance between"), and three betweens during the death-rebirth process ("death-point," "reality," and "existence" betweens). *Thos pa* refers to one of three types of wisdom or understanding, those developed by learning, reflecting, and meditating. The words *thos grol* mean that this book's teaching "liberates" just by being "learned" or "understood," giving the person facing the between an understanding so naturally clear and deep that it does not require prolonged reflection or contemplation. So the most common Tibetan title of the work is *The Great Book of Natural Liberation Through Understanding in the Between (Bardo thos grol chen mo).* It is itself a subsection of a larger work called *The Profound Teaching of The Natural Liberation Through Contemplating the Mild and Fierce Buddha Deities.*

I became inspired by such reflections. I decided to try to produce a version that would be simple and useful, easy for bereaved relatives to read, and easy for lost souls to hear in the room where they anxiously hover about their corpses and wonder what has happened to them. At the same time, I would put in the commentary a technical description of the death process gleaned from the larger Tibetan literature on Unexcelled Yoga.

The result is this book. As I was working on the text, I found other Tibetan editions that seemed more reliable and often clarified obscurities in the edition printed in India my teacher had given me. I also found some previously untranslated sections of the larger work, which clarified the teaching; I have included them here as appendices. Working on this text has been a fascinating and rewarding experience—I am once again grateful to my late teacher. I hope you also will find it useful.

ROBERT A. F. THURMAN
*Ganden Dekyi Ling*
*Woodstock, New York*
*August 1992*

*Note:* In the work below, I have avoided the footnote form altogether, in order to keep the text simple for the general reader, and to keep everything readers need on the page they're on. There are of course a number of unfamiliar terms and concepts. I have included these in a glossary at the back of the book, with brief explanations of all special terms and important names, places, and objects.

In the writing of Sanskrit and Tibetan names I have written them phonetically as pronounced by English readers, not observing the conventions of scholarly transliteration: Shakyamuni, not Śakyamuni; Vairochana, not Vairocana, and so forth. I have omitted long marks on vowels, and write the vowel *r* as "er."

PART
ONE

# PREPARATIONS
# FOR THE
# JOURNEY

# CHAPTER 1

# BACKGROUND

## AN OUTLINE OF TIBETAN HISTORY

The Tibetans have always called their own country Bö, on some occasions adding Khawajen, "Land of Snows." Their own recorded history dates back some 2300 years, to the time of the Macedonian Greek empire in the west, the Mauryan empire in India, and the late Chou empire in China. During Tibet's first eight centuries, it was ruled by a military dynasty. It had an animistic religious system, run by a priesthood of shamans adept in divination, sorcery, and sacrifice. Its polity centered on a royal family believed to have descended from the heavens. The first seven kings came down to rule on a magical ladder hanging in space, up which they would return when their time had come to die. Due to some conflict in the palace, the eighth king cut the sky rope, and the kings thereafter, like the pharaohs of Egypt, were interred in large burial mounds, along with possessions and companions.

The early dynasty was centered in the Yarlung Valley, a river valley running south from the eastward flowing Tsang-chu (the Brahmaputra), near present-day Tsetang. Gradually, over the centuries, the dynasty added tribes and territories to its domain, uniting the lords of neighboring kingdoms in a feudal, military network. The tribes they unified were already tied by three main common bonds: their territory, language, and religious tendency. They all inhabited the approximately one-million-square-mile Tibetan plateau, with an average altitude of 13,000 to 14,000 feet. Living successfully at such an altitude involves a complex physiological adaptation. To be comfortable there, you really have to be born there from a lineage long acclimatized. The Tibetan language belongs to the Tibeto-Burman language family, a family distinct from the Indic, Dardic, Turkic, Mongolian, and Sinitic language families of the surrounding lowland areas. Religiously, Tibetans tended to deify elements of nature, especially mountains and sky, and shared a complex set of rituals of sacrifice, divination, and propitiation of a diverse pantheon of underworld, landscape, and celestial deities.

The high-altitude culture was distinguished from those around it by its more "spiritual" orientation. Lifespans at high altitude are somewhat shortened, and the stark and spectacular mountain landscape is conducive to reflection and contemplation. In the early centuries, this spirituality was practical in outlook. Like most shamanisms, it sought mundane success, victory, health, wealth, and progeny. During the period of military expansion, it seems to have focused on a cult of kingship, run by shamanic adept priests. Since the king had descended from heaven as a divinity on earth, he guaranteed power and order. The shaman assisted this order by inviting the king's descent, celebrating his presence, securing the cooperation of the deities in the heavens, lands, and underworld, and managing the transition from the old king to the new. The shaman was required to travel to the land of the dead and back, in order to gain personal experience of the period of chaos between reigns. His role was to draw on the power of chaos while keeping it in its place, assuring its continuing separation from the land of the living, the realm of order.

The Tibetan dynastic culture was quite successful for many centuries. Rival kingdoms from surrounding lowlands could not intrude for long on the high plateau, so it was allowed to develop without interference. The Tibetans' struggles with their natural environment and with each other strengthened them, and by the sixth century they had unified the highland and become an empire to be reckoned with. They began to mount campaigns in all directions into the lowlands. At this time they developed a fearsome reputation among the Chinese, Turkish, Mongolian, Persian, and Indic peoples.

In the early seventh century, an emperor named Songzen Gambo reached the militaristic empire's natural limits. Unity among warlords is always tenuous, and the high-altitude Tibetans had no interest in further expansion outward into the lowlands. He began transforming the civilization from feudal militarism to something more peaceful and spiritual, based on the people's cultivated moral outlook. In working on this transformation, Songzen Gambo investigated the major civilizations of outer (from his perspective) Asia, and noted that Universalist (Mahayana) Buddhism provided the cultural backbone of the Pala and post-Gupta dynasties of India, the silk route city states of central Asia, and the T'ang dynasty of China. So he began a systematic process of cultural adaptation. He sent a team of scholars to India to learn Sanskrit, create a written language for Tibetan, and begin to translate the vast Buddhist literature. He married nine princesses from different surrounding countries, including Nepal and T'ang China, requesting each to bring Buddhist artifacts and texts with her to Tibet. He built a geomantic system of imperial temples, centered on the Jokhang and Ramoche cathedrals in his new capital at Lhasa, with a network of branch temples creating a pattern of sacredness to contain the nation.

For the next two and a half centuries, his successors continued his work of cultural transformation, sponsoring translations, holding research conferences, building institutions, and educating their subjects. This process reached a high point during the 790s, in the reign of Emperor Trisong Detsen, who, with the help of the Indian adept Padma Sambhava and the Indian Buddhist abbot Shantarakshita, built the first monastery at Samye. Here the Indian Buddhist university structure and curriculum were transplanted, and a sixty-year process of collecting all the useful knowledge then available in Asia was begun. Mathematics, poetry, medicine, the art of government, art and architecture—all these branches of learning were cultivated, not only Buddhist philosophy and psychology. Scholars were invited from Persia, India, Uighuria, Mongolia, the silk route states, and T'ang China, and Tibetans became skilled at comparison and combination, in their quest for the best understanding of man and nature. For example, during the 830s, hundreds of scholars from all over the known world spent a decade comparing the medical systems of India, China, Persia, Mongolia, and Uighuria, creating a Tibetan medical system that integrated the best available psychology, anatomy, neurology, surgery, botany, chemistry, and nutrition with Buddhist spiritual technology.

After this high point of Samye's ascendancy, a period of confusion ensued, precipitated by excessive pressure from the emperors in their injection of Buddhist perspectives and practices into all facets of life. There was a revolt within the royal family itself. A series of assassinations and coups ended with the collapse of the dynasty, the regional fragmentation of the nation, and the temporary suppression of Buddhism. Within a century, however, Buddhist insights and institutions reemerged, now rooted among the people, with sponsorship from regional rulers. For the next three centuries, Tibetans more and more turned their interests toward Buddhist education, and monasteries were built all over the country. The vast work of translation was completed and a voluminous indigenous literature was developed. No new royal dynasty emerged to control the whole country. Tibetan militarism was unable to return due to the power of Buddhism and its morality of nonviolence. Local noble families still ruled regional areas, but more and more they shared even their social and political power with the rapidly developing monastic institutions.

During the thirteenth and fourteenth centuries, the Mongolian empire unified most of Eurasia, and Tibet was formally incorporated within the Pax Mongolica. In reality, it was very little changed, divided into thirteen main administrative regions, each run by a combination of a local ruling family and a local monastic hierarchy. The Sakya hierarchy and the Khon family were formally put in charge over all by Khubilai Khan, but the Sakya hierarch was more of a spiritual figurehead than an active administrator. Toward the end of the fourteenth century, the Mongol empire fell apart, and the native Tibetan dynasty of Pagmodru asserted control over Tibet. At the same time, a spiritual renaissance was ushered in by the life work of Lama Jey Tsong Khapa. The new era of national dedication to the practice of Buddhism as the main aim of life was sealed by his founding the Great Prayer Festival in Lhasa in 1409. He offered celestial ornaments to the Jowo Rinpoche image of Shakyamuni Buddha enshrined in the Jokhang cathedral, to symbolize the nation's realization of the eternal presence of the Buddha. A tradition thus began for the whole nation to come together for two weeks of prayer and celebration every lunar new year. The keys of the city were turned over to the monastic abbots, and all ordinary business was suspended. This festival was a core event for all Tibet from 1409 until 1960, when the Chinese occupation stopped it by force.

During the fifteenth and sixteenth centuries, the renaissance initiated by Tsong Khapa transformed the spiritual, social, and physical landscape of Tibet. In region after region monastery building intensified, as more and more men and women became determined to dedicate their "precious human lives endowed with freedom and opportunity" to fulfill their evolution and attain enlightenment. The social climate became more and more peaceful, as fewer and fewer individuals were available for the armies of the remaining local warlords. One of Tsong Khapa's younger disciples, Gendun Drubpa, led the new Geluk Order during a long and creative life of inspiring teaching, writing, and building. After his death, a beautiful young boy in another region claimed to be Gendun Drubpa from the moment he could talk. After many tests and miraculous recognitions, he was accepted by the community as the actual reincarnation of the great master, and he was raised and educated to fulfill the same leadership role, as the Lama Gendun Gyatso. His subsequent reincarnation, discovered through similar miracles, tests, and demonstrated abilities, Sonam Gyatso, led the order in the sixteenth century, until during an historic visit to Mongolia in 1573, he was named "Dalai Lama" ("Oceanic Master") by the Mongolian emperor

Altan Khan. Including his two predecessors retroactively, Sonam Gyatso became known as His Holiness the Third Dalai Lama.

During Sonam Gyatso's time and that of his successor, the warlord rulers of Tibet had begun to feel too constrained by the steady wave of spiritual renaissance, popular dedication to enlightenment education, and money- and time-consuming monastery-building. A period of turbulence ensued around the turn of the seventeenth century, with the fate of the country in the balance. Would the secular forces of the remaining militaristic aristocratic warlords prevail, curtailing the ascendancy of the monastery-centered lifestyle, in parallel with what was happening at the time in northern Europe, China, and Japan? Or would they give up their ways of violence, lay down their arms, and, once and for all, themselves embrace the path of spiritual evolution?

In 1642, almost exactly a thousand years after the building of the Jokhang cathedral, His Holiness the Fifth Dalai Lama (1617–1682) was crowned king of Tibet, founding the Ganden Palace Victory Government that Tibetans still consider their legitimate government today. The "Great Fifth," as he is known, created a unique form of government eminently suited to Tibet's special society. It was almost completely demilitarized, acknowledging the centrality of the monastic institutions in the national life and the priority given to nonviolence. The nobility was virtually expropriated, retaining the use and income from parts of their hereditary estates only as salary for service to the Ganden government. They were completely deprived of their private armies, losing their feudal power of life and death over their peasants, who up to then had closely resembled the medieval serfs of Russia and Europe.

Internationally, Tibetan independence and national integrity were guaranteed by the new pan-Asian emperors of the era, the Manchus. A Tungusic people from the forests north of Korea, they conquered northern China in 1644 and wished to conquer the rest of East Asia undisturbed by any rivals. Due to his authority over the fearsome Mongols, the Dalai Lama was seen as a potent ally by the new Manchu emperor. In 1651, an alliance was formed between the Manchu Shun Chih emperor and the Great Fifth. The Manchus recognized the Dalai Lama's secular authority over Tibet and his spiritual authority over the world as they knew it. The Dalai Lama recognized the Manchus as legitimate rulers of Manchuria and China and as international protectors of the Buddhist Dharma, its practitioners, and institutions. The bottom line was that the Dalai Lama agreed to encourage the Mongols to practice Buddhism, and the Manchus agreed to protect the peace for the demilitarized Buddhist societies. The Tibetan pacification of the Mongols, the demilitarization of that most militarily powerful society, is one of the remarkable social transformations in history, though it is no more astonishing than Tibet's self-transformation over the previous millennium.

# TIBET:
## A SPIRITUAL CIVILIZATION

During the three centuries of Tibet's modern period, the national priority was on monastic education, literary and philosophical creativity, the practice of meditation, the development of ritual and festival arts, and so forth. Spiritual adepts were accepted as the highest level of Tibetan society, considered to have become perfected Buddhas through their practice of the Tantras (spiritual technologies) of Unexcelled Yoga (self-cultivation). They were inner-world adventurers of the highest daring, the Tibetan equivalent of our astronauts—I think it is worth coining the term "psychonaut" to describe them. They personally voyaged to the furthest frontiers of that universe which their society deemed vital to explore: the inner frontiers of consciousness itself, in all its transformations in life and beyond death.

In Western culture, the last frontiers of our material conquest of the universe are in outer space. Our astronauts are our ultimate heroes and heroines. Tibetans, however, are more concerned about the spiritual conquest of the inner universe, whose frontiers are in the realms of death, the between, and contemplative ecstasies. So, the Tibetan lamas who can consciously pass through the dissolution process, whose minds can detach from the gross physical body and use a magic body to travel to other universes, these "psychonauts" are the Tibetans' ultimate heroes and heroines. The Dalai Lamas and the several thousand "reincarnate" Lamas (also called "Tulku," which means "Buddha Emanation") are these heroes and heroines. They are believed to have mastered the death, between, and rebirth processes, and to choose continuously, life after life, to return to Tibet out of compassion to lead the Tibetans in their spiritual national life and to benefit all sentient beings.

Thus the modern Tibetan civilization was unique on the planet. Only such a special civilization could have produced the arts and sciences of dying and death transmitted in this book. I describe the unique psychological character complex that corresponds to the modern Tibetan society as "inner modernity." It should be understood to contrast with the modern Western psychological character complex, which can be described as "outer modernity." The Western character complex is usually contrasted with a premodern "traditional" character. It is often described as a complex of traits such as individualism, openness and flexibility of identity, restless reflectiveness, and adherence to rationality. This modern Western character complex is connected with a peculiar perception of all things—including psychic or mental things—as ultimately reducible to quantifiable material entities. This is what gives it its "outwardness." The modern Tibetan character complex shares the modern traits of individualism, openness and flexibility of identity, reflectiveness, and rationality. But the Tibetan character is bound up with its peculiar perception, derived from Buddhist civilization, of all things as infused with spiritual value, as interconnected with mental states. In contrast to Western ideas, the Tibetan view is that the mental or spiritual cannot always be reduced to material quanta and manipulated as such—the spiritual is itself an active energy in nature, subtle but more powerful than the material. The Tibetan view is that the "strong force" in nature is spiritual, not material. This is what gives the Tibetan character its "inwardness." Thus while Western and Tibetan personalities share the complex of modernity of consciousness, they are diametrically opposed in outlook, one focused outward on matter and the other inward on mind.

This difference of personality underlies the difference between the two civilizations. While the American national purpose is ever greater material productivity, the Tibetan national purpose is ever greater spiritual productivity. Spiritual productivity is measured by how deeply one's wisdom can be developed, how broadly one's compassion can exert itself. Tibetan Buddhists believe that outer reality is interconnected with inner mental development over a beginningless and endless series of lives, so they see no limit to how far the self and the environment can be transformed for the better. The self can become a Buddha, a being of perfect wisdom and compassion; and the environment can become a perfect Buddha-land, wherein no one suffers pointlessly and all are there for the happiness of all.

The ultimate example of the inwardly directed rationality of the modern Tibetan mind is precisely our present concern, the Tibetan exploration of death. The outwardly directed Western mind long ago dismissed the topic of death and future lives as archaic, of concern only to the superstitious traditional mind. Materialistic habits of thought reduce the mind to matter and eliminate the soul. Ruling out the possibility of future lives, death is merely a physiological condition, equated with a "flatline" on an electroencephalograph. There is no interest at all in the states of the person or condition of the mind after death. Scientific investigation restricts itself to the material quanta perceivable by the physical senses, augmented by machinery, during this one bodily life. At the same time, Westerners have set about exploring the outer world, the farthest continents, the macro realms of the outer galaxies, and the micro realms of the cell, the molecule, the atom, and the sub-atomic forces.

Tibetan inwardly directed reason put the material world second on its list of priorities. Its prime concern was the world of inner experience, the waking, gross realm of causality, relativity, sensation, percept and concept, and the subtle realm of image, light, ecstasy, trance, dream, and finally, death and its beyond. The Tibetans considered the inner, subtlemost, experiential realm the important point at which to assert control of all subjective and objective cosmic events. And so they set about exploring this inner world, using analytic insight and contemplative concentration to extend their awareness into every crevice of experience. They used the manipulation of dreams and inner visions to visit lucidly the territories of the unconscious. They used focused dis-identification with coarse subjectivity to gain access to the subtlest level of sentience. And they used an augmented sense of mindfulness and memory to gain access to past life experience, including the dreamlike experiences of the between states traversed from death to birth.

## TIBET'S PRESENT PLIGHT

In spite of some neglect of its material progress, Tibet developed during its modern period into a relatively happy land. Tibetan society was organized to maximize the individual's potential for inner development, economic pressure was mild, and conflict within and warfare without were rare. However, it was still far from a perfected Buddha-land. In modern geopolitical terms, it became highly vulnerable during our century as a result of one positive quality and one negative quality. Positively, it was long demilitarized and therefore no match for the modern armies first of the British and eventually of the Chinese. Negatively, it had become too isolated from other nations, locking them out as Buddhism disappeared from them. Consequently, the only two nations with a little knowledge of Tibet, the British and the Chinese, were able to misrepresent Tibet to the rest of the world in any way that suited their immediate need. When the British wanted to enact trade agreements with the sovereign Tibetan government, they dealt with Tibet as the independent nation that it was. Meanwhile, they let the world at large think of Tibet as under China, to keep the Russians out and to keep the Chinese happy, pleased for the British to retain possession of Hong Kong and its valuable trade opportunities. The Chinese likewise knew very well they did not control Tibet, that Tibetans had no sense of being Chinese, and that no Chinese person had ever had the slightest feeling that any Tibetan was a kind of Chinese. Meanwhile, they still pretended to the world that they owned Tibet (which they call *Shitsang,* "the Western Treasury"), that it had always been a part of China. Thus when the Maoist government invaded Tibet in 1949, they told the world they were "liberating" their own country's Tibetan province from foreigners (there were half a dozen Europeans in Tibet). But since Tibetans considered the Chinese to be foreigners, they resisted being "liberated" to the death. The full force of the Red Army overwhelmed the Buddhist Tibetans, and the Chinese occupation ever since has only endured by brute force. Over a million Tibetans have died unnaturally, and the entire Buddhist culture has been shattered. Not a single Tibetan does not dream and pray to be free and independent of the invaders.

In order to transform Tibet into a part of China, the Chinese have attempted to suppress the Tibetan language, Buddhism and the culture based on it, and all vestiges of Tibetan national identity. Such a project is doomed to failure, as the Tibetans simply cannot make themselves into Chinese. Therefore the attempt to make Tibetans into Chinese ends up killing off the Tibetans. Fortunately, during this time His Holiness the Fourteenth Dalai Lama has succeeded in maintaining a healthy community in exile, with the patronage of the government of India. And there is a hope that the nations of the world, if they learn about Tibet in time, will not let the genocide of the six million Tibetans be completed in the 1990s.

## BUDDHISM IN SUMMARY

What is Buddhism? This *Great Book of Natural Liberation Through Understanding in the Between* will be supposed by readers to be a "Buddhist" approach to death and dying. But if it were merely "Buddhist," it would be relevant only for "Buddhists." There would be no point in translating it for the general public. The long-standing Western interest in this "Book of the Dead" would be inexplicable. But only one aspect of the *Book of Natural Liberation* is "religious" in the usual sense, that is, concerned with a particular system of belief. For that matter, only one aspect of Buddhism itself is religious.

Buddhism is a teaching originated by Shakyamuni Buddha about 2500 years ago. It is not based on, or a reform of, any religion existing in ancient Indian culture. Nor was it based on a revelation received from any sort of deity. The Buddha flatly rejected the contemporary Indian form of the religious belief in an omnipotent world Creator. He did not "believe in God" as Westerners understand God. To many Westerners, he would appear an atheist (although he did accept the presence of nonomnipotent, superhuman beings he called "gods"). He did not even consider belief or faith an end in itself, as many religious people do, although he accepted reasonable beliefs as practically useful to people. He encouraged people to question authority and use their power of reason, and not to accept irrational traditions. In his personal quest of truth, he was often quite unreligious.

Shakyamuni was called a "Buddha," an "Awakened" or "Enlightened" person, because he claimed to have achieved a perfect understanding of the nature and structure of reality. After a normal education as a warrior prince of his era, he devoted six years of concentrated study, yogic discipline, and meditative contemplation to the quest for reality. He considered the human mind capable of reaching a full understanding of everything, given enough native ability, the correct education, and heroic effort. Having reached that full understanding himself during his thirty-fifth year, he felt that other humans would also be able to achieve it. He dedicated the next forty-five years to teaching all kinds of people. History records that large numbers of his contemporaries did succeed in reaching high levels of realization. They formed a broad-based movement that gradually spread through the countries of the Indian subcontinent, and eventually throughout most of Asia. This movement often did have a religious dimension; but it had equally important social and intellectual dimensions.

The Buddha used the Sanskrit word "Dharma" to designate his Truth or Teaching. In the process he added a new dimension of meaning to the word. "Dharma" was derived from the verb /dhr, "to hold," and had a range of important meanings associated with holding. It could mean a distinct phenomenon, one that held a particular character, or also the particular character itself. It could mean a custom, duty, or law that held human behavior in a particular pattern. It could also mean religion, in the sense of a held pattern of belief and ritual. But the core of the Buddha's discovery was the essential reality of freedom—that underlying the lived reality of existence is the immediacy of total freedom, especially freedom from suffering, from bondage, from ignorance. This essential freedom can be realized by the human mind as its own deepest and most true condition. This realization makes it possible for freedom to prevail over the habitual suffering of personal experience. So the realized individual is thenceforth *held apart* from suffering; not *held in* anything, but *held out* of binding patterns. Thus the new range

**Figure 1. Structure of the Buddha Dharma**

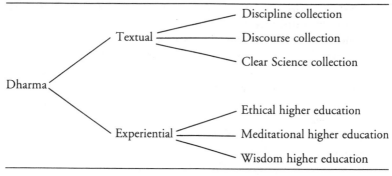

Dharma
- Textual
  - Discipline collection
  - Discourse collection
  - Clear Science collection
- Experiential
  - Ethical higher education
  - Meditational higher education
  - Wisdom higher education

of meanings of "Dharma" concerned being *held away from* suffering. Dharma came to mean the Teaching, the path of practice of the Teaching, the virtue of that practice, the reality or Truth taught in that Teaching, and the freedom of that reality or Truth, nirvana itself. This Dharma as "Teaching" is divided into two branches: the Textual Dharma and the Experiential Dharma (the Teaching and its practice). Each of those is in turn divided into three: the Textual into three types of verbal teachings, the Discipline, Discourse, and Clear Science collections, and the Experiential into three types of higher learning, the Ethical, Meditational, and Wisdom higher educations. See figure 1.

The Buddha taught the Dharma far and wide throughout India for over forty-five years. Numerous people found his teachings beneficial, and they began to form a new community within the old society. This new community was called the "Sangha"—simply "the Community"—and it formed around a new institution at its core, a monastic order of monks and nuns. Before Buddha, there had been wandering ascetics and hermits in India, but he was the first to organize suburban communities of settled monastics. The community became very important in the history of Buddhism, as it was the protective structure around the individual who followed the Buddha's example and educated him- or herself in the teachings. These three main aspects of Buddhism, the Buddha, the Dharma, and the Sangha—Teacher, Teaching, and Community—came to be known as the Three Jewels (Skt. *triratna*) of Buddhism, that is, the three most precious things for the individual seeking liberation from ignorance and suffering. Through the millennia since its founding, people have been considered Buddhists when they "take refuge" in these Three Jewels. They take refuge by trying to follow the Buddha's example and teachings, trying to understand the Dharma, and becoming a member of the Sangha.

Thus, the Buddha founded an educational movement that developed historically on three levels: the social (and so, inevitably, political), the religious, and the philosophical or scientific. The essence of all three movements lay in his realization of the relativity and interdependence of all things, mental as well as physical. Rather than a founder of a religion, he was primarily a critic of religion. He critiqued its absolutist tendencies, its devaluation of human reason, and its legitimation of unreasonable, arbitrary, and oppressive structures of authority. Reality, as Buddha saw it, is beyond dogmatic theories, while freely open to unprejudiced experience. The human life form is extremely well adapted to reality, and is extremely close to full understanding of it, which, when attained, results in an extraordinary liberation and happiness.

During the Buddha's time, there were many views of the nature of life, ranging from spiritualistic soul theories embedded in elaborate theistic belief-systems, to a strikingly modern, materialistic nihilism. The Buddha rejected all absolute soul theories, postulations of a rigidly fixed identity or static personal essence, with his cardinal doctrine of selflessness, or soullessness (*anatma*). He taught that the psychological habit of assuming a fixed subjectivity, an unchanging identity, was a key obstacle to a good life. But the Buddha never rejected the relative presence of a living self. He insisted on the continuity of the changeable, fluid soul from life to life. He explicitly rejected the contemporary nihilism that reduced even the *relative, conventional, lived* soul, self, or identity to a random epiphenomenon of matter. He insisted on the relative self's reality, vulnerability, responsibility, and evolutionary potential. In fact his teaching of the universal relativity of the self opened up a widely popular vision of a vast interconnectedness of the individual with the boundless forms of life. This vision of inevitable interconnectedness inspired the popular determination in Buddhist societies for persons consciously to evolve toward realizing their highest potential and transforming the whole world into a positive environment.

The Universal Vehicle (Mahayana) Buddhist scriptures, which became popular in India about four centuries after the Buddha's time, teach that a Buddha is a cosmic being whose state of achievement can be described as consisting of Three Bodies. First, a Buddha's perfect wisdom becomes a Truth Body, a Body of Ultimate Reality, in that an enlightened being experiences the whole universe as one with his or her own being. Second, a Buddha's perfect compassion becomes a Form Body, a limitless embodiment that reaches out from the enlightened being's blissful oneness with the ultimate reality of freedom to help countless other beings escape from suffering by realizing their own oneness with freedom. This Form Body is itself divided into two. There is a Beatific Body, which is a sort of subtle or ethereal body made of a Buddha's sheer joy at being free of suffering, at having realized the absolute nature of reality. It is as infinite as reality, a subtle radiant omnipresence of a Buddha's joy throughout all things. Then there is an Emanation Body, which arises out of the background energy of the Beatific Body when a Buddha wishes to interact with ordinary beings, who cannot perceive the Beatific presence around them, who feel suffering and alienation. Buddhas emanate—magically create—whatever gross embodiments are appropriate to relate to beings, to liberate them from their suffering, and ultimately to inspire them to discover their own enlightenment and their own beatitude. Shakyamuni Buddha, the historical Buddha, is an Emanation Body Buddha, but the Buddha who emanated himself as Shakyamuni is believed to have an inexhaustible power to emanate himself in infinite other forms according to the needs of beings. Thus, all Buddhas are understood to have these Three Bodies: Truth, Beatific, and Emanation. These categories provide a useful framework for us to understand the Tibetan sense of the inconceivable reality and presence of enlightened beings.

The Buddha taught that humans should investigate the relative world of material and mental nature, in order to understand it thoroughly and improve the lives of all beings. They should investigate not only through their senses, but also through an intensified use of the subjective human mind itself, using reason and introspection, and cultivating critical thought and focused concentration to degrees of acuity unimaginable to the normal, untrained individual.

The Buddha founded and greatly furthered the tradition of Inner, or Mind, Science (*adhyatmavidya*). It is called "science," because it is an organized discipline for seeking knowledge of the mind in an exact manner, with a view to freeing individuals from its negative potentials and enabling them to realize its positive potentials. The Buddha set up lifelong educational and research institutions, which eventually developed into what came to be called monasteries and convents. These institutions, dedicated to higher education, spread widely throughout India and the rest of Asia over the centuries after Buddha's time. They became a permanent presence in all Asian societies, until the advent of either Islam or international secularism wiped them out. The study of the death, between, and rebirth processes in particular was conducted by researchers within these Mind Science institutions, the results being contained in a huge, cumulative scientific literature on the subject. This scientific literature on death is unique in world civilizations. It is the ultimate source of the *Natural Liberation.*

## TIBETAN IDEAS ABOUT DEATH

The Tibetan attitude toward death and the between is neither mystical nor mysterious. This guidebook for the journey through the between shows how the reality of death fits into the Tibetans' world, vividly picturing the continuity between former, present, and future lives. Their multilife perspective is no more (and no less!) a religious belief system than our modern sense of the structure of the solar system, or of the pattern of the cycle of seasons in a year. Tibetans considered it a matter of common sense and scientific fact that animate beings exist along a continuum of lives, and that the death, between, and rebirth processes follow a predictable pattern. They have credible accounts by enlightened voyagers who have gone through the between experience consciously, preserved the memory, and reported their experiences. Tibetans accept these reports of their psychonauts just as we do those of astronauts who report what happened on the moon. Tibetans also believe that most people can recover memories of their former lives by a fairly elementary regime of meditation. Tibetans act on this Buddhist perspective in a practical manner, using their lifetimes to educate themselves to understand the world and to prepare for death and future lives by improving their ethical actions, emotional habits, and critical insight.

Tibetans share our Western view of death in some ways, and in other ways see death very differently. On a human level, they see it as we do, as a tragedy at the end of life. They have methods for anticipating and warding off untimely death, for cheating even timely death and for prolonging the precious human life. On this human level, they are even more afraid of death than we modern materialists or humanists, who expect an automatic, painless oblivion. Tibetans see an anesthetic oblivion as very improbable, understanding death rather as a door to a transition that can be worse than fatally dangerous for those unprepared or badly misdirected by negative habits and attitudes. They thus naturally see death as a malevolent, powerful nihility that is lurking out there, that will come for them at any time. In harmony with their inheritance from India, they envision this terror as the ferocious, terrifying God of Death, Yama, king of the underworld and judge of the dead. He is portrayed as blue-black in color, with a buffalo head and two arms, holding a white spinal-column-and-skull club and a noose, phallus erect, standing naked on the back of a fire-breathing buffalo. He is sometimes with his consort, the fearsome Chamunda, who can also be considered a female personification of his energy. He has numberless hordes of minions who do his bidding and roam around collecting the souls of the dying. When he comes to call, a person cannot say no, they must go with him down to the underworld. And there in his iron hall that is windowless and doorless, their good and evil deeds are weighed in the balance. Yama judges them and then sends them on, to the various heavenly realms if their virtue predominates, to the animal and hellish realms if their sins predominate. If they are most fortunate and their virtue includes great sensitivity, generosity, and intelligence, they will be able to return to the human realm, which is considered better than heaven for spiritual practice. Tibetans are terrified of Yama, and they look to the Buddhas and Bodhisattvas to save them from judgment at his hands. They dramatize his presence at festivals and masquerades as a fierce deity who is danced by a giant monk wearing a terrifying mask and a colorful costume. He is always shown as ultimately tamed by the Buddha, by the Wisdom Bodhisattva Manjushri, or by the Compassion Bodhisattva Avalokiteshvara in his form of Padma Sambhava, the great adept and first historical savior of Tibet.

Though the personification of Death is vivid in the Tibetan imagination, we notice at once that it is not Yama himself that is so awful, but rather his judgment and the possibly negative fate he metes out. Tibetans have the commonsense view that life is boundless, that we did not come out of nothing and cannot become nothing. We are both beginningless and endless. Since we will always be involved in the relational realm, we must know our inner freedom as well. If we do not, and are forced in our ignorance to experience our inevitable involvement as an endless bondage, as a perpetual suffering, our lives will be boundless torment.

Human life is characterized as being midway between states of excessive pain and states of excessive pleasure. A being assumes human rebirth from life in other forms by accumulating a vast amount of merit, through deeds of giving, moral interacting, and tolerating, and an equally vast amount of intelligence, through long efforts of developing critical wisdom and penetrating concentration. The human form is relatively free of rigidly programmed instinctual reactions. Thus human beings are uniquely endowed with the ability and opportunity to understand fully their situation, reprogram themselves completely positively, attain the unexcelled perfect enlightenment of Buddhahood, and become boundlessly happy, alive, radiant, and helpful to other beings. To die unenlightened and lose the liberty and opportunity of human embodiment before attaining enlightenment, and then to be reborn involuntarily in extremely miserable conditions innumerable further times—this would be the ultimate tragedy. Once human life is understood as providing the liberty and opportunity for evolutionary freedom and altruistic enlightenment, its loss is far worse than is the loss of life assumed to be either sheer obliteration into nothingness or secure passage to heaven. It is something like expecting loss of life to result in a passage into hell or purgatory. This is a danger that is more than fatal. It is a doorway to nearly limitless torment. Thus, the Tibetan sense of the beginningless and boundless nature of life, of beings as endlessly reborn, does not palliate the fear of death at all. It lends an intensity to this life that is quite compelling. It is what really underlies the strong religiosity and spirituality of the Tibetans, which does not come from their environment of highland wastes and snowy mountains.

On the more spiritual level, however, Tibetans have learned to view the ordinarily fearsome death as a strong force close to life, a powerful impulse to the good, an intensifier of positive attitudes and actions. They tend not to get caught in the reification of death as a force of pure evil, some sort of radical, insensate, arbitrary malevolence. They rather learn to see it as nonexistent as a thing in itself apart from life. This sense of the relationality of even death encourages them to view death on the highest level as the immediate, omnipresent realm of freedom, not merely part of life but the ground of life.

Tibetans observe that anyone can die at any time in any place. Our sense of the concreteness of the life situation, of the solidity of the waking world of the five senses and their objects, is a complete error. Nothing that we think we are, do, feel, or have has any essence, substance, stability, or solidity. All the somethings in and around us with which we preoccupy ourselves from morning to night are potentially nothing to us. If we died, they would dissolve in our tightest grasp, forgotten if they were in our mind, lost if they were in our hand, faded into blank numbness if they were our mind and body. Surprisingly, once we become accustomed to the omnipresent possibility of death in life, we feel greatly liberated. We realize we are essentially free at all times in all situations. We realize that all compulsion is only based on the illusion of substantial continuation, enduring substance, binding essence. We become completely immersed in the medium of freedom. Our participation in relationalities is, in reality, totally voluntary. This sense of the immediacy of freedom is exhilarating. This higher understanding of death is associated with Yamantaka, the Terminator of Death, who is the most terrifying personification of the wisdom of selflessness, the realization of the emptiness of nothingness.

People have noticed that Tibetan culture is highly colorful, that the Tibetans are on the whole a cheerful, vibrant, and lively lot. They are individualistic and unpredictable. They cherish freedom in all respects and on all levels. They have used their independence to practice the enlightenment teaching of the Buddha, not just to develop materially or militarily. They have lived intelligently by their lights, have used human life well and extracted its fullest potential for evolutionary, not just material, progress. A great measure of the unique beauty of their civilization comes from their vivid awareness of the immediacy of death and the freedom that awareness brings.

# CHAPTER 2

# THE TIBETAN
# SCIENCE
# OF DEATH

## WHAT IS DEATH?

What is death? The question is a scientific one. Western science holds that a "flatline" on the EEG means cessation of heartbeat and brain activity, and therefore represents death. The illusion of the subjective "I" in the individual consciousness, assumed by materialists to correspond with the presence of brain wave activity, should cease with the cessation of brain waves. Yet the picture of death as a nothing in consciousness is not a scientific finding. It is a conceptual notion. There are many cases of people being revived after "flatlining" for some time, and they report intense subjective experiences.

In the popular imagination developed by a modern scientific education, death is most often supposed to be a terminal state, a nothingness, an oblivion, a void that destroys life, that swallows it up forever. It is aligned with sleep, darkness, and unconsciousness. It is feared by those who feel happy, or feel they should be happy. It is sought after by those who are in misery, filled with unbearable pain and anguish, as a blessed final anesthesia. But science should not neglect to question this picture. In fact, inner science begins with the analysis of nothingness. Nothing is after all just nothing. It cannot be a place that resembles an idea of nothingness. A place involves area, or extension. It is defined by coordinates and boundaries. It is not nothing. It is room. Nothing has no room, nor can anything be located within nothing. Nothing cannot have an inside or an outside. It cannot destroy, swallow, or terminate. As nothing, it can have no energy or effect. As nothing, it cannot be a thing, a realm, a state, or anything. It is absolutely nothing to fear. It is nothing to hope for.

This ultimate end of everything, this diametric opposite of all, is nothing in itself. And yet we think of nothing as something. Clearly, "nothing" is that conceptual entity that shows most clearly the illusory status of all conceptual entities. To use the verb "exist" about it is a misuse of language. To refer to nothing as "it," "this," "that," or whatever, without quotes, is a mistake, as only the concept can be referred to. "Nothing" is categorically unimaginable, so it is incorrect to picture nothing as a destination. It is wrongly imagined to be a ground state giving off no reading, which appears as an EEG flatline. It is incoherently imagined to be an anesthesia following a loss of all sensation. It is wrongly conceived to be a place of quiet within which consciousness can slip. It cannot be entered.

When we do imagine nothing in the above ways, we are actually doing nothing more than comforting ourselves. We are building our image of the state of nothingness on our habitual sense of deep sleep. We lose concerns, worries, sensations, and finally consciousness itself as we fall asleep. We "fall" asleep, having a sense of relaxing into a ground state. We may have a last moment of awareness of slipping away, we may have a first moment of waking up complete with a memory of having been in a dream, or, less easily, of waking up in a dream or losing consciousness out of a dream. But we do not have any direct experience of being unconscious, so we cannot remember having been unconscious. Thus our sense of having rested in a state of nothingness of consciousness is an inference based on the last and first moments of threshold awareness.

We associate sleep with refreshment, rest, peace, and quiet. Someone with a mental or physical sickness who cannot sleep is considered to suffer torture, and sleep deprivation will destroy anyone's body before too long. We love sleep. Actually sleep does not correspond with a flatline, absolute lack of brain activity. Our brains can be more active during dreaming than in some waking states. Sleep is thus materialistically very different from the death state of a corpse. When we imagine death as entry into nothingness, we are merely comforting ourselves. Our sense of death as a sleep is a mere analogy even from a materialistic perspective. It is also likely that the dualistic model of "liberation" that motivates Individual Vehicle Buddhism and mystical forms of Hinduism, Taoism, and Western monotheism—a model of liberation as a state of absolute aloofness from the world of life—is derived from this universal human experience of sleep. In most cultures, sleep is accepted as a blissful withdrawal into an aloof state of peace, a restful separation from troubles, worries, pains, and entanglements. So religious ideals of nirvana, conceived as a state apart, ultimate liberation from pain and sorrows, or a supreme release, may be nothing but guaranteed states of permanent, gloriously unconscious sleep!

When we see this equation, we can understand at once why materialists scoff at spiritual or religious forms of liberation. Why would they need it? They have already guaranteed themselves permanent rest. They have a guaranteed nothingness waiting for them, attained without the slightest effort on their part, without ethical sacrifice, without realization, without developing any skill or knowledge. All they have to do is fall asleep, a skill they have already cultivated during thousands of nights.

But what is it that provides them the guarantee of a restful nothing awaiting them after death? Do they have any credible evidence? No one has ever returned to report entry into nothingness. They have no recorder, no viewer, no extension of their senses into the subjectivity of a dead person. They cannot physically probe into the brain-dead state of any being. They have no convincing description of nothingness, which obviously has no attributes. They have never observed even one material thing become nothing. Why should the energy reality of a state of awareness, be it even a minimal awareness of pure rest, be the exception to the law of physics that energy is conserved and only transformed? What makes the materialists believe so powerfully in the nothingness of that one energy continuum?

The answer is, obviously, that they have no grounds at all for this belief. It is merely a belief based on brave assertion, corroborated by many other believers, all without a shred of evidence, reinforced by constant repetition and dogmatic insistence. It provides ultimate comfort, satisfying the religious urge to have a complete sense of reality. This comfortingness might give rise to suspicion or doubt, so it is disguised for the materialist by the pretense that nothingness is something frightening, something undesirable, a bitter pill that he or she, the brave modern human grown-up, has learned to swallow.

This is why materialist scientists are so dogmatically dismissive of evidence about the postdeath continuity of consciousness. They cannot consider the evidence even casually, because this would generate questions about their own belief. Like any religious dogmatism, since it is a logically weak belief, often admittedly irrational, based on no credible evidence, it cannot allow even the slightest questioning, for fear that the resulting doubt could not be withstood.

In fact, a considerable body of credible evidence supports the probability of postdeath existence of consciousness and sentient future life continuity. First, it is the natural thing to expect, since everything else in nature exhibits continuity through changes. Second, many credible witnesses report that they died and experienced certain adventures. Some died clinically and were revived. Some remember as children details and circumstances of former lives, and some of their memories are corroborated by other people, standing up to the investigation of reputable researchers. Some codify the data collected in various ways and present it in manuals in traditions of dying used in many cultures. And the majority of humans in most civilizations feel they must have some concern for the state of their awareness in the future lives they will be obliged to face.

No sane person fears nothingness. It might be boring. It might not be delightful. But at least it should be restful, peaceful, and painless. And relative to all the troubles of wakefulness, it is pleasant and much sought after by every one of us. What we do fear, and should fear rationally, are pain and suffering. We work hard in life to avoid pain and suffering for ourselves and those dear to us. So we are afraid of death, not because we know it *is* nothing, but because we know in our bones it *cannot* automatically bring us nothing. We fear the many painful somethings it might bring us. So our sensible human caution wants to know what it will bring, how we can prepare to avoid the bad and gain the good—what to expect and how to prepare for it. We know that falling asleep tonight will not prevent tomorrow and its challenges. So we prepare for tomorrow as best we can. The better we are prepared, the more happily we fall asleep. We know that the sleep of death will not automatically prevent new situations for consciousness. So we prepare for those new situations. And the better prepared we are, the more relaxed we will be when we have to die.

For even the most diehard materialist, Pascal's famous "wager" is still compelling: If we become nothing after death, we will not be there to regret having prepared for something. But if we are something after death, and we have not prepared at all, or are badly prepared, then we will long feel bitter, painful regret. So we have everything to lose by not preparing, and nothing to gain; we have everything to gain by preparing, and nothing to lose. Should our preparation be for nothing, a little time spent on it in this life will not be regretted for eternity. Should our preparation be for something, the time taken away from it for the sake of this life's business or pleasure will be deeply regretted for eternity as the waste of a vital resource.

So, those of us who have either the prudence or the adventuresomeness to deal with a life situation of total relativity in space and time can safely proceed. There are no boundaries to our interconnectedness with limitless dimensions and universes. And there are no limits to our continuity of development, bad or good. A very powerful commitment—to ameliorate the situations in which we find ourselves along with others—arises from the understanding of the inevitability of being situated in infinite relativity and continuity. The abandonment of any reification of nothingness leaves us with an absolute preoccupation with the quality of relative situations. This preoccupation demands that we use every means at our disposal to improve them.

To fall back on particular religious beliefs supported by no rational evidence or plausible inference is not sensible, given the fact that our choices of actions might have unlimited consequences. Having cured ourselves of the temptation to reify nothingness, why would we reify some improbable soul-state that reproduces the characteristics of a pleasant nothingness—a blissful anesthesia, aloofness from connection to conditions, permanent isolation from experience, and all guaranteed by an absolute, nonrelative power that controls the relative yet is unaffected by it? Here, rather, we should use Pascal's wager in reverse. If, due to an inevitable destiny of soul, an Omnipotent Being will save us no matter what we do, we will not regret having spent a bit of time preparing unnecessarily to save ourselves. But if there is no such Being, or if there are divine Beings more powerful than us who can help us if we are prepared to accept their help, then we will deeply regret for a very long time our failure to prepare ourselves.

There is no reason for a sound faith to be irrational. A useful faith should not be blind, but should be well aware of its grounds. A sound faith should be able to use scientific investigation to strengthen itself. It should be open enough to the spirit not to lock itself up in the letter. A nourishing, useful, healthful faith should be no obstacle to developing a science of death. In developing such a science, it behooves the investigator to consider all previous attempts to do so, especially those traditions with a long development and a copious literature. Of all these, the science of death preserved in the Indo-Tibetan tradition is perhaps the most copious of all.

Given the boundless interconnectedness of living forms, beginningless and endless, and spread throughout an infinity of space, the materialist picture of evolution as natural selection operating purposelessly, yet efficiently developing life forms through random mutation from a definite beginning point within a finite theater of planetary environment, needs some revision. First of all, postulated definite beginnings and finite settings are always suspect. The materialist account describes reasonably the material, causal development process, but why should not mind as well as body develop and mutate?

The Buddhist view of all this, the psychobiological evolutionary account known as the "theory of karma," is very like the Darwinian idea of evolution. The karma theory describes a "great chain of be-ing," postulating a kinship between all observed species of beings, and a pattern of development of one life form into another. Hu-mans have been monkeys in the past, and all animals have been sin-gle-celled animals. The difference in the karma theory is that individuals mutate through different life forms from life to life. A subtle, mental level of life carries patterns developed in one life into the succeeding ones. Species develop and mutate in relation to their environments, and individuals also develop and mutate from species to species. This karmic evolution can be random, and beings can evolve into lower forms as well as higher ones. Once beings become conscious of the process, however, they can purposively affect their evolution through choices of actions and thoughts. Although there are undeniable differences, the karma theory gives an evolutionary explanation of how beings are the way they are. So I have translated *karma* throughout as "evolution" or "evolutionary action."

Karma means action that causes development and change, and so is close to what we mean by evolution. There is no need to retain the Indian word *karma*. Some translators do so because of a factor of mystification; they feel that nothing in the target language can re-produce the unique meaning of the original term. Some Westerners who delve into Eastern thought also keep the term because they are thinking of *karma* mystically, as a kind of fate. But in Buddhist sci-ence, it has nothing to do with fate—it is an impersonal, natural process of cause and effect. Our *karma* at a given moment of life or death or the between is the overall pattern of causal impulses result-ing from former actions connected with our life-continuum. These form a complex that impresses its effects on our bodies, actions, and thoughts. In turn, our ongoing actions of body, speech, and mind form new causal impulses, which determine the nature and quality of our lives in the future. This complex can be called our *evolution-ary momentum*. There is an old Tibetan saying, "Don't wonder about your former lives; just look carefully at your present body! Don't wonder about your future lives; just look at your mind in the present!" This expresses the sense that our present body has evolved from a long evolution driven by former actions, and our future em-bodiments will be shaped by how we think and what we decide to do in our present actions.

The time of the between, the transition from a death to a new rebirth, is the best time to attempt consciously to affect the causal pro-cess of evolution for the better. Our evolutionary momentum is tem-porarily fluid during the between, so we can gain or lose a lot of ground during its crises. Tibetans are highly aware of this. It is why they treasure the *Book of Natural Liberation* so much as a guide to bettering their fate.

# THE SIX REALMS

Buddhists have schematized the possible life realms into six main categories. Negative possible experiences can increase limitlessly, leading to forms and embodiments of experience that are utterly hellish, as those realms have been imagined by Eastern as well as Western imaginations. Buddhists have developed elaborate pictures of the eight hot hells, the eight cold hells, the eight crushing hells, and the eight cutting hells, moving out imaginatively from the painful experiences of heat, cold, compression, and dissection. There are mentally excruciating hell depictions as well, infinite in their terrifying variety and experiential negativity. These hells are produced by negative evolutionary actions driven predominantly by hate. They are the feedback constructions and magnifications of limitless continua of hate. Fortunately, no sojourn in hell can logically be eternal, though they seem of infinite duration to the agonized sufferer in them. I have called the beings in these realms "hell-beings."

Next there are the realms of the pretans, often called "hungry ghost realms." Pretans are certainly hungry and thirsty, but they are not ghosts. They are considered living beings caught in realms of extreme frustration. I have anglicized their Indian name *preta* and call them "pretans." Greed, the desire to incorporate, is magnified and fed back to produce the pretan realms, just as hate creates the hells. Pretans undergo infinite permutations of the tortures of Tantalus. Some have giant stomachs the size of Yankee Stadium, narrow throats miles long and the diameter of pin holes, and insatiable hunger and thirst. When they find something resembling food, it is hard to get, hard to eat and swallow, and it burns on its way down and creates inconceivable pain instead of giving satisfaction. Pretans are incarnations of hunger, thirst, craving, and frustration.

As the hell-beings are incarnations of hate and the pretans of greed, animal life forms are created by accumulated ignorance, folly, or stupidity. Animals are more familiar to us, being close to the human life form. They suffer from relative lack of intelligence and limited ability to communicate. They are bound mainly to involuntary, instinct-driven reactions to situations. Their potential for freedom is extremely limited. They are not looked down on by Buddhists as intrinsically inferior to humans; they also have souls, they also suffer, and they also will attain enlightenment. But their situation is not well suited to intensive positive development, due to the fixity of their instinctual ignorance. They need a special kind of care and assistance to help them evolve, care that a human must almost become a Buddha to provide effectively.

Humans, in their realm nearby the animals, are also incarnations of all the negativities, but have become free of the extremes of hate, greed, and ignorance that bind the hell-beings, pretans, and animals. The human life form is the evolutionary product not only of these negativities, but also of their opposites, patience, generosity, and intelligent sensitivity. Over long evolutionary periods prior to taking life as a human—over billions of lifetimes—infinitesimal quanta of patience have diminished the force of hell-producing hate, arising in the form of slight decreases of hate-reactions at being hurt. Infinitesimal quanta of detachment or generosity have diminished the force of pretan-producing greed, arising as slight decreases of attachment-reactions to habitual objects of desire. And both tolerance and generosity are stimulated by infinitesimal quanta of heightened sensitivity to other beings, which counteracts the self-centered delusions that dominate the animal existence and arise as slight decreases in self-preoccupied absorption in the pursuit of instinctual programs, and hence in momentary noticings of the needs of other animals. The cumulative effect of these tiny voluntary departures from the push of the instincts of beings in the three "bad estates," or "horrid realms" (hell, pretan, and animal), develops the evolutionary momentum to loft a being into the human life form. And this is why the human life form is considered such a precious treasure, a hard-won, magnificent achievement, not to be wasted carelessly. Relatively speaking, human life has freedom from necessity of involuntary drivenness by instinctual reactions, and the opportunity to use that freedom with intelligence and sensitivity to attain ultimate freedom and reliable happiness.

Beyond the human life realm is the life realm of the antigods, or titans, as I have translated their Indian name *asura*. They have freedom and opportunity beyond that of the human being; indeed, they have risen to their estate from the human level, usually, but they have invested their generosity, tolerance, and sensitivity in the pursuit of power. They have been caught in the thrall of competitiveness and are driven by jealousy. They want to outdo other beings. They love to fight. They live in heavenlike realms near the heavens, and they are constantly trying to compete with the gods, attempting to take the heaven realms away from them. Since their lives of constant fighting and killing and dying habituate them to rage, they tend eventually to fall down into the hells.

The highest egocentric life forms in terms of sheer merit and intelligence are those of the gods. Due to their long evolutionary practice of generosity, sensitivity, and tolerance, coupled with their mastery of mind control, they ascended from the human life form through various paradises. They have more freedom and opportunity than humans, but the very richness of their endowment is their greatest danger: They feel so great and grand, they have such comforts, pleasures, powers, and glories, their lifespans are so long, and the lower realms and the possible sufferings of egocentric lives seem so far away from them, that it is very hard for them to use their freedom creatively. They are dominated by pride, and tend to fall back below the human level when their extremely long lives lose the evolutionary momentum that created them.

There are three regions within the god realm, the desire, pure form, and formless regions. The desire region consists of six heavens, two of them terrestrial though invisible to humans, and four celestial heavens that still have a kind of landscape for the deities within them. The deities of these heavens experience a paradisiacal existence, but as a result they lose the drive for ultimate freedom and happiness in a seemingly never-ending round of high-quality pleasures. Above the six desire heavens are the sixteen pure form heavens, within which deities exist in bodies of pure energy. They are said to be "Brahma-bodied," meaning they are like transgalactic energy clouds of bliss and brilliance. Their self-delight is their chief failing, and though they have vast intelligence, they tend to ignore the memory of their past as weaker, suffering beings, their sense of the plight of infinite other beings around them throughout the multiverse, and the possibility of their future vulnerability. "Beyond" these pure form heavens—though the spatial term "beyond" loses meaningfulness here—are the four formless heavens, those of infinite space, infinite consciousness, absolute nothingness, and beyond consciousness and unconsciousness. In these heavens dwell countless trillions of gods who have withdrawn from involvement in forms, driven by the pursuit of the absolute. Aiming at the ever more peaceful, the ever more subtle, and the ever more real, they are not safeguarded by the critical awareness of the constructedness of all states, their emptiness and relativity. They remain within realms of dead calm for extremely long periods of time, untroubled by any concern, secure in their sense of having achieved final ultimacy, of having become one with the absolute. They are most subtly locked by pride and delusion into the ultimate self-constructed world of alienation and self-preoccupation imaginable. Buddhists consider these heavens and the life forms of the gods to be the most dangerous pitfall for meditators, because they are so close to what the philosophically uneducated expect the absolute to be: an infinite objectivity, an infinite subjectivity, nothingness, and an infinite indefinability. Only the understanding of voidness, the relativity of all things and states, provides the critical defense against succumbing to the apparent calm and transcendentality of these heavens and becoming reborn there for a very long time.

The "six realms of migration" are graphically represented everywhere throughout Tibet and elsewhere in the Buddhist world in the "wheel of life" often found on temple walls. This figure represents the experience of the dying person, who flies into the "mouth of Death" (the deity Yama, holding the wheel in mouth and hands and feet), and lands on the wheel of egocentric life according to his or her evolutionary momentum (see color insert, plate 4).

The *Book of Natural Liberation* presupposes this cosmological context as the setting for the deceased person's journey through the between. Once one has felt the boundless interconnectedness of all life forms, the inspiring infinite horizon of positive evolution toward Buddhahood is accompanied by the terrifying infinite horizon of negative evolution or degeneration toward the animal, pretan, or hell-being life forms. The horrid states are truly frightening and definitely to be avoided. Nothingness would be far preferable. Awareness of the possible horrid states is a powerful motivator toward positive development for oneself, and an intense catalyst for compassion for others. It is indispensable for developing the messianic drive to save other beings from suffering that is called the will to, or spirit of, enlightenment. This is the spiritual conception that changes an ordinary egocentric being into an altruistic bodhisattva.

Some Asian teachers have said in recent decades that the horrid states are simply metaphorical and not to be taken literally, that they merely indicate states of mind to be avoided. There is some truth to that, of course, especially since the whole universe also consists of states of mind. It was also practical of those teachers in that their students, Westerners with a certain background and education, might have been frightened away from an edifying path of learning and meditation by the prospect of the crackling brimstone fires of hell they thought they had long ago escaped. But in the final analysis the metaphorical approach is misleading. And it no longer is quite so necessary. All the world is in some sense created by the mind, from the infinitely positive to the infinitely negative. If you step out in front of a freight train, its painful crushing of you is all in the mind as well. A liberated person, viscerally aware of the precise sense of "just being in the mind," would have no problem standing in front of such a train if there were any benefit for beings from doing so. But it takes a person of such ability to ignore the possibility of hell, the pretan realm, the animal realm, or even the worse forms of human life without liberty and opportunity. It is more healthy for the rest of us to fear being crushed by freight trains—it gives us energy to get out of their way. It is healthy for us to fear letting negativities go unchecked because of the infinitely negative consequences they can produce—it gives us energy to nip negativities in the bud.

If we are going to use the science of death to develop the art of dying well, we must realize that all these realms need to be considered just as real as our present lives in the human realm. Those who have remembered their own previous lives have reported this to be the case. And it makes logical sense that the life forms in the ocean of evolution would be much more numerous than just the number of species on this one tiny little material planet we can see around us nowadays. So, the encouragement provided by the "it's all in your mind" approach can be useful. But we should remember that it cannot be applied selectively to those aspects of reality we do not like. All of reality is in the mind, and the mind has us experience it as "out there." So we should still take care to see to it that "out there" is beautiful and not horrible, to prevent the horrible and develop the beautiful.

## THE THREE BUDDHA BODIES

The six realms scheme gives a static cross section of the ordinary Buddhist cosmos. We need also a sense of the Buddhist view of the boundless process of existence experienced by the enlightened. A soul's continuing life-process endlessly goes through the phases of death state, between state, and life state. These phases are parallel within a single life to deep sleep, the dream state, and the waking state. And within the waking state there is a third parallel cycle, the deep trance state, the subtle body-mind state (a consciously directed out-of-body state, known as magic body), and the gross body reentry state. These sets of three are connected with the standard analysis of the Buddha state into the Three Buddha Bodies, the Truth Body, the Beatific Body, and the Emanation

**Figure 2. The Three Buddha Bodies and their analogues**

| Truth Body | Beatific Body | Emanation Body |
|---|---|---|
| Death | Between | Life |
| Sleep-state | Dream-state | Waking-state |
| Waking Trance | Waking Magic Body | Waking Gross Body |

Body. The practice of Tantric yoga aims to align and transmute ordinary death, the sleep state, and trance into the Buddha Truth Body; the ordinary between, the dream state, and the waking subtle, magic body-mind state into the Buddha Beatific Body; and ordinary life, the waking state, and the integrated gross body into the Buddha Emanation Body.

In the context of practices such as those presented in the *Book of Natural Liberation,* oriented toward preparing for a successful use of the ordinary between state to accelerate progress toward Buddhahood, the processes of the sequence of lives, daily life, and the single lifetime can also be described as the "six betweens," the life, dream, trance, death-point, reality, and existence betweens. This scheme is used to create in the practitioner a sense that all moments of existence are "between" moments, unstable, fluid, and transformable into liberated enlighten-ment experience. Thus, the life between is normal living, understood as existing between birth and death. The dream between is the period between deep sleep and the waking state. The trance between is the state between the waking state of dualistic consciousness and the en-lightened awareness of transcendent wisdom. The death-point between is the momentary flash or several-day period of unconsciousness be-tween life and the reality between. The reality between is the prolonged conscious state (sometimes as long as a fortnight) between the death-point and existence betweens. The existence between is the second pro-longed, conscious state of the between traveler, consisting of the experiences of encountering various birthplaces in a womb, egg, mois-ture, or lotus; it occurs between the reality between and conception, or birth into the life between. This way of describing all aspects of the normal life cycle can be schematized as in figure 3.

These six betweens are designed to emphasize the transitional na-ture of all moments of existence anywhere on an individual's life-continuum. The schemes of the Three Bodies and the six betweens are used to create a context supportive of efforts to transmute the ordinary

**Figure 3. The life cycle as the six betweens**

| *The Six Betweens* | *Experienced Between* |
| --- | --- |
| life | birth and death |
| dream | sleep and waking |
| trance | dualistic consciousness and enlightened awareness |
| death point | life and reality |
| reality | death point and existence |
| existence | reality and birth |

round of suffering of persons locked into egocentric self-preoccupation into an experience of love and happiness.

## THE BODY-MIND COMPLEX

Having laid out the outlines of the cosmos underlying the *Book of Natural Liberation,* what is the Tibetan model of the body-mind complex? The Buddhist sciences put forth a number of models for different purposes. The schemes we need to understand here are those of the three levels of gross, subtle, and extremely subtle body and mind, the five aggregates, the five elements, and the six senses. Before describing them, we should bear in mind that all such schemes in Buddhist sciences are heuristic devices, patterns easy to remember. There need not absolutely be only five or six of this or that. In each case, one could analyze things into more or fewer categories. The sets used by the Tibetans are those that they have found most useful in their long experience. Conceptual schemes are like lenses in a camera. A scene with a 105 mm. lens looks different than it does with a 35 mm. lens. There is no need to argue over which is more true to what is out there. They are merely different levels of magnification.

The three levels of the body-mind complex are used to provide a framework for Buddhist practitioners to integrate their subtle, contemplative experiences with their ordinary experience. This enables them to alter their habitual self-identification process, in order to enter usually unconscious states consciously. Thus, when we see something or feel a sensation, we are normally conscious only of the surface level of the experience, the tree over there or the ache in here. We are not conscious of the photons of light striking the neurons of sensitivity in the microscopic workings of the optic nerves. We are not aware of the neurotransmitter chemicals flashing signals through the central nervous system to let the brain know there is an ache in the stomach. But the Buddhist inner scientist or psychonaut seeks to become conscious of such normally unconscious processes. She thus needs the equivalent of a microscope for this inner exploration. So, she develops a subtle model of the self, with which she trains herself to identify, in order to experience directly the subtler inner processes.

The body-mind complex is analyzed into three levels: gross, subtle, and extremely subtle. The gross body is the body of flesh, blood, bone, and other substances that can be further analyzed into the five main elements of earth, water, fire, wind, and space. Further analysis down to the level of modern elemental chemistry is considered too fine for this context, reaching a level of differentiation that is out of touch with the self-identifying imagination. The gross mind that corresponds to this body is the mind of the six sense-consciousnesses, the five that correspond to the physical senses of the eyes, ears, nose, tongue, and body, and the sixth, mental sense-consciousness that operates within the central nervous system coordinating all the input from the senses with concepts, thoughts, images, and volitions.

The subtle body roughly corresponds to what we think of as the central nervous system. It is not as much the "wet-ware" (brain-matter) of the system as it is the pattern structuring it into a vessel of experience. The nerve channels are a structure of energy pathways that consist of thousands of fibers radiating out from five, six, or seven nexi, called wheels, complexes, or lotuses, themselves strung together on a three-channel central axis that runs from midbrow to the tip of the genitals, via the brain-crown and the base of the spine. Within this network of pathways, there are subtle "drops" of awareness–transmitting substances, moved around by subtle energies called winds. The subtle mind corresponding to these structures and energies consists of three interior states that emerge in consciousness the instant subjective energy is withdrawn from the gross senses. These three are called luminance, radiance, and imminence (the deepest state of the subtle mind), and are likened to pure moonlight, pure sunlight, and pure darkness. In unenlightened persons these three are mixed with normally subconscious instinctual drive-patterns, called the eighty natural instincts (a long list including various types of desires, aggressions, and confusions).

The extremely subtle body is called the indestructible drop; it is a tiny energy pattern existing normally only in the center of the heart wheel or complex. The extremely subtle mind that corresponds to it is the intuition of clear light, called transparency. At this extremely subtle level, the body-mind distinction is abandoned, as the two are virtually inseparable. This indestructible-drop transparent awareness is the Buddhist soul, the deepest seat of life and awareness, whose continuity is indestructible, though it constantly changes while moving from life to life. To achieve conscious identification with this body-mind, to experience reality from this extremely subtle level of awareness, is tantamount to attaining Buddhahood. And this is the real goal of the *Book of Natural Liberation.*

Another important way of analyzing the gross body-mind complex is the scheme of the five aggregates, or processes: the material, sensational, conceptual, volitional, and consciousness processes of the individual life. The Sanskrit word for these, *skandha,* literally means heap. "Aggregate" is standard for Buddhist translations, though in some re-

**Figure 4. The gross, subtle, and extremely subtle body-mind complex**

| Level | Body | Mind |
|---|---|---|
| gross | five-element body | six sense-consciousnesses |
| subtle | nerve channels, neural energies, neural drops | three luminance-intuitions, involved with eighty instincts |
| extremely subtle | energy carrying the clear light in indestructible drop | mind of clear light energies, or indestructible drop |

spects I prefer "process," indicating their dynamic quality. The first of these processes corresponds with the gross body, and the latter four analyze mind and its functions into conceptually and introspectively manageable levels. The original purpose of the aggregates scheme was to explore the body and mind in order to locate that which is habitually experienced as the fixed self; to discover the unfindability of anything mental or physical which can serve as that fixed self; and through that insight to attain liberation from bondage to the habitual sense of fixed identity. The following figure summarizes this scheme of the five aggregates, or processes, of the body-mind complex.

In these schemes, the gross body-mind complex begins at birth and ceases at death, except for mental consciousness, which changes for the between-being since it is no longer embedded in gross matter and preoccupied with the input of the five physical senses. Dream consciousness is an instance in normal life of mental consciousness operating independently of the gross physical senses. It is an important analogy or even precursor of the between-consciousness: The five gross senses cease operating in sleep, and mental consciousness continues more subtly. During most dream experiences, mental consciousness produces out of itself a simulation of eyes and ears and even an environment, in order for the dream being to hear sounds and see sights and colors. The sense of having a body that sometimes emerges in a dream is an important analogue of the sense of self of a between-being. Normal people without special training rarely have such a sense. Many rarely remember dreams, almost none remember the first arisal of the dream or the dissolving out of the dream, and very few are capable of lucid dreaming—dreaming while being aware they are dreaming, without waking up. The development of such abilities is of primary importance in developing the ability to *die lucidly,* to remain self-aware of what and where one is during these transitional experiences.

An important first step toward the ability to die lucidly is developing a sensitivity to the transitions between these various states. The

Figure 5. The five aggregates of the individual life

| Aggregate | Constituents |
| --- | --- |
| matter | five elements (earth, water, etc.), or five sense objects and senses |
| sensation | pleasure, pain, and indifference associated with five senses |
| concepts | all images and words used to organize experience |
| volition | desires, hates, delusions, and many other emotions |
| consciousness | five sense consciousnesses and mental consciousness |

subtle body-mind schemes are designed specifically for that purpose. The subtle-body scheme of channels, winds, and drops can be employed by mental consciousness in the process of unfolding special types of inner sensitivities. The channels include the 72,000 circulatory passages within the body, which are structured around a central axis of three main central channels running from midbrow via the crown down in front of the spine to the tip of the sexual organ via the coccyx, with the five nexus wheels at brain, throat, heart, navel, and genitals. There are various pictures of these wheels and channels, because the practitioner can visualize them in a variety of ways, depending on the specific inner sensibilities he is trying to unfold.

The energies that flow within these channels, the subtle winds, are schematized into five main and five branch winds, which have specific bases, ranges, colors, functions, and characters. The details of this are not essential in this context. It is enough to emphasize that becoming aware of the body's functions in terms of these energies is the key technique for the processes of gaining control over the life and death functions. Finally, the drops are the awareness-transmitting substances, chemical essences associated with genetic materials. They form the base of specific consciousnesses located in specific centers at different times in different states. For example, in the Kalachakra system, there is a special system of four kinds of drops. Waking-state drops form at brow or navel during waking activity, providing the focus of awareness or the center of the sense of self during waking experience. Dream-state drops form at the throat or the base of the spine during dreaming, providing the central focus for awareness during dream experiences. Sleep-state drops form in the peripheral heart center or mid-genital center to give focus to deep rest experiences. Finally, fourth-state drops form deeper in the heart center or at the genital tip center, providing the focus for bliss awarenesses during advanced enlightenment or orgasmic experi-

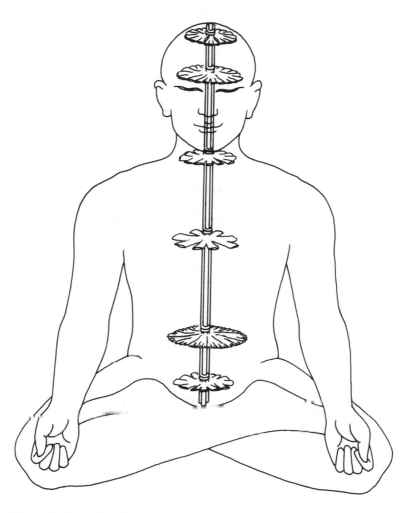

**Figure 6. The subtle body's wheels and channels**

This depicts in general the physiology of the channels of the subtle nervous system. There is the triple central axis, with five or six or more nexi ranged along it. From these nexi energy fibers expand out all over the body, numbered as 72,000 (not depicted here). Thus the self-image cultivated by the practitioner during subtle yogas is that of a sensitive, gyroscopelike structure, within which energy and awareness circulate in a dynamic way.

**Figure 7. The subtle mind's intuitions, experiences, and instincts**

| Subtle Mind Intuitions | Experiential Analogy | Associated Instinctual Pattern |
|---|---|---|
| luminance | moonlight | 33 instinct patterns; desire emphasis |
| radiance | sunlight | 40 instinct patterns; aggression emphasis |
| imminence | dark-light (darkness) | 7 instinct patterns; ignorance emphasis |

ences. Understanding the workings of the drops enables practitioners to focus awareness and to intensify experiences and realizations.

The subtle mind is the subjectivity that corresponds to the subtle body patterns of channels, winds, and drops. The above figure summarizes its analysis into three main states, associated with eighty instinctual patterns or "natures." These states occur when specific subtle physical events happen in the subtle body.

The Tibetan view is that everyone has such a subtle mind, and everyone traverses these experiences. But it takes a special training to develop awareness of them, to experience them lucidly.

Finally, there is the extremely subtle body-mind, where the body-mind duality itself is abandoned. This is the indestructible drop, called "the energy-mind indivisible of clear light transparency." Very hard to describe or understand, and not to be misconstrued as a rigid, fixed identity, this subtlest, most essential state of an individual being is beyond body-mind duality; it consists of the finest, most sensitive, alive, and intelligent energy in the universe. It is a being's deepest state of pure soul, where the being is intelligent light, alive and singular, continuous yet changing, aware of its infinite interconnection with everything. It is beyond all instinct patterns of lust, aggression, or delusion, beyond all duality, one with reality, and one with the Truth Body of all Buddhas. It is what is referred to by "Buddha nature," and its actualization in experience is the goal of the *Book of Natural Liberation*. It is the key to the special method of relaxing into one's deepest natural state that is taught at the highest level in the Nyingma Order of Tibetan Buddhism as the "Great Perfection" (see glossary and chapter 8). Each living being is really just this indestructible drop at the extremely subtle level. This is the living soul of every being. It is what makes the boundless process of reincarnation possible. It is the gateway into liberation, always open, essentially free, though the being evolved around it may identify itself with intensely turbulent states of suffering. It is peaceful, translucent, trouble-free, and uncreated. Knowing it is what made the Buddha smile. It is what makes Buddhas and living beings the same.

This extremely subtle indestructible drop is very similar to the Hindu notion of the Self (*atman*) or Supreme Self (*paramatman*), which is reached as the absolute negation of all petty, individual, personality selves. The Buddha was never dogmatic about formulae, even about his most powerful formula known as "selflessness." He emphasized self-lessness when talking with absolutists, and he emphasized self when talking with nihilists. So it is not a question of early Buddhism having no self, and Tantric and Tibetan Buddhism later returning to a self. Buddha always taught a soul as what reincarnates, as a selfless continuum of relative, changing, causally engaged awareness. To get down to lucid experience of the extremely subtle indestructible drop of soul requires the full realization of voidness or selflessness. It is, in the words of the author Maitreyanatha, a Supreme Self of Selflessness. However, the point here is not the philosophical niceties of the extremely subtle, but the clear exposition of these schemes, themselves important tools for the yoga of dying creatively.

## STAGES OF DEATH

Now that the three levels of body and mind have been outlined, we can turn to the scheme encoding the stages of the death process. This is central in the *Book of Natural Liberation*, since the deceased is presumed to be traversing these stages as we are reaching out to him or her. This scheme is called the eight stages of the dissolution process. Tibetan explorers have reported that a dying person goes through the following stages and tends to have the following experiences. Each dissolution expresses a certain sequence of subjective experiences.

This model of the death process has been found by generations of yogis and yoginis—male and female practitioners of Buddhist yoga, the linking of one's life energies to one's knowledge and understanding—to be extremely useful in developing understanding and control of the death transition. The first four stages are further elaborated by a scheme known as the "twenty-five gross elements," in which they are associated with the five aggregates and with the basic wisdoms or enlightenment energies corresponding to each aggregate.

Combining the first four of the eight dissolutions with these twenty-five gross elements, we get a more complete description of the death process. When earth dissolves into water, one feels sinkingly weak

Figure 8. The stages of death: dissolutions and experiences

| Dissolution | Experience |
| --- | --- |
| 1. earth to water | mirage |
| 2. water to fire | smokiness |
| 3. fire to wind | fireflies in the sky |
| 4. wind to consciousness | clear candle flame |
| (sometimes "wind to space"; end of gross body-mind experience) | |
| 5. gross consciousness to luminance | clear moonlit sky |
| 6. luminance to radiance | clear sunlit sky |
| 7. radiance to imminence | clear pitch-darkness |
| 8. imminence to translucency | clear light of clear predawn sky |

and melting, the material aggregate dissolves as the body seems to shrivel, the mirror-wisdom (which is the transmuted energy of delusion) dissolves as forms become indistinct, the eye sense deteriorates and sights are blurred; everything seems like a mirage of water down a highway. When water dissolves into fire and bodily fluids seem to dry out, sensations cease as one becomes numb, equalizing wisdom (which is the energy of attachment) dissipates as sensations disappear, the ear sense goes and one can no longer hear; one feels surrounded in smoke. When fire dissolves into wind and one feels cold, individuating wisdom (the energy of desire) fades as notions dim out from one's mind, inhalation weakens and the nose cannot smell anything; one feels surrounded by a swarm of fireflies or a burst of sparks. When wind dissolves into space or consciousness and breathing stops and energy circulations withdraw into the central nervous system, volitional functions disappear along with wonder-working wisdom (the energy of competitiveness), the tongue thickens and tastes are forgotten, the body sense fades and textures are lost; one feels enveloped in a candle flame in its last moment.

From this time, one might be pronounced clinically dead. The gross physical elements have all gone, and there is no movement in brain or circulatory system. But gross consciousness, with its mind sense and its eighty instinct-patterns that agitate the three realms of the subtle mind, dissolves only at the fifth stage. The winds that drive the eighty patterns dissolve into the central channel, and the white awareness-drop (or male essence, the white "spirit of enlightenment") from the brain descends down the central channel toward the heart complex; one inwardly perceives within the mind-space a vast sky full of white moonlight. Next, the red awareness-drop (or female essence, the red "spirit of enlightenment") rises from the genital wheel toward the heart com-

Figure 9. The aggregates and wisdoms corresponding to
the early stages of death

| Aggregates | Wisdoms | Elements | Media | Objects |
|---|---|---|---|---|
| matter | mirror | earth | eye sense | sights |
| | (gone in first dissolution) | | | |
| sensation | equalizing | water | ear sense | sounds |
| | (gone in second dissolution) | | | |
| conception | individuating | fire | nose sense | smells |
| | (gone in third dissolution) | | | |
| volition | wonder-working | wind | tongue sense | tastes |
| | | | body sense | textures |
| | (gone in fourth dissolution) | | | |
| consciousness | ultimate-reality | | mind sense | |

plex; one perceives a sky full of orange sunlight. In the seventh dissolution, the stage of imminence, the two drops meet at the heart and enclose the consciousness; one perceives the sky full of bright dark-light, or pure darkness, and then one loses consciousness. Finally, one passes into the realm of clear light translucency, gaining an unaccustomed kind of nondualistic consciousness.

At this point a key structure of ordinary life, what is known as the sixfold knot at the heart complex, unravels. The right and left channels have tightly enclosed the heart complex center from the moment of our conception in this life, and subsequent development of the central nervous system occurs around this sixfold heart-knot. When it unravels totally, our extremely subtle consciousness flies out of its location, driven by our evolutionary orientation. This is the real moment of death; this is the death-point between. It is the subtlest state possible for a being. Anything said about it does not do it justice. Extremely subtle clear-light consciousness is beyond dualities of finity and infinity, time and eternity, subject and object, self and other, consciousness and unconsciousness, even ignorance and enlightenment. It is a state so transparent that one unprepared for it will see right through it and not even notice it. One will experience the loss of consciousness in the latter part of the imminence state, and the return to the consciousness of darkness when reversing back up through the imminence state toward reembodiment, without any sense of having been in any other state, or feeling disoriented and uncertain, as we sometimes are when we awaken too suddenly. The whole science and art of navigating the between-state bears down on this moment, assisting a person to use the transition between habitual lives to enter this extremely subtle awareness that is naturally at one with blissful freedom, total intelligence, boundless sensitivity— that is, perfect enlightenment.

Many persons spend a number of days in this juncture, but often in a state of complete unconsciousness. Confusion about what has happened to them, residual unconsciousness from the stage of imminence, and terror at being cut loose in the universe prevent them from recognizing their deepest home in this clear light translucency, their spiritual oneness with the most loving, powerful, and secure beings in the universe. This is the time when the *Book of Natural Liberation* traditions are of greatest impact. Ideally, the deceased will have learned and practiced them before dying. Otherwise they can be taught at the time of death, though it is unlikely that the totally untrained person can overcome the egocentric instinctual drives and the fear and terror during this high energy crisis and achieve total liberation. Especially because of the difficulty of unraveling the sixfold heart complex knot, it must have been gradually worked on and loosened up during a person's life for its sudden loosening in the death process not to cause an overwhelmingly distracting trauma at this point.

Most people traverse these dissolutions without recognizing what is happening to them, not being able to rest in the clear light, not realizing their essential freedom, happiness, and natural and joyous boundless participation in the lives of all beings. They will mentally shoot through the void's clear light and rise back up into gross embodiment through the eight dissolutions in the reverse order. They will faint again at imminence, then rise through dark-light, radiance sunlight, and luminance moonlight into instinctually dominated consciousness, then reassociate themselves with wind, fire, water, and earth, structured by the imagery they retrieve from the evolutionary patterns encoded by their own actions in their spiritual genes (the genes the individual brings from former lives). These structures will remain fluid in their dreamlike existence in mental bodies in the between-state, only becoming solidified at the grossest physical level when they take rebirth in a lotus or womb or egg or moist cavity. During the between-state time, due to its fluidity and the subtlety of their energy embodiment, their consciousness is magical in power and extremely intelligent, so they can make excellent use of the *Book of Natural Liberation* if it is read or mentally transmitted to them. Here, in the process of safeguarding the quest of a rebirth—defending beings against falling into really destructive states of existence, and guiding them into advantageous life situations—the *Great Book of Natural Liberation Through Understanding in the Between* serves the magnificent purpose its author intended.

During the between-state, the consciousness is embodied in a ghostlike between-body, made of subtle energies structured by the imagery in the mind, similar to the subtle embodiment we experience in dreams. Though subtle, it is an embodiment of consciousness; it arises through the stages of dissolution in reverse, and when the individual leaves it to enter a gross body at conception in a womb, she dissolves out of it in a kind of minideath process. The eight dissolution processes are followed downward from the between-state embodiment into the clear light consciousness and again upward in reverse from clear light to the new embodiment. Indeed, even when a being falls asleep, wakes up in a dream, dissolves out of a dream, and wakes up in the gross body again, these dissolution stages can be discerned, usually compressed into a rapid succession of unnoticed instantaneous phases. The meditative practices associated with between-state training are crucial for sharpening attention so you can become aware of the process, slow down the transitions, and remain lucidly aware of the changes as they occur. It is vital to master and hold in mind these schemes, developed over the centuries in the Tibetan science of death.

## THE REALITY OF LIBERATION

The science of death is the foundation of the art of dying, just as the science of medicine is the foundation of the art of healing. To use this *Book of Natural Liberation* to best advantage, we must understand clearly the opportunity afforded by a conscious approach to the death process. What does "liberation" mean in the phrase "natural liberation"? What does it mean to say that the basic and ultimate reality of all things is emptiness, or freedom? What does the *Book of Natural Liberation* mean when it promises "natural liberation" (Tibetan, *rang grol*), mentioning attributes such as "perfection," "natural bliss," "no more rebirth," and "cessation of suffering"? Is Buddhism after all an escapist system? Is the *Book of Natural Liberation* a prescription for escape?

It can seem so sometimes. There is more than one idea about liberation and freedom within Buddhism. In the Buddha's original teaching of the Four Noble Truths, the third Noble Truth is that of *nirodha,* which literally means "cessation," meaning cessation of suffering. Nirvana, the name for the final reality realized by an enlightened being, literally means "extinguished," "blown out," or "gone out." The spiritual climate in Buddha's time was derived from numerous movements of ascetic intellectuals, who were sick of the fettered, unenlightened life, who saw it as unendingly miserable, and who sought annihilation of mind as well as body through intense, transcending samadhi. To help them, the Buddha presented the nirvana he had found in a slightly dualistic light, as if it were the final extinction they so fervently desired. He was already a Buddha, and as a Buddha was undivided from nirvana while walking and teaching all over India, still being present in some sense while transcendent in some sense. Yet, he called his eventual death parinirvana, or "final nirvana," to keep up the allure of a goal beyond all life for the strongly individualistic, dualistic seekers of freedom conceived as obliteration.

In fact, the person addicted to egocentrism, who is habitually oriented toward an isolated center of being that seems to be the real him or her, who feels aloof when up and alienated when down, who feels intuitively the correctness of "I think therefore I am!"—that is to say most of us—does have a secret craving for oblivion. Oblivion after all is only the full entry into a withdrawn reality of total separation from hassles. To be sure, we expect no fun there, we may miss the few people we really care about, we may forego our few real pleasures, but at least we feel sure of no severe pain or agony. There is no unlimited horizon of danger and vulnerability. Some moderns, who most vigorously reject the suggestion that they might be emotional annihilationists, closet cosmic escapists, and who most bravely assert their existential commitment to unrelenting involvement, may dare to do so only because they basically feel secure that oblivion awaits them no matter what. Indeed, they might think they were terrified of that oblivion, thereby proving to themselves that the possibility of hell was not the issue. Among humanity as a whole, vast numbers of lemminglike people seek cessation through suicidal wars, through becoming heroin addicts, through persisting in cigarette and alcohol addiction. There is no question that annihilationism flourishes abundantly in our world.

Therefore, allowing nirvana to appear as if it were the supreme of blissful oblivions is not a useless teaching tactic. It is adroit and beneficial. Especially since it turns out that the seeker who embraces nothingness, who blasts off into the samadhi of the void, finds that what ceases is not all life, but is his or her ignorance, misknowledge, egocentric addiction, the subjective and objective self-addictions. Fortunately, liberation—the cessation of self-addiction—results in a powerful and durable happiness, a vibrant and sustaining bliss. That special overflowing of joy makes the small worldly joys previously knowable in the tight trap of self-addiction seem paltry and pathetic. And the final bonus is that this relatively ultimate bliss, this supreme beatitude of the happiness of real freedom, naturally realizes that the lack of isolated, fixed, and independent self is just equivalent to the presence of all totally interrelated things and beings, inconceivably intertwining endlessly throughout unmeasurable eternity and unencompassable infinity. Free from all craving for nothings and oblivions, there is a personal destiny of endless involvement with limitless others. All this spurs you to share your happiness and to release the flow of your love, without the slightest diminution of your ultimate nirvana of indivisible bliss and freedom.

Although this kind of freedom spontaneously invested in total involvement, individual bliss indivisible from loving union with all others, is inconceivable in its real meaning within dualistic conceptual terms, it is clear enough what is being claimed. Cessation, extinction, termination of, and freedom from self-addiction are a most plausible doorway to real happiness, true love, and boundless bliss. Once this is clear, it becomes easier to understand what the author means by liberation. If we are not clear about this, there is some risk of misunderstanding the Great Perfection language as simply urging us to sink into a liberation of the kind of automatic oblivion seemingly awaiting every materialist, with absolutely no need for any sort of scientific foundation or transformational teaching.

In order to clarify this essential focus of these teachings, I have translated a short philosophical text that belongs to the Natural Liberation literature, the *Natural Liberation Through Naked Vision, Identifying Intelligence* (see chapter 8). In the passage below from that text (see pages 230–231), Padma Sambhava has just been mentioning that the reality of freedom, nirvana, Truth, and so forth—This Itself—is the highest goal intended in every sort of Buddhist teaching.

> *To introduce the three-point entrance to this itself—*
> *Realize past mind as trackless, clear, and void,*
> *Future mind as unproduced and new,*
> *And present awareness as staying natural, uncontrived.*
> *Thus knowing time in its very ordinary way.*
> *When you nakedly regard yourself,*
> *Your looking is transparent, nothing to be seen.*
> *This is naked, immediate, clear intelligence,*
> *It is clear voidness with nothing established,*
> *Purity of clarity-voidness nonduality;*
> *Not permanent, free of any intrinsic status,*
> *Not annihilated, bright and distinct,*
> *Not a unity, multidiscerning clarity,*

*Without plurality, indivisible, one in taste,*
*Not derivative, self-aware, it is this very reality.*

This introduces the ultimate reality of nirvana, the Great Perfection, the Truth realm, the final freedom, the evolutionary perfection of Buddhahood. This realization is the aim of all the teachings of the *Book of Natural Liberation*. It is accessible in principle because it is already the deepest reality of the present, the actual condition of even the most ordinary. You must look "nakedly" at yourself, reversing the aim of seeing back upon itself. You look for that fixed, independent, isolated self that feels like the kernel within you, out of which your drives and thoughts emerge. But when you turn 180 degrees to look within the looking, you find nothing that has intrinsic status, nothing standing independent in its own right.

Even Descartes found that too: he found that he could find nothing at the point of origin of thought. He erroneously asserted that it was because a subject could not be an object. And he then went wild and said that this subject, this one thing he could not find, demonstrate, establish in any way, was *the one thing he could be foundationally certain of*! He could doubt everything, but he could not doubt that he doubted! So: I think, therefore I am. Only the laziest Buddhist philosopher would make such a statement.

Not making his mistake, we look nakedly and see nothing established there as a fixed thing in itself. Remember, this is in our seeing itself. We cannot even see anything substantial behind the seeing of nothing. We turn again and again, whirling around pointing to the point of origin of the pointing. Our looking becomes transparent to itself. Nothing is to be seen as independent or objective. And this transparency spreads infinitely. Descartes was right, in one way: the subjective cannot be found. But, subject gone, how can objects remain substantial? A subjectivity that cannot find itself cannot indulge in finding objects out of a sense of certainty in itself. Subjectivity and objectivity both dissolve under penetrating observation of this kind, and all that remains is free, clear transparency. This transparency itself is naked, pure intelligence. It is clarity, immediacy, nonduality, and voidness of all intrinsic status including any intrinsic status of voidness itself. This bright and clear intelligent awareness is not annihilated, it is not obliviously sunk in union, and it is not rigidly, fixedly dependent, not stuck in a plurality of interrelated yet intrinsically independent entities. Experientially, we enjoy the one taste of freedom without getting lost in isolation. This is the Diamond Reality of Clear Light, this is the real nature of each of us that makes natural liberation possible. Our true nature, our Buddha essence, is not something that needs laboriously to be created—it is already overwhelmingly present as our very soul.

This soul, furthermore, is not established intrinsically in itself, as a realm of voidness wherein all contents have disappeared. It is rather a realm of voidness wherein all beings and things are transparently present, none independently established in itself, but each present relatively in the inconceivable network of beauty and bliss that is the void. Thus, our Buddha Truth Body of our freedom-wisdom is simultaneously our Buddha Beatitude Body of bliss, and our Buddha Emanation Body of love, that reaches out to help other beings rediscover their own free, luminous, blissful, loving natures. As the *Natural Liberation Through Naked Vision* says (page 231):

> *This objective identification of the actuality of things*
> *Contains complete in one the indivisible Three Bodies.*
> *The Truth Body, the voidness free of intrinsic status,*
> *The Beatific Body, bright with freedom's natural energy,*
> *The Emanation Body ceaselessly arising everywhere—*
> *Its reality is these three complete in one.*

I trust it is clear by now that nirvana, the freedom intended by the *Book of Natural Liberation,* is not oblivion. The Truth Body is not some absolute aloof transcendence far beyond us. It is the infinite radiance of blissful wisdom energy, beauty enjoying itself unboundedly. And it is simultaneously beauty overflowing in itself as love and goodness, enfolding all beings, who pathetically feel themselves apart and alienated in self-addictive isolation. Beings like us.

The *Book of Natural Liberation* itself is the words of Padma Sambhava, the lotus-born master, who himself is believed to be the Buddha Truth-Beatific-Emanation Bodies reaching out to us. He does not just sail above us in poetic evocation of his own bliss, he reaches into our present situation tirelessly, seeking to find us where we are, giving us a practical access to our freedom. He challenges our habitual self-alienation from our own reality, as in another passage (pages 231–232) from the *Natural Liberation Through Naked Vision*:

> *To introduce the forceful method to enter this very reality,*
> *Your own awareness right now is just this!*
> *It being just this uncontrived natural clarity,*
> *Why do you say, "I don't understand the nature of the mind"?*
> *As here there is nothing to meditate upon,*
> *In just this uninterrupted clarity intelligence,*

*Why do you say, "I don't see the actuality of the mind"?*
*Since the thinker in the mind is just it,*
*Why do you say, "Even searching I can't find it"?*
*Since here there is nothing to be done,*
*Why do you say, "Whatever I do, it doesn't succeed"?*
*As it is sufficient to stay put uncontrived,*
*Why do you say, "I can't stay still"?*
*As it is all right to be content with inaction,*
*Why do you say, "I am not able to do it"?*
*Since clear, aware, and void are automatically indivisible,*
*Why do you say, "Practice is not effective"?*
*Since it is natural, spontaneous, free of cause and condition,*
*Why do you say, "Seeking, it cannot be found"?*
*Since thought and natural liberation are simultaneous,*
*Why do you say, "Remedies are impotent"?*
*Since your very intelligence is just this,*
*Why do you say, "I do not know this"?*

These words, each expression simple enough in itself, enable freedom to interlock with our ordinary worries. Like the between-guides in the *Book of Natural Liberation,* they make each gap in our addictive self-obsession a potential doorway into selfless freedom. They proceed by challenging our self-indulgence in self-pitying, artificial remoteness from our salvation. They offer forceful reassurance to lift us up from self-loathing and the fear and trembling it promotes. They cannot harm us—unless we misunderstand them as reinforcing the spiritual nihilism so perniciously ingrained within our culture, which misunderstanding we have taken pains to guard against above, by carefully distinguishing between voidness and nothingness, freedom and oblivion.

On this secure foundation, let us move on to the Tibetan art of creative dying.

# CHAPTER 3

# THE
# TIBETAN ART
# OF DYING

## INTRODUCTION

It is important to understand the inner scientific dimension of the *Book of Natural Liberation Through Understanding in the Between,* in order to approach it practically and use it effectively. The original is useful to Tibetans in two main ways. First, it is considered a scientific handbook on the realities and experiences of death. It provides guidance on what the death process is, how their present actions can affect it, and how they can manage it as it happens. This guidance also helps them understand, prepare for, and manage the deaths of those dear to them. Second, it is considered a guidebook for spiritual practice on two levels: It helps the yogi and yogini develop the abilities they need to traverse the death crisis with skill and confidence; and it gives those who feel unable to prepare fully for death, and are not confident of their abilities, a religious sense of how to seek help from enlightened divine and angelic beings. No intelligent tourist would depart for a foreign land without a good guidebook giving instructions on basic preparations, necessary equipment, dangers, and obstacles. No intelligent Tibetan would depart the known territory of this life without a good guidebook for the between.

In the previous section, I have described the Tibetan analysis of the realities of the death process. In the following, I introduce the preparations for death, how to develop the ethical momentum, contemplative skills, and realistic insight required to traverse the between successfully. Staying mainly within the framework of the *Book of Natural Liberation,* I occasionally introduce clarifying ideas from other Tibetan teachings.

## ORDINARY
## PREPARATIONS FOR DEATH

*Hey! Now when the life between dawns upon me,*
*I will abandon laziness, as life has no more time,*
*Unwavering, enter the path of learning, thinking, and meditating,*
*And taking perceptions and mind as path,*
*I will realize the Three Bodies of enlightenment!*
*This once that I have obtained the human body*
*Is not the time to stay on the path of distractions.*

(*The Root Verses of the Six Betweens,* page 115)

The art of dying begins with preparations for death. As for any journey, there are innumerable preparations one can make. The *Book of Natural Liberation* suggests at least five main types of preparation while still living: informational, imaginational, ethical, meditational, and intellectual.

The primary preparation is the development of a clear picture of what to expect. This we can do by studying the inner scientific descriptions of death, mastering the main patterns, and practicing their remembrance until we are ready for the crisis at any time.

The second kind of preparation, which the *Book of Natural Liberation* joins the broader Buddhist tradition in encouraging, is the development of a positive imagination of potential future realms. Buddhist texts, due to the relatively nonsuppressive social milieu of Buddhist countries, especially India, are rich in visionary descriptions of heavens, celestial realms, hidden paradises, and so forth. These descriptions certainly exist in all religious traditions, but mainly in the esoteric province of the mystics of those traditions. The authoritarian, militaristic, and production-oriented societies of the West and the Far East tended to suppress the individual imagination of heavenly realms of pleasure, persecuting visionaries who experienced celestial beauty. Only in recent times, as modernization has brought greater wealth and a corresponding relaxation of social control to parts of the West and Far East, has the tight control of the popular imagination been lifted, and secular and sacred arts that open the imagination to bliss have become more widespread.

An important preparation for death should be the reading of the Buddhist sutras and treatises that describe the heavenly Buddha-lands, such as the Buddha Amitabha's Sukhavati, the Pure Land of Bliss. A Buddha-land refers to the environment of a Buddha, signifying that the evolutionary transmutation of the finite individual into an infinite body of awareness takes the environment with it, so that self and other are indistinguishable. You must have tried to imagine in detail one of the celestial realms described in the sutras for it to mean something to you when, in the *Book of Natural Liberation,* a particular Buddha is said to emerge from a particular direction to invite you into his Buddha-paradise. The Buddha-land descriptions are incredibly lush and imaginatively stimulating. They open up for us the possibility of unearthly beauty and happiness. The mere reading about and imagining of these realms will open the imagination to be prepared for magnificence that might otherwise be frightening in its glory.

Those with strong roots in other religious traditions should read up on the visions of their own mystics, to ready themselves for the extraordinarily beautiful pearly gates of heaven. And the secularists should look into the literature on life after death, especially reflecting on the accounts of those who actually report near-death or postdeath experiences. The science-fiction literature contains rich descriptions of worlds of exquisite beauty, among the more dramatic realms of danger and adventure.

A third type of preparation is ethical. It involves selective management of your living habits in the light of impending death. This need not be a morbid shivering in the corner. It can make you enjoy life more, live it more intensely, bring happiness to those about you. When you die, you will lose not only all your property and relationships, you will lose even your own body. So right now, why not practice a little bit by becoming a bit more detached about all the things you tend to get obsessed about?

The three main ethical practices are to build up generosity, sensitivity to others, and tolerance. They are all-important preparations for death. They are not directly mentioned in the *Book of Natural Liberation,* because their necessity is taken for granted in Buddhist societies. Western religions teach the same virtues. And secularists can recognize them as common sense, improving the quality of life as well as preparing for confrontation with the ultimate.

Practice giving things away, not just things you don't care about, but things you do like. Remember, it is not the size of a gift, it is its quality and the amount of mental attachment you overcome that count. So don't bankrupt yourself on a momentary positive impulse, only to regret it later. Give thought to giving. Give small things, carefully, and observe the mental processes going along with the act of releasing the little thing you liked.

Practice being more relaxed in your relationships. Remind yourself that you could be dead and not there, and that your main concern for your loved one is their happiness, not just what you are getting out of them. Observe feelings of jealousy that arise for no good reason all the time, and realize how imprisoning they are, how uncomfortable you feel and how oppressed your loved one feels. Concentrate on actions that make your friends and loved ones happy, really happy, not just superficially entertained. Think about others before yourself. Realize each relationship is temporary, so put as much good energy into it as possible while it is there.

Practice being more relaxed about your body. Don't fuss so much about it, wasting time and money on things and treatments you don't really need. Remember you tend to be most beautiful and dashing when you forget about how you are looking. When you look at yourself in the mirror, remember that you might be dead and your skin turn blue, your lips shrivel, your flesh sag and decompose. Don't dwell on this morbidly, but breathe a sigh of relief that you are alive and well right now. Worry less about minor blemishes. Take care of your body, but don't be obsessive about it: be sensible but not fanatic. And develop a greater tolerance of difficulties. Don't mind so much if someone hurts you in an accident. Don't be angry with a mosquito if it bites you. It does it by nature. Defend yourself from injury, but don't get carried away. You can practice using pain and hardship to build your tolerance and patience, the better to be able to face greater hardships; but build up bit by bit, as self-mortification tends to backfire, resulting in ever greater self-obsession.

The fourth kind of preparation you can make is meditational. While it is good to have a knowledgeable teacher, it is not necessary to go out and join a group, convert to another religion, give up your normal pursuits and life-style, and so on. In fact, in any campaign of self-discipline, extreme measures are likely to be short-lived and not to achieve their goals. Previous translations of the *Book of Natural Liberation* do not give any real way to meditate. The sections translated are those designed to be used right at the moment of death and for some time after. The meditational preparations should be made from the time one first decides it makes sense to do them. Again, the *Book of Natural Liberation* presupposes that most members of Tibetan society will have some kind of meditation practice, so it does not spell the basic ones out in much detail.

The first type of meditation you can begin with is the calming meditation, called one-pointedness. You learn to sit comfortably in a balanced position—the cross-legged position is actually quite easy and healthful, but any balanced position will do. You practice in short sessions, five or ten minutes at a time, starting with observing your breaths, counting them, relaxing and calming, letting your thoughts go their own way without dragging you with them. Always stop the sessions while you are enjoying them—never prolong them until you are tired. The idea is to condition yourself to enjoy them and to want to go back to them. Once you have come to enjoy this practice, you can choose a meditation object. If you are a Buddhist, a small image of Shakyamuni Buddha is recommended. If you are a Christian, an icon of Christ. If you are a Moslem, a sacred letter. If you are a secularist, a Mona Lisa, a flower, or a satellite picture of the planet. You then devote short sessions to keeping your attention on that object without distraction. You learn to disidentify from thoughts and emotions, let them take off here and there in the mind field, while you bring your attention back to your object. At first, you feel discouraged at your great distractedness. But you relax about it, try to keep focused an instant longer, bring attention back to the object an instant sooner, and so forth. Bit by bit is the watchword. The main point is to improve your ability to monitor your mind, to use it effectively to concentrate on something, and to develop more control of emotions and reactions. Along the way, it is a proven way to lessen stress on your system, improve your health, improve your ability to get things done, and so forth. If you get involved in this practice, there are more elaborate instructions in a number of recent books.

Doing calming meditation is like developing a tool. It does not necessarily lead to higher realization. The next important type of meditation, crucial for one's preparation, is insight meditation. Insight meditations use the calmed and focused mind to better understand reality, the environment, and the self. They begin from developing mindfulness or alertness by observing oneself without reacting. This practice is like calming, except that the object is your whole mind-body process. You scan over it slowly, observing all that is going on, without reacting to anything. After the initial phase of heightening familiarity with your various processes, you use a scheme like that of the five aggregates listed above. Using such a mental map of your being, you look everywhere for your real self. You soon discover there is no fixed identity within yourself, no independent point of subjectivity. This discovery becomes the insight into selflessness, the doorway to liberation. This meditation becomes extremely complex and there are extensive teachings on it. The point here is to develop a greater mindfulness of one's whole system and how it works; this can be very helpful in developing the ability to be aware at all times. It might lead to attaining lucid dreaming, for example, which is a very important preparation for the attempt to become lucid in the between. Importantly, insight meditations increase the ability to cease identifying with cognitions, thoughts, and emotions, realizing that what seems like an absolute "I" is only a temporary construct. Whatever degree of this ability you develop will become extremely important at the death point. The many promptings of the *Book of Natural Liberation* not to fear this or that, not to be carried away by this or that perception, and so on, are all calling for some aspect of the ability to disidentify, some flexibility of the habitual sense of self.

The third type of meditation one can practice is therapeutic, intended to condition your mind to a positive orientation. For example, there are meditations on love, wherein you reflect on your connectedness to other beings, how kind they have been and are to you, how much you benefit from relating to them, how beautiful they are, and so forth. You decondition your aversions and reinforce your enchantments. In this way you can intensify your loving attitude toward others. Then there are meditations on patience, in which you decondition your anger habit and reinforce your tolerance. There is the meditation on detachment, in which death is a major theme, through which you become freer and freer of obsession with possessions and mundane activities.

Fourth, there are imaginative meditations, visualizations of positive places or events, which can be most useful in developing openness to the unprecedented situations one may face at death. These range widely: cultivating an imagined home, a place of safety, peace, and quiet; developing self-confidence in facing any situation; overcoming subconscious defeatist attitudes; and achieving the adamantine self and the exalting environment of the esoteric mandala realm, a perfected environment or Buddhaverse.

Finally, there are meditations that can be used in daily life, to combine a spiritual orientation with daily activities, utilizing time and effort that is otherwise wasted on this life only, from the Natural Liberation perspective. The most ordinary occasions can become opportunities for contemplative practice.

> *Hey! Now when the dream between dawns upon me,*
> *I will give up corpselike sleeping in delusion,*
> *And mindfully enter unwavering the experience of reality.*
> *Conscious of dreaming, I will enjoy the changes as clear light.*
> *Not sleeping mindlessly like an animal,*
> *I will cherish the practice merging sleep and realization!*
>
> (*The Root Verses of the Six Betweens,* page 115)

This involves using sleep as a time for practice. You can convert the process of falling asleep into a rehearsal of the death dissolutions, imagining yourself as sinking away from ordinary waking consciousness down through the eight stages into deep-sleep clear-light transparency. And you can convert the dream state into a practice of the between-state, priming yourself to recognize yourself as dreaming when in the dream. This is quite difficult to do all at once, but not so hard if you can remember to persist, making a little progress bit by bit. It is very important, for if you can become self-aware in the dream state by the practice of lucid dreaming, you have a much better chance of recognizing your situation in the between after death.

Another very simple type of daily life meditation is the common Tibetan practice of recitation of a mantra. OM MANI PADME HUM is the mantra of great compassion. Literally, "Om—the jewel in the lotus—hum," for a Tibetan it means that all is well with the universe, the force of good and love is everywhere and competent to help all beings out of every difficulty. The mantra thus resonates with the most positive possible outlook. Tibetans develop the ability constantly to repeat the mantra silently or in a low voice. They learn about the mantra and about Avalokiteshvara, the Lord of Compassion, feel close to his positive energy, and practice repeating the syllables in sessions of meditation. Thus abandoning a level of habitual mental rumination, they use that layer of the mental bandwidth for the stream of the mantra—omanipaymeyhum. Some of them can combine it with a visualization in which they see the six jeweled syllables, on a turning wheel in the heart center, radiate the rainbow light rays of the five wisdoms to bless all beings throughout the universe. The stream of the mantra then connects with a constant vision of radiant color streaming forth and back in loving energies. Other mantras can also be used in the same way. If the mantra is Jewish, Christian, or Moslem, you can use it to create the same kind of positive stream in your mind. Such a practice will be especially valuable in the death crisis. By learning to let it flow automatically, it will easily carry you over rough spots in the dying and between transitions.

Another kind of daily-activity meditation is the conscious association of an ordinary activity with a spiritual practice. When you wash dishes, associate their cleansing with clearing away mental addictions, making the washing into a prayer. When you build a building, associate it with building a pure land mandala. When you observe a person in the subway, associate the encounter with being there for him or her when you are a Buddha. When you open a door, associate it with opening the door to enlightenment.

The fifth type of preparation is intellectual. Contrary to some contemporary misconceptions, Buddhism is not at all anti-intellectual. The intellect is a vehicle of liberation; it is the source of wisdom, after all, and wisdom is the only faculty that can enable you to achieve liberation. Meditation, love, ethics, none of these alone can bring about enlightenment without wisdom. Learning should be life-long. No one finishes their education just in a few years of school. Really, school only teaches you how to learn; it is only the beginning. Numerous texts enable us to learn about the nature of life, the nature of liberation, the nature of self, and the nature of the environment. Especially important are the teachings of emptiness, selflessness, and relativity, as well as those on the spirit of enlightenment of love and compassion. Reading the sutras in general also has the virtue of being itself a form of the third type of meditation, therapeutic, as the extensive descriptions therein of the pure lands, the inconceivable realizations of the Buddhas and their disciples, all these have an immersion effect on your consciousness. If you are more interested in another religion or philosophy, study its literature regularly, looking especially into its descriptions of death and afterlife, other realms, and the methods of developing the ethical, religious, and intellectual higher self. Secularists can get great benefit from the sciences, especially those that are critical and opening, and from the self-development literature of modern psychologies.

## EXTRAORDINARY PREPARATIONS

*Hey! Now when the meditation between dawns upon me,*
*I will abandon the host of distracting errors,*
*Focus in extreme-free experience, without releasing or controlling,*
*And achieve stability in the creation and perfection stages!*
*Giving up business, now one-pointed in meditation,*
*I won't surrender to the power of erroneous addictions!*

(*The Root Verses of the Six Betweens,* page 115)

Some people will feel so moved by a new consideration of death and the spiritual aim of life that it raises that they will not be satisfied with the normal preparations just described, which can be integrated within a conventional lay life, focused on family, career, and consumption. They will want to change their lives, treat them as "life-betweens," and dedicate everything to accelerate their positive evolution. In Buddhist societies they might become monks or nuns to devote themselves full time to the pursuit of enlightenment, minimizing their concern for what are called the "purposes of this life," family and friends, food, drink, houses, clothes, wealth, fame, power, and other ordinary pleasures. In modern society, however, there are few facilities or social supports for the renunciant, so full-time, extraordinary practitioners will have to make special, individual arrangements in order to devote themselves totally to transformative spiritual development.

The procedure the Tibetan tradition would have them follow involves four stages: first, the preliminary stage of exoteric enlightenment teachings; second, the development of a relationship with a qualified teacher and the obtaining of initiation in the advanced, esoteric practices necessary to accelerate personal evolution; third, the development of the visualization ability taught on the creation stage, the stage of cultivating the creative imagination; and fourth, the mastery of the perfection stage—the stage where the transformational journeys actually begin—with its yogic disciplines that simulate and rehearse the death transitions. The *Natural Liberation* literature only alludes to the first and second of these four stages, since it assumes that all Tibetans are familiar with them. In terms of the third stage, it contains an elaborate mandala visualization practice, which I have translated for the first time (see *The Dharma Practice, Natural Liberation of the Instincts,* page 203). It does not contain specific instructions for the perfection stage practices, except as embedded in the between-process instructions themselves and in the general Great Perfection philosophy (see *The Natural Liberation Through Naked Vision, Identifying the Intelligence,* page 225). However, numerous other esoteric traditions in Tibet contain full instructions on all four stages. Most important of these are the Unexcelled Yoga Tantras, the traditions of death-transcending, transformative discipline believed to derive from the Buddha's esoteric teachings, which were developed and brought to Tibet by the great adepts of ancient India such as Padma Sambhava, the practitioners of Tantra who attained Buddhahood in their ordinary bodies and remained in association with their gross bodies in order to help others attain liberation. Without going into these in great detail, I provide an overview of their main practices to inform you of the full inventory of possible preparations for the voyage of the between.

*THE PRELIMINARY STAGE*

This is the stage of the intensive practice of the usual, exoteric Buddhist teachings, performed in the context of preparing to embark on the subtle esoteric practice of the Unexcelled Yoga Tantras. In most of the Tibetan orders, there are arduous preliminaries to esoteric practice, usually the "four hundred-thousands"; these are a hundred thousand each of four practices: formal prostrations, repetitions of the hundred-syllable purification mantra of Vajrasattva (one of the archetypal mild Buddha-deities, the archetypal male form adopted by the Buddha when he teaches Tantra), ritual offerings of the entire universe to the enlightened beings, and mentor-yoga contemplations. These are usually performed before receiving initiation into any practice. In the Geluk Order, a practitioner can be assigned nine sets of "hundred thousands": refuges, prostrations, water offerings, mandala offerings, clay Buddha-image-making, Vajrasattva mantras, vow-purifying mantras, fire offerings, and mentor-yoga contemplations. However, the more important foundational preliminaries are the practices of the Individual and Universal Vehicles, the main monastic and messianic Buddhist paths. Tibetan masters have specially formulated these into the three principal paths to enlightenment: those of transcendent renunciation, the spirit of enlightenment of love and compassion, and the transcendent wisdom of selflessness. The first is an emphasis of the Individual Vehicle, the second an emphasis of the Universal Vehicle, and slightly different forms of the third are the keys to liberation for both.

Transcendent renunciation is developed by meditating on the preciousness of human life in terms of the ocean of evolutionary possibilities, the immediacy of death, the inexorability of evolutionary causality, and the sufferings of the ignorance-driven, involuntary life cycle. Renunciation automatically occurs when you come face-to-face with your real existential situation, and so develop a genuine sympathy for yourself, having given up pretending the prison of habitual emotions and confusions is just fine. Meditating on the teachings given on these themes in a systematic way enables you to generate quickly an ambition to gain full control of your body and mind in order at least to face death confidently, knowing you can navigate safely through the dangers of further journeys. Wasting time investing your life in purposes that "you cannot take with you" becomes ludicrous, and, when you radically shift your priorities, you feel a profound relief at unburdening yourself of a weight of worry over inconsequential things.

The spirit of enlightenment of love and compassion is the energetic and cheerful aura you create for yourself by shifting the orientation of your life away from self-preoccupation to preoccupation with becoming an enlightened being in order to bring happiness to all others. It is developed on the basis of your astonishing relief and happiness at the initial experiential taste of real liberation from all troubles, gained from the first realization of transcendent renunciation. At the beginning, you systematically meditate upon your connectedness with all sentient beings, generating a deep feeling of intimate familiarity with all of them equally by going back into your infant memories of tender cuddling affection and diffusing that toward all beings, while reflecting on your mutual evolutionary beginningless and personal interconnection. Once you feel close to all beings in such a visionary network of blood and milk connections, you realize how they constantly suffer, life after life; you remember the relief you now feel at the prospect of liberation; and you generate a powerful ambition to liberate them as well. At the conclusion of this meditative process, you lock in this ambition with the heroic vow to serve all beings. You turn your aspiration to help the world into a solid determination. At that time, you will have generated the spirit of enlightenment of universal love and compassion: you become a bodhisattva, a messianic hero or heroine. The spirit of enlightenment is all a matter of orientation and determination.

The wisdom that is essential for your actual liberation systematically develops through the meditation of the twofold selflessness. The two kinds of selflessness are subjective selflessness and objective selflessness. You begin by cultivating awareness of subjective selflessness, observing your habitual sense of having a solid self-center, a fixed, definite, unchanging identity that is you. You take some care in noticing how absolute and undeniable this self seems, how your drives and impulses and thoughts seem to come from it, how unquestionable it seems. When you really become aware how deeply you feel such a center, you begin a process of digging deeper to find it, to put your finger on it, to really know it, to know who and what you really are. There are many subtle systems of investigation that have been developed to help you with this difficult task. You learn them and you meditate with them. You analyze your inner constituents of body and mind, sensations, emotional and conceptual mechanisms, and the complex of consciousness itself. You need to develop heightened powers of concentration systematically, to stay with this analysis as it goes deeper and deeper. Through your studies, you can have the help of millions of previous investigators, who have left clues and methods from their quests over centuries. You don't have to be a philosopher; you just have to want to know who you are.

Eventually, the investigation leads you to realize that you are going to fail to find that hard-core identity of the self. You realize that it does not exist at your center in the way that it seems to. You have moments of feeling that you perhaps don't exist at all, but you realize that that sense of nonexistence is also not itself a hard-core identity. As you go along, you must rely on the help of the wisdom literature to deal with this failure to be able to pin down any intrinsically identifiable mode of either existence or nonexistence. You must also take your time, and persevere without expecting spectacular breakthroughs and feeling discouraged if none occur. Gradually, your sense of absoluteness begins to erode, while your sense of just being there relatively becomes more and more liberated. You realize that identity is a construct, a relative fabrication, and you begin to understand objective selflessness. You look out at others and at the objects of the world, realizing that they too are mere relativistic entities, with no hard-core identities either. Finally, you realize that this interdependent network of nonabsolute, relative beings and things is fluid and malleable, open for creative development. If it's all a mutual construct, let's make it more beautiful. Everything is open for transformation. Once things are not fixed by rigid core structures that constitute their identities, their openness to transformation implies some danger that they can degenerate into negative configurations, causing suffering to living beings. But that danger is more than offset by the possibility that everything can be transformed toward limitlessly positive configurations, realms of joy and fulfillment for living beings.

This meditation can go as deep as full enlightenment itself. But at this preliminary stage of the path, preparing for the special context of the tantric art of traversing the betweens, you need to use inference and experience to reach the certainty that any sense of absolute anything is only relative, and that anything you can sense at all is only relative. This is to realize the equivalence of voidness and relativity, no longer looking for an absolute void beyond the world, no longer depreciating the relative world as lacking ultimate value. You integrate this certainty into your daily experience by a twofold process. You let experience affirm absolute voidness, knowing that anything you can experience is relative and void of intrinsic identity. And you let absolute voidness affirm your relative experience, since knowing a thing's voidness makes its relative presence undeniably important. From there on it is a matter of deepening this realization by pushing it inward, to overlay your instinctual misknowledge that still habitually gives you a feeling of an enduring hard-core identity. The more you can bear down through focused concentration on this specific identity feeling, the more free you will become. This is where meditation is really needed: after you have a sound realization. This is where you realize how deep your instincts go. This is where you begin to desire a higher technology of deepening your realization and expanding your liberation. You decide you cannot bear to delay liberation for many lives. You want to complete the process in this one lifetime. You become determined to seek initiation in the Unexcelled Yoga Tantra, to recognize your life as the life between, to learn the art of reenvisioning your entire self and world on the creation stage, and to learn the interior voyages of the trained psychonaut on the perfection stage. It is not that you seek a different teaching to provide a shortcut previously unavailable, for the wisdom aspect of these paths does not vary; whether viewed from an exoteric or an esoteric perspective, voidness is the same. But the method is different; the technique is accelerated, the art is more developed. You seek a way of accelerating your evolution, compressing the development achieved through many conscious deaths and many lives of practice into one life, death, and between, if possible; or at most a few.

The esoteric subtle practices of the Tantra are thus approached on the basis of an already clear but incomplete understanding, as a method of compressing eons of lives into one life, eons of deaths into one death, and eons of betweens into one between.

## MENTOR AND INITIATION

While it is possible to practice the three principles of the ordinary path from a book, it is considered much more efficient to have a spiritual teacher, or mentor, to apply the various themes and techniques specifically to you. The teaching of selflessness is made especially easier when learned from a teacher who herself or himself already understands selflessness. Many people will already have a spiritual teacher by the time they get serious about seeking initiation and entering the advanced stages of practice. However, sometimes you will select a different mentor for tantric initiation. It is quite common to have several spiritual teachers. To practice the transformational teachings of Unexcelled Yoga Tantra, the personal relationship with a spiritual mentor is foundational.

A large literature discusses the choice of a mentor. It is no simple matter. You should have a good intuitive feeling about a teacher, of course, but you also should examine the teacher's life-style, her words of teaching, the quality of her other disciples. You can find fault with anyone. It is asking too much to ask for what looks like perfection right away to your habitual critical gaze. But you should use common sense as well. A spiritual teacher who does not seem clear on teachings, whose opinions often contradict the traditional texts, who does not practice what he preaches—who uses disciples for his own wealth or fame, who indulges himself with little self-control—is most probably to be avoided, no matter what his title and background. The reliable mentor should be lucid in teaching, be usually in agreement with the traditional texts, and most often behave accordingly; make effort to benefit others; be concerned with the needs, not the uses, of the disciples; be unconcerned about wealth or fame, whether comfortable and well known or not; and be moderate in life-style, though all fun need not be poison. Such a mentor, even without great title or lineage, even if not exotic in background, is most probably reliable.

Once you have chosen a mentor, that mentor may impose further preliminary practices upon you, such as the "four hundred-thousands" or others deemed necessary specifically for you. But once a mentor has accepted you as a disciple and agreed to provide initiation and instruction, you can approach a mandala of Unexcelled Yoga Tantra.

Unexcelled Yoga begins by developing a creative meditation that harnesses the imagination to visualize an enlightened self, body, and environment. The exercise is to imaginatively transform your ordinary self and universe into what you are taught an enlightened person and environment would be like. The purpose of this is to develop an archetypal model for your actual transformation. In order to create something, first you have to imagine it. And imagination can be extremely powerful in life-between reality. Once you have understood ultimate reality to be empty of any sort of intrinsic substantiality, reality, identifiability, or objectivity, you become aware of its actual apparent nature at any level of experience as utterly conventional, merely structured by the collective imagination of the world of beings.

Driven by ignorance, ordinary beings structure their universe into an ordinary world maintained by their ordinary imaginations, encoded in language and imagery. Liberated through wisdom, enlightened beings are free to restructure their universe to respond to the needs of the many beings, transforming entire worlds into Buddha-lands. The Unexcelled Yoga Tantra practitioner imitates this ideal by cultivating a purified perception of the environment as the Buddha-land mandala, and a purified perception of the self as the actual body, speech, and mind of Buddhahood.

Initiation is the doorway that opens upon this practice of imaginative transformation. The tantric path begins with the encounter with the vajra, or "diamond," mentor. This can be misunderstood to mean that Tantra is the path of "guru devotion," thinking that having found the vajra mentor, you merely sit at her feet and worship. A good mentor rarely lets her capable disciples sit around indulging in mere devotion. True, you must open your imagination to envision the mentor as the actual Buddha, whose body is the Emanation Body quintessence of the countless Buddhas of the three times, whose speech is the Beatific Body, quintessence of the Dharma, and whose mind is the immutable, all-pervading, and inconceivable body of Truth. You must imaginatively approach the mentor as the living embodiment of the Sangha, Dharma, and Buddha Jewels. You must submerge your own imperfect imagination and perception in the mentor-Buddha's perfected vision. But then you must immediately adopt the mentor's vision, which sees you yourself as a Buddha, sees your potential as actualized in you. The mentor's enlightened vision is communicated to you through the ritual of initiation, which is a kind of anointment as a vajra crown prince of enlightenment. You are formally installed and exalted on the majestic lion-throne of royal Buddhahood, granted an imaginative foretaste of the goal of your spiritual quest.

Such initiation is conferred at the outset of tantric practice as the indispensable entrance, but the first initiation rarely fully empowers the beginner. This is because it requires a highly disciplined visualization ability actually to enter the mandala palace, perceive the building and ornaments in all their vivid details, see the mentor-Buddha within, with his or her retinue, and experience yourself as an archetype deity with many faces and arms. The real mandala constitutes its own perfected universe, and is not within the ordinary world. It is an achievement even to glimpse it with the imagination, using the objects, symbols, and personages in the temple where the consecration is conferred. Further, you must understand all the vows and pledges involved in the tantric ethic, and you must have the ability to keep them, which itself requires a high degree of yogic mastery of mind, senses, and body. However, the first initiation empowers you according to your ability, and permits you to engage in the study and practice that will enable you eventually to attain full initiation.

Initiation rituals are immensely complicated. The Unexcelled Yoga Tantras use four main categories of initiation: the "vase initiation," which focuses on the body and empowers you for creation stage visualization practice; the "secret initiation," which focuses on speech and empowers you for the initial stages of the perfection stage transformation practice; the "wisdom-intuition initiation," which focuses on the mind and empowers you for the higher stages of the perfection stage; and the "precious word initiation," which focuses on body, speech, and mind indivisibly, and empowers you for the highest integration level of the perfection stage, which corresponds to the Great Perfection teachings.

The text for the initiations into the mandala of the mild and fierce deities who are invoked in the *Book of Natural Liberation* is not included in the generally printed editions of the work. This is according to the esoteric tradition that a qualified mentor is the first requirement for initiation. There is no need to circulate a text that cannot be used without the mentor. However, the first text of the Natural Liberation literature, the *Three Body Mentor Yoga*, expresses contemplatively an initiation sequence (I quote in the order of the initiations):

> *To the ineffable self-created Emanation Body Mentor*
> *In the palace of the flawless perfect lotus,*
> *I pray ardently with reverent devotion!*
> *Self-freed without abandoning misconceiving hatred,*
> *I freely accept the effortless blessing of the Emanation Body,*
> *As self-evident wisdom's introspective self-illumination!*

Here the mentor is invoked as the Emanation Body Buddha. You, the initiate, then receive his blessing in the form of white light rays radiating from a diamond OM—the seed mantra of the body of all Buddhas—on your crown. They enter the crown as diamond light, blessing the body, conferring the vase initiation, and empowering you to practice the creation stage.

> *To the deathless, great bliss Beatific Body Mentor,*
> *In the palace of bright, pure wisdom's universal bliss,*
> *I pray ardently with reverent devotion!*
> *Self-freed without abandoning lust and longing,*
> *I freely accept the effortless blessing of the Beatific Body*
> *As the automatic liberation of inner wisdom's universal bliss!*

Here the mentor represents the Beatific Body Buddha, emitting ruby light rays from a red AH—the seed syllable of the speech of all Buddhas—at his throat center, which enter your throat center, filling you with ruby light, blessing your speech, conferring the secret initiation, and empowering you to practice the magic body practices of the perfection stage.

> *To the birthless, nondeveloping, Truth Body Mentor*
> *In the palace of the perfect, all-pervading Realm of Truth,*
> *I pray ardently with reverent devotion!*
> *Self-freed without abandoning misknowing delusion,*
> *I freely accept the perfect blessing of the Truth Body*
> *As the effortless, nonartificial, primal wisdom!*

Here the mentor represents the Truth Body Buddha, emitting sapphire light rays from a deep blue HUM—the seed syllable of the mind of all Buddhas—at his heart center, which enter your heart center, filling you with sapphire light, blessing your mind, conferring the wisdom-intuition initiation, and empowering you to practice the clear light practices of the perfection stage.

> *To the impartial great bliss Triple Body Mentor,*
> *In the palace of authentic clear light introspection,*
> *I pray ardently with reverent devotion!*
> *Self-freed without abandoning subject-object dualism,*
> *I freely accept the great bliss Three Body blessing,*
> *As original wisdom's Three Body spontaneity!*

Here the mentor represents the Buddha as the integration of all three bodies, emitting diamond, ruby, and sapphire light rays from his OM AH HUM seed syllables, which enter your three centers, filling you with red, white, and blue light, blessing your body, speech, and mind, conferring the precious word initiation, and empowering you to attain supreme Buddhahood as perfection stage integration, the Great Seal, or the Great Perfection. The mentor then dissolves entirely into the three light rays and wholly merges within you, and you become indivisible with the mentor.

The essential outcome of initiation is that, on both conscious and subconscious levels, you are imaginatively exalted in the actuality of your own potential enlightenment, physically, verbally, mentally, and intuitively. While you may still be far from full realization, your subsequent practice proceeds with that imaginative orientation. You meditate within the imaginative understanding that perfect enlightenment is fully immediate and your practice is gradually removing impediments to your realization of that fact; you no longer assent to the idea that your enlightenment is somewhere beyond, "out there" in place or in time, to be reached later. This is called "using the result as the vehicle," contrasted with exoteric practices, where the vehicle is considered the cause of an eventual result. Result-vehicle practice proceeds in the stress situation of a paradox or a focused cognitive dissonance. Your ordinary mind knows that you are not enlightened, but your cultivated imagination envisions your state of enlightenment as it appears to other enlightened beings, represented by your mentor. Your visualization of enlightenment thus exerts a powerful critical pressure on your habitual perception of unenlightenment, while both are made more flexible by the awareness of the voidness of both.

This special result-oriented approach is important to understand, not to be misled by the Great Perfection teachings in the *Natural Liberation* collection. If you do not understand precisely how a special cognitive dissonance is being cultivated, when you hear, "Everything is naturally perfect, just relax and clear light will shine, you're already a perfect Buddha!" you will oscillate between two unhealthy responses. At first you may feel good, thinking that your real "I," the assumed hard-core self you habitually sense within, is none other than the Buddha mind; this will lead you deeper into self-addiction, reinforcing the instinctual self-habit. Later, when you recognize that you don't really feel that much better than you did before the text told you you were perfect, you will conclude that Padma Sambhava was wrong, and you will feel depressed about your practice and cynical about any practice. This will deprive you of the benefit of the *Natural Liberation*, the marvelous spiritual technology of the Tantras, and the sophisticated and beautiful Great Perfection teachings.

So when you hear that you are in the Great Perfection, recognize this statement as essentially initiatory, as placing you in the context of your goal and highest imaginable possibility, opening for you the task of critically removing all the impediments to your experience of your own reality. And when you feel discouraged, realize you have been overeager, don't let yourself go in cynical self-pity, and then disidentify from the hard-core self that wanted enlightenment yesterday or it's not worth working for. And when you hear the Great Word of the Great Perfection in the between, when you are detached from your heavy encasement in a habit-encoded body, you can break free of impediments much more immediately, more naturally, so the encouragement that your goal is the clear light within can be crucial in helping you to let go, and not to hide in self-indulgence, not to dodge and doubt. Remember, in that critical moment, hesitation and self-seeking can be worse than fatal. They can lead to lifetimes spent in uncomfortable embodiments in unpleasant environments.

## THE CREATION STAGE

Something similar to a creation stage practice for the *Natural Liberation* system is taught in *The Dharma Practice, Natural Liberation of the Instincts,* a text translated in full in chapter 7. The basic goal of the practice is to harness the imagination to transform the perception and conception of ordinariness into the vision and experience of enlightenment. All the elements of the ordinary world—the ordinary subject and the

Figure 10. The Five Buddhas, and the corresponding aggregates, poisons, colors, and wisdoms

| Aggregate | Poison | Buddha | Color | Wisdom |
|---|---|---|---|---|
| form | anger | Akshobhya | diamond | Mirror Wisdom |
| sensation | pride | Ratnasambhava | gold | Equalizing Wisdom |
| conception | lust | Amitabha | ruby | Discriminating Wisdom |
| emotion | envy | Amoghasiddhi | emerald | All-accomplishing Wisdom |
| cognition | delusion | Vairochana | sapphire | Reality Perfection Wisdom |

ordinary object—are imaginatively reenvisioned as pure wisdom energy. Death, the between, and life are imaginatively converted into the Three Buddha Bodies, Truth, Beatitude, and Emanation, respectively. The five body-mind aggregates are envisioned as the five Buddhas, and the five poisons as the five wisdoms. Every other being is imagined to be a Buddha-deity. Every subtle instinct is imagined a micro Buddha-deity. Every form is imagined as part of the mandala jewel palace. There are different systems of doing this. Since it is a creative, imaginative association that is taking place, it is not necessary to make a rigid correspondence between the impure and purified elements. We will use the system of the *Natural Liberation.*

The five aggregates of matter, sensation, conception, creation, and consciousness, along with their five poisons—hate, pride, lust, envy, and delusion—are reenvisioned as five Buddhas and five kinds of wisdom: Akshobhya and mirror wisdom, Ratnasambhava and equalizing wisdom, Amitabha and discriminating wisdom, Amoghasiddhi and wonder-working wisdom, and Vairochana and ultimate perfection wisdom, respectively. The most ordinary things and the most negative emotions and notions are associated with specific Buddhas, wisdom energies, colors, precious substances, and symbols, in order to simulate the actual consciousness of a realized Buddha, who actually sees things as configurations of blissful and intelligent energies.

You may feel confused, and that feeling of confusion *is* Vairochana; you may feel angry, and that anger *is* Akshobhya. The stuff of your body and objects around it *are* Akshobhya, your sensations *are* Ratnasambhava, your conceptual cluster *is* Amitabha, your emotions *are* Amoghasiddhi, and your consciousness *is* Vairochana. No longer can there be dependency on the mentor, since the mentor has imaginatively been fused with the Buddha-deity, and you have also imaginatively become a Buddha-deity, and a mentor, under the pressure of all beings' need for help and liberation. In the initiation, you have been consecrated with the glory and bliss of enlightenment, and entrusted with the responsibility of enlightenment to understand the universe and all beings in it, to care for them, and to see to their ultimate happiness.

Another way of expressing creation stage visualization is in terms of imagining the five perfections: the perfections of environment, enjoyments, companions, body, and self. The environment is imagined as the mandala palace of Buddha majesty; any sense of being in an ordinary environment is corrected by such visualization. Enjoyments are experienced by enlightened faculties; ordinary objects are perceived only by impure habit. Companions may seem to be ordinary beings, but they are actually Buddhas and Bodhisattvas, there to help you realize your own enlightenment. Your body may seem to be ordinary flesh and blood, but it is actually made of the wisdom stuff of all Buddhas. You choose an archetypal Buddha-deity to model your self-image upon, assuming a mild-deity form if that suits your temperament, or a fierce-deity form if you need that to stir up your deeper energies (see glossary under Archetype Buddha, or Deity, p. 245). Your ordinary self-sense of yourself as an alienated individual is critiqued as an impure self-conception; you now visualize yourself as the manifestation of the diamond of the wisdom that realizes voidness.

This is the creative, aesthetic context in which you practice Unexcelled Yoga. This creation stage is a sustained creative meditation using the imagination to shape the materials of inner vision into a universe of fulfillment. It is structured around the scheme known as the "three conversions," conversion of death into the Body of Truth, conversion of the between into the Body of Beatitude, and conversion of life into the Body of Emanation. These conversions emerge from two main foundations: the critique of the habitual perception of the outer environment as the ordinary world of suffering, which leads to the emergence of this world's Buddha-land perfection; and the critique of the concept of the ordinary unhappy self, which leads to the emergence of its Buddhahood perfection. These pure perceptions and conceptions are systematically cultivated by the yoga of visualization. A developed "pure perception" and a "Buddha-self-image" open the door to the outer world of great bliss, where all beings are fulfilled, and to the inner "diamond self of selflessness," which is great compassion *actually become able* to help all beings, through perfect mastery of the cosmic situation. This pattern of the imaginative conversion of death, between, and life to the Three Buddha Bodies is clearly evident in the *Natural Liberation* in the *Three Body Mentor Yoga*, there presented in the form of a prayer.

*The Dharma Practice, Natural Liberation of the Instincts* (see chapter 7, page 205), is the closest thing in this literature to a creation stage practice, through the archetypal Buddha-deities visualized in miniature mandala patterns in the body of the practitioner, in what is called a "body mandala" pattern. An arrangement of the Buddha-deities in a large-scale mandala environment appropriate for the *Book of Natural Liberation* is not given in the literature available to me. However, based on the *Dharma Practice,* I can construct a standard creation stage practice for the hundred Buddha-deities of the *Natural Liberation,* in order to give an idea of how to cultivate in practice a greater familiarity with the symbolism of the *Natural Liberation.*

You sit upon your meditation seat, before an icon of any or all of the hundred Buddha-deities, or of the prime Buddha Samantabhadra, or of the original mentor Padma Sambhava. You set up a modest altar for symbolic offerings, using little bowls of water, flowers, votive candles, and incense. You place before you a vajra scepter and a vajra bell, and whatever other implements you may need. You visualize the entire lineage of Buddhas and mentors as present in the imagined sky before you, from Samantabhadra (All-around Goodness), Amitabha, and Padma Sambhava, right down through history to your own personal mentor. You take refuge in them, invite the hundred Buddha-deities, request them to stay with you, salute them, make offerings to them, confess your sins and faults, rejoice in the merit of all others, request the teachings from the Buddhas and mentors, request the teachers not to depart into nirvana, and dedicate the merit of your practice to the ultimate enlightenment of all beings.

Next you visualize yourself emerging from the truth realm as the Buddha Vajrasattva, white in complexion, with two arms and peaceful mien, adorned in royal garb and jewel ornaments, as described in the *Dharma Practice.* You then recite the hundred-syllable purification mantra—OM VAJRASATTVA SAMAYA . . . —and so on, 21 or 108 times (see chapter 7). This mantra recitation is believed to have the greatest power to purify sins and remove emotional and intellectual obscurations. Up to here, these ten branches of preliminary practice follow the *Dharma Practice* closely. Now, we must interpolate some sequences standard for creation stage practice, before continuing with the *Dharma Practice*'s body mandala.

You then invite all mentors and Buddha-deities to merge with you, and you yourself dissolve into absolute voidness. You pronounce the mantra OM SHUNYATA JNANA VAJRA SVABHAVA ATMAKO HAM! (OM, I am the essence of the intuition of voidness). From that void you visualize the emergence of a perfect universe, in the center of which towers a measureless mansion made of five jewel substances, radiant with jewel light. Within it you arise as indivisible with the Three Bodies of Buddhahood, as the central deity of the mandala, Samantab-

hadra in union with your consort, your archetypal male or female counterpart. You then dissolve as Samantabhadra and arise as Buddha
Vairochana in union with your consort, as depicted in the *Dharma
Practice*. One by one you visualize the Buddhas of the four directions,
their Buddha-goddess consorts, their attendant Bodhisattvas, their door
guardians, all surrounded by the hosts of Buddha-deities. Once you
imagine this whole community present within the mandala palace, you
invite the real Buddha-deities to send "wisdom-being" duplicates from
their actual Buddha-lands, which merge within the icon you have imagined. Then you visualize yourself and all these deities as receiving con-
secrations from all the deities of the mandala, who are streaming around
you as a vast host of blessing. The overflow energy radiates out
from you as rays of blessings to all beings around you in the universe.
These beings are drawn into the mandala by the magnetic tractor-beam
jewel light rays of your great compassion, where they, too, become
consecrated, arise as Buddha-deities, and stream back outward to establish their own mandalas and bless beings infinitely throughout the
universe.

You then dissolve again into the Body of Truth and arise again,
now with your body itself containing two measureless mansions within
it: one at the level of the heart, with forty-two lotus-moon-sun disc
seats, and one at the level of the brain, with fifty-eight solar discs. In
those mansions you visualize the hundred deities as radiantly present,
being your own emotions, instincts, and genetic energies manifest in
microdivinity form.

From here you can follow the visualization text of the *Dharma
Practice*. You visualize each of the deities mentioned in that text, and
you see it take its place in your body. At the end of the visualization,
you pray that it will emerge during your future voyage through the
between to conduct you to liberation, which really means to return you
to the deepest essential reality of yourself. At first this visualization process will seem extremely cumbersome and confusing and frustrating,
but persistent, careful repetition will make it seem more and more familiar, until after a few months of practice with the proper guidance
from your personal mentor, you will feel quite at home with it. It is
mandatory that you consult works of art—any of the exquisite Tibetan
tangka icons that depict these hundred Buddha-deities of the *Natural
Liberation* between-mandala—as it is too difficult to visualize them just
from verbal, linear descriptions.

Finally, this creation stage pattern could be used by non-Buddhist
practitioners who seek to mobilize the Tibetan art of dying to prepare
for their own between-transition, while deepening their sense of contact

with the images and deities of their own religion. The specific pattern should be designed to suit the individual imagery. But the Tibetan sequence could be helpful: an invocation of the deity or deities, the angelic figures, and the lineage of great patriarchs of your tradition; a merging with you of these symbols of benevolence and power; a channeling of the benevolence through you toward all others; a locking in of the sense of the presence of the divine within every aspect of the body, the mind, and the ordinary world; a focus on the sense of complete calm in the divine reality of peace and love; a prayer for the deities chosen to appear to you at the beginning of the between; and finally a dissolving of the purified universe within a renewed ordinary, but fortified, person and reality.

## THE PERFECTION STAGE

The creation stage imaginative manipulation of the jewel plasma of Buddha forms continues in extravagant detail, getting ever more subtle, until it reaches a point where one becomes capable of visualizing the entire mandala palace and occupants as contained within a shining drop at the tip of the nose, heart center, or genitals, and of holding that precise hologram stable for several hours. At that point, one is ideally ready for the perfection stage yogas. The creation stage meditation sessions always end with the dissolution of whatever visionary realms have been created into the clear light of universal emptiness. They also rehearse at a certain point, in the process of offerings, the experience of the four ecstasies, which are offered to all the assembled Buddha-deities. These ecstasies are central in the perfection stage, and will be briefly described below.

The perfection stage can be approached as having five stages, though there are various ways of arranging them. These stages are called: one, body isolation, isolation of the body from all impurity of ordinariness; two, vajra repetition, isolation of speech from the ordinary by the unification of energy-wind and mantra; three, mind isolation or self-consecration, full dissolution of all energies and structures of consciousness into the central channel and arisal of the subtle energy-body as the magic body; four, clear light, repeated voyaging of the magic body through the clear light reality, which deepens the experience of nonduality; and five, integration, perfect Buddhahood as the indivisibility of clear light Body of Truth, magic body Body of Beatitude, and the former ordinary body as Body of Emanation.

There are numerous Tantras used in the different Tibetan Buddhist orders, all inherited from the creative pioneer work of the great adepts of India. Each one has its own way of understanding and expressing the path, the creation stages, the perfection stages, and the final goal itself, Buddhahood. All these Tantras emerge from the same path of transcendent renunciation, the enlightenment spirit of universal love, and the wisdom of selfless voidness. All of them accelerate the deepening of wisdom and the development of compassionate evolution to make possible the achievement of Buddhahood within the single well-endowed human lifetime. All of them employ the imagination to approximate the goal state and reach it more quickly. All of them mobilize the subtle mind as great bliss wisdom to realize ultimate reality and shape its energies for the happiness of all beings. That they present the process of achieving this one goal of supreme integration of Buddhahood variously as Great Perfection, Great Seal, bliss-void indivisible, and so on is a difference of conceptual scheme and terminology, not a difference of the path or its fruition.

The creation stage terminates in a preliminary form of "body isolation," which occurs when your body becomes isolated from all ordinary appearances and self-images. You actually experience yourself as the deity, feeling as yours the faces and eyes and arms—just as you sense your ordinary body now—perhaps with other miniature Buddha-deities located at vital points throughout your body, in some form of body mandala. This is still a gross level, though blissful, of body perception. Body isolation enters the perfection stage realm when the discrete sense of a gross body is transcended, when every atom of every part of the body and senses is experienced as a Buddha-deity in an explosion of visualization beyond the organizing capacities of the gross imagination. The model of the body is no longer anthropomorphic, the subtle body being perceived as nerve channels, neural wind-energies, and subtle drops. The mind is the subtle instinctual consciousness of the three luminances, as already sketched above, along with the system of nerve centers, winds, and drops.

The mandala palace and deity body visualizations are gross imagination patternings, which are intended indirectly to open up internal sensitivities in the subtle body-mind. The perfection stage consciously pursues this internal opening process. To refer back to the scheme of the gross and subtle body-mind described above (see page 35), the neural wind-energies are enumerated as tenfold: five main energies—vital, respiratory, digestive, muscular-motor, and evacuative—and five branch energies that power the five senses. These are now perceived as Buddha-deities. The drops of subtle structure are the male hormonal essence as in semen, the female hormonal essence as in ovum, called white and red "spirits of enlightenment," respectively. The extremely subtle mind of the indestructible drop is locked in the center of the heart center section of the central channel. This is the ultimately subtle "self" of selflessness, the ultimate subjectivity of innate ecstasy that realizes the objective clear light of universal emptiness, already discussed above. The extremely subtle body is the energy within this drop, although at this level of fineness there is no longer any body-mind, or even subject-object, dichotomy.

Through various focusing techniques used in the body-isolation perfection stage, you reach a point of stabilized concentration, where you can rehearse the process normally experienced only at the time of physical death. Respiration becomes shallow and then stops entirely. You experience the four stages of melting, of earth into water, water into fire, fire into air, and air into gross consciousness (identified with space in some systems), accompanied by the subjective signs called "mirage," "smoke," "fireflies," and "candle flame" (see page 42). This practice must be based on a fully stable Buddha-confidence—an imaginatively cultivated Buddha-self-image—and purified perception, isolated from all ordinariness. Otherwise, the involuntary terror and unconscious resistance to death will disrupt the delicate neurological poise required for you to traverse the dissolutions.

Next, your gross consciousness dissolves into your subtle consciousness, which is composed of the eighty natural instincts. These are the subtle, instinctual potentialities, rather than gross emotions, that obstruct the three intuitions known as luminance, radiance, and imminence (see page 40). The fourth state is the extremely subtle mind, clear light, or transparency. The subjective signs of the progressive dissolving of one state into another are called "moonlit sky," "sunlit sky," "pitch-dark sky," and "predawn sky."

Great stability is required throughout this process, since the instincts swirl around as they dissolve, and there is danger of becoming unsettled by identifying with them. The dissolution of gross consciousness through luminance intuitions into clear light is accompanied by entrance of all the wind energies into the central channel. They carry with them all the white and red life-drops, withdrawn from the outer nerves and the left and right channels, entering the central channel usually through the midbrow aperture up into the brain center. If you were not carefully prepared by initiation, instruction, and practice, you would actually die at this point, and your vital energies would leave the gross body, once your normally closed central channel was opened. But because the knots around your central channel have been carefully untangled ahead of time, you easily avoid this danger, and the subjective

**Figure 11. Movement of energy through the subtle body**

| Subtle Body Movement | Ecstasy | Voidness | Reverse Movement |
| --- | --- | --- | --- |
| brain to throat | ecstasy | voidness | genital to navel |
| throat to heart | supreme | extreme | navel to heart |
| heart to navel | intense | great | heart to throat |
| navel to genital | orgasmic | universal | throat to brain |

death experience becomes your doorway to the opening of the inner bliss-world of enlightenment.

Within the stable subjective sense of being a subtle body of channels and centers, energies, and drops, you concentrate all your energy at the navel center, on a red-hot seed syllable visualized there with great vividness and stability. Heat blazes from it and shoots up the central channel. When the consciousness-structuring drops melt down from the brain center and permeate the throat center, you experience ecstasy and voidness. When they melt further and descend to the heart center, you experience supreme ecstasy and extreme voidness. When they reach the navel center, you experience intense ecstasy and great voidness. When they reach the genital center, you experience orgasmic ecstasy and universal voidness. You are immersed in the clear light, here called the metaphoric clear light. You then experience the four ecstasies and four voidnesses in the reverse order, as the energies and drops move back up gradually through navel, heart, throat, and brain centers, where reverse order orgasmic ecstasy merges with universal emptiness a second time. The four ecstasies are summarized in figure 11.

After enjoying these first tastes of orgasmic ecstasy and universal voidness clear light, you rearise through the three stages, experiencing the eight signs—predawn sky and so on—in the reverse order. The energies then emerge from the central channel and circulate in the gross body, which you experience as if being reincarnated in your old body, entering it from the top of your head.

This attainment is still far from total Buddhahood, since although the central channel has been opened, it is still constricted here and there, especially in the heart center, which has prevented the internally orgasmic permeation process of drops and energies from reaching the intensity needed to embody the highest wisdom of total Buddhahood. So you begin the next stage, the stage of vajra repetition, with the precise aim of unraveling the heart-center knot, through which right and left channels constrict the central nexus of the whole system and imprison the extremely subtle body-mind.

It has seemed to most scholars of this subject that the opening of the central channel is a single event; once it's open, it's open, so to speak. It has been hard to distinguish between Hindu kundalini yoga, Taoist energy yogas, and the Buddhist Tantric yogas. The fact is that the opening of the central channel, like any surgical operation (the scalpel in this case being critical wisdom coordinated with creative imagination), can be more or less complete. There are numerous ecstatic experiences, which affect the central nervous system in a variety of ways.

The vajra-recitation practice cultivates the transcendence of the ordinariness of time, as the body isolation transcended ordinariness of space. The root of time is respiration, and so the wind energies are united with mantras, especially OM AH HUM, the vajras, or diamonds, of body, speech, and mind. The other wind energies are perceived as Buddha-deities, and this is cultivated in an extremely refined meditative technique until you become a living OM AH HUM, alone in the center of an empty universe. When complete concentration develops in this way, the normal respiration ceases, and the dissolution process outlined above ensues, with the difference that the four ecstasies and four voidnesses occur when the energies and drops in the central channel penetrate the central chambers of the heart center in a certain sequence.

The opening of the heart center is a delicate untangling process, highly dangerous if forced, and therefore the vajra recitation can take many years for even the most capable yogi or yogini. Its goal is reached when all impediments in the heart center are gone, and the dissolutions can lead to the orgasmic ecstasy that engages the indestructible consciousness-energy drop in the center of the heart. This is then called the "mind isolation," as the mind is isolated from any nonexperience of great bliss. The subtlest mind becomes the mind of great bliss, which becomes the ultimate subjectivity for the cognition of the still metaphoric clear light of universal voidness or of selflessness.

This achievement of mind isolation is a deeper form of orgasmic ecstasy, of universal voidness clear-light samadhi. You then arise in the subtle magic body with the signs and marks of Buddhahood. This magic body is made of pure neural energy flashing up from the clear light. It is like the between-body, and like the body you have when you arise in a dream, its eyes are like the eyes you see with in the dream, its ears and other senses like the between or dream senses. If you choose, although you no longer involuntarily need to reenter your ordinary gross body, you may, for the benefit of beings, reactivate that body. Subsequently, when you fall asleep, you enter the clear light automatically.

When you dream, you arise in the sleep Beatific Body. When your dream body returns and you wake, you experience it as the sleep Emanation Body. If you decide to leave your ordinary body due to some circumstance, you will employ the dissolution and arisal processes to achieve the death Body of Truth, the between Body of Beatitude, and the reincarnation Body of Emanation.

Self-consecration proceeds from mind isolation's opening of the heart-knot, which brings the extremely subtle body-mind of the indestructible drop into play as the ultimate subjectivity of orgasmic ecstasy for the ultimate objectivity of the clear light. The practice proceeds with the inner condition of the dissolution-compression process and the outer conditions of union with a consort. Respiration ceases, the eight signs emerge, the emergent and reverse orders of four ecstasies and four voidnesses are experienced. Now, when resurrection from the clear light occurs, the subtlest subjectivity controls the neural energies as the fivefold rainbow light rays of the five Buddha-wisdoms and shapes them into the actual magic body. It is technically called "impure" at this stage, and is described by five similes: dream body, Vajrasattva's mirror image, moon in water, phantom, and bubble. It is a dream body, in that it exists as if apart from the gross body, emerging from it yet reentering it. It is like Vajrasattva's mirror image in that it appears with the hundred-and-twelve superhuman signs. It is like the moon in water in that the one moon appears wherever there is a body of water to reflect it, as the magic body manifests wherever beings need it. It is like a phantom in that it appears substantial yet lacks any substantiality. And it is like a bubble in that it irrepressibly bubbles forth from the clear light ground.

The fourth stage, clear light, ensues after six to eighteen months of practice of the third stage of magic body. You constantly immerse yourself in clear light, returning to your gross body, teaching beings, developing the field of beings in society, and so forth. The depth of the immersion increases, and finally you reach the actual, objective clear light, no longer the metaphoric clear light. In the objective clear light, your third stage magic body merges like a rainbow fading in the sky, attaining the irresistible path that directly remedies addictive obscurations. You have the usual series of ecstasies and voidnesses. At the moment of emerging from the objective clear light into the reverse-order imminence intuition, you become a saint, gain the pure magic body, gain the liberation path abandoning the emotional obscurations, and achieve the learner's integration.

The fifth stage, integration, is accomplished after further immersion practice conquers the intellectual obscurations, the obstructions of omniscience that prevent even the highest Bodhisattva from understanding perfectly all the levels of causality of the superficial worlds of living beings, hence impede his or her mastery of liberative art. This integration is the integration of the pure magic body, the perfection of compassion as orgasmic ecstasy, with the objective clear light, the perfection of wisdom as universal voidness intuition. The great Indian adept Nagarjuna's *The Five Stages* describes integration (my translation):

> Abandoning the two notions of the samsaric life-cycle and the nirvanic liberation, there, where they become the same, that is called "integration." Knowing the addictive and the purificative both as the absolute itself; who knows them as just the same, knows this integration. Knowing wisdom and compassion as the same, who acts in such a way is said to have attained integration. Freedom from the two notions of subjective selflessness and objective selflessness is the nature of integration. Free from mindfulness and carelessness, having a constantly spontaneous character, the yogi who acts as he pleases abides in the stage of integration. . . . The perfectly pure deity and this so-called "imperfection," who understands them as inseparable, he is the integrated one. . . . Thus, the yogi who abides in such a place abides in the stage of integration. He sees the reality of omniscience, and is called the "upholder of variety." Buddhas quite as numerous as the sands of the Ganges realized this very thing and, abandoning being and nothing, attained the essence of the Great Seal. So knowing, the intuitive one does everything without hesitation, achieving all by the hidden discipline, attaining all perfections. By the merit gained from teaching this supreme fifth stage, may the whole world sport in this samadhi of integration!

These processes of perfection stage yoga are breathtaking. This sketch would never enable you to practice them in any way. The point of providing it is to let you know what remarkable arts are available to prepare for every possible contingency of death, between, and life. It inspires us to master the possibilities, if not in this life, in another.

The *Natural Liberation Through Understanding in the Between* does not, at least in the texts provided in the usual collection, provide instruction in the complete perfection stage. The great world of Great Perfection, describing the culminatory realities of the fourth and fifth stages, is given as a goal. And the newly deceased adept Lamas are given the brief instruction that they should practice the teachings they have mastered and they will be liberated in the death-point beginning of the reality between. But the *Book of Natural Liberation* is mainly aimed at those of us unable to reach the heights of the psychonauts.

On the other hand, there is a way in which all the aspects of these perfection stages are subtly available to the audience of the *Book of Natural Liberation*. The between is after all a time of crisis after death, when the soul (the very subtle mind-body) is in its most highly fluid state. Naturally much of the art of Tantra is designed to work with precisely that totally transformable subtle state. If the good person, who has a strong momentum of good evolutionary action, is unprepared for the between, he or she can lose an enormous amount of evolutionary progress in the twinkling of an eye by becoming frightened and hiding in darkness. Similarly, a bad person, who has a great weight of negative evolution, if well prepared for the between, can overcome immense eons of wretched lives by bravely shooting for the light. After all, a tiny achievement on the subtle plane can have a powerful impact on the gross. The soul in the between can directly modify, just with creative imagination, what the Buddhists call "the spiritual genes" it carries with it. The between voyager has temporarily an immensely heightened intelligence, extraordinary powers of concentration, special abilities of clairvoyance and teleportation, flexibility to become whatever can be imagined, and the openness to be radically transformed by a thought or a vision or an instruction. This is indeed why the between-traveler can become instantly liberated just by understanding where he or she is in the between, what the reality is, where the allies are, and where the dangers. So, no matter how advanced the perfection stages and Great Perfection may seem to those of us embedded in the pursuits of ordinary life, beings in the crisis of the between would do well at least to know about it from study. This surely underlies Master Padma Sambhava's intention in composing this unique work, which, without compromising esoteric strictures, communicates the perfection stage possibilities to the ordinary people of Tibetan society, as the Tibetan lamas do today to us ordinary people in global society.

It is hard to make suggestions about how a non-Buddhist yogi or yogini might learn about the perfection stages and design parallel processes that fit with his or her worldview. There are certainly adept traditions in all the great literate and earth religions, and all of these certainly deal with the basic realities of life and death. The genuine shaman knows of the dissolution process, knows of divine allies and demonic interferences, and usually finds a ground of benevolence and trust, some sort of Lord of Compassion. The monastics of all ages have experimented with journeys of the soul, and some have lived to recount their experiences in useful works. Sufi and Taoist adepts have given instructions and maintain living traditions. The Tibetan tradition can be used by any seeker in any of these traditions for its systematic technologies and its penetrating insight.

# CHAPTER 4

# THE
# NATURAL
# LIBERATION
# LITERATURE

## THE HISTORY OF THE TEXTS

According to the texts themselves, the *Book of Natural Liberation Through Understanding in the Between* was composed by the great adept Padma Sambhava, and dictated by him to his Tibetan consort, the yogini Yeshe Tsogyal. It was probably written in the late eighth century C.E. Padma Sambhava is a semilegendary figure, whose mythical biography contains some episodes similar to the life of Buddha Shakyamuni and others similar to those of the eighty-four great adepts. Padma Sambhava's name is one of the root mantras of the fierce form of Avalokiteshvara, the horse-head-crowned Hayagriva. (Fierce deities are still compassionate, but in a "tough-love" way.) Padma Sambhava is said to have issued from the tongue of Amitabha Buddha in the western Pure Land of Bliss in the form of a rainbow-trailing meteor. This was Amitabha's answer to an appeal from Bodhisattva Avalokiteshvara to do something more for beings on earth in the kingdom of Udyana, who were about to suffer a catastrophe due to the frustration of their king, who could not beget an heir. The meteor raced to earth and plunged into a lotus lake in a pleasant valley in the northwest Indian subcontinent, in what is now Pakistan. Where it landed a giant lotus grew, within which, in due time, a beautiful boy was seen sitting in the midst of rainbow auras. When asked his origin, he said, "My mother is wisdom, my father compassion, my country the Dharma of reality."

Padma Sambhava is something like the Tibetan Superman. He is the great adept's adept. He is an Emanation Body Buddha, able to teach about the between because he can travel through it at will himself. After living for centuries in India accomplishing beneficial wonders, he went to Tibet at the invitation of emperor Trisong Detsen, to help him and the Indian abbot and philosopher Shantarakshita build the first monastery ever to take root in that warlike land. He tamed many demons in Tibet, gave many teachings, including the *Natural Liberation*, and eventually disappeared to his own paradise on earth, the Copper Glory Mountain, which is somewhere in Africa or Arabia. He still lives there, according to Tibetan mythic vision.

Anticipating the great persecution of the ninth century that was to destroy much of early Tibetan Buddhism, Padma Sambhava hid numerous texts throughout Tibet, including the *Book of Natural Liberation*. After the eventual restoration, traditions of spiritual "treasure-discoverers" (Tib., *tertoen*) emerged, who exhibited extraordinary powers of clairvoyance, including X-ray vision. They were often thought to be reincarnations of aspects of Padma Sambhava himself, or of his twenty-five major tantric disciples. There are numerous accounts of their finding texts in caves high on cliffs, underground, in rocks and trees. Sometimes they found treasures in their minds, hidden there by the master during their former lives, sealed in the memory codes of their spiritual genes, and discovered at the right moment when people had need of them in some later life and century. This tradition was in keeping with ancient Indian Buddhist precedent, especially in the world of the great adepts. After all, the entire Universal Vehicle sutra and Tantra collection itself was believed to have been discovered during the first century B.C.E. by the adept Nagarjuna, in the palace of the dragon king at the bottom of the Indian Ocean!

A famous treasure discoverer of the fourteenth century was called Karma Lingpa. He is claimed by some to have been an incarnation of Padma Sambhava himself. He discovered the *Book of Natural Liberation* collection in a cave on the Gampo Dar mountain in central Tibet. There have been numerous disputes, in Tibet as well as in the West, about the authenticity of such "treasure-teachings." These disagreements are not very important for us, since the best way to judge a text such as the *Book of Natural Liberation* is by its content, not by its cover. If its content contradicts the mainstream of the Buddhist tradition, if it seems incoherent, if it seems ill-founded, and so forth, then it can be dismissed as a crude fabrication. If its content is in keeping with the Buddhist intellectual, psychological, and spiritual tradition, if it is reasonably presented, lucid, meaningful, and useful, then it should be accepted as an authentic Buddhist teaching, an authentic treatise of Buddhist science and a testament of Buddhist faith. Once that is established, if the tradition itself claims it was authored by Padma Sambhava, then we might as well accept that too.

As for exactly who Padma Sambhava was—was he really a spiritual

Superman, is he still alive, and so on—we do not need to pass judgment on these articles of religious faith in order to study and use the text. Naturally, we moderns are not predisposed to expect such things to be true; though secretly, most of us are still hoping.

What is relevant, though, is why Karma Lingpa discovered the text when he did. The fourteenth century saw a great spiritual, institutional, and social renaissance in Tibet, generated by the many outstanding lamas of the Kadam, Sakya, Kagyu, and Nyingma orders, and culminating in the great synthesis achieved by Lama Jey Tsong Khapa around the year 1400 C.E. All these lamas were scholars, saints, scientists, and psychonaut explorers. A great many of them are believed to have attained the ability of what we can call "lucid dying." They had practiced the perfection stage yogas we have outlined during a lifetime of total focus on enlightenment and had achieved success in the inner moonwalks, sun-shots, and ultimate-clear-light-shots of that yoga—every bit as challenging and significant as the outer moon-walks of our astronauts! Thus when they died, they often manifested wondrous signs to those left behind, they maintained their own conscious continua of awareness, and they used the death occasion to enjoy and solidify their attainment of the Three Bodies of Buddhahood. On top of all that, they consciously chose to reemanate from the clear light foundational reality to take reincarnation in the meeting of parental genes in the womb of a Tibetan mother. They gave clues to their followers as to where to find them. They spoke up as small children and demanded to be returned to their home monasteries and circles of disciples. And they used life after life to develop their own enlightenment abilities, to develop those fortunate enough to be their disciples, and to continue to develop Tibetan, Himalayan, Mongolian, Manchurian, and Chinese societies toward fully enlightenment-oriented human civilizations. These lama adepts became so successful and commonly accepted that Tibetans became accustomed to the presence of many reincarnations, so much so that they almost refused to accept the spiritual authority of any lama who was not working through his or her third or seventh or eleventh enlightened life. These lamas were the most advanced research scientists, the most charismatic holy men and women, the most respected social leaders, and the most beloved members of Tibetan society.

Thus the era of the fourteenth century was ripe for teachings to emerge that made the death-rebirth transition plain and clear to the wider society. The fact and phenomena of the between had long been known and fully described in the vast sutra collection and its commentarial literature, translated from Sanskrit during the first five centuries of Tibetan Buddhism. The technologies of traversing the between, such as those taught in the *Book of Natural Liberation,* had long been available in the vast literature of the Tantras. The original collections of basic Tantras and their Indian commentaries by the great adepts formed a total of several hundred 2000-page volumes of works (in English translation equivalent) translated from Indian language originals. A rich Tibetan secondary literature was rapidly proliferating, created by the hundreds of thousands of Tibetan scholars and adepts educated in the thousands of monastic universities of all the orders established during these centuries of renaissance.

So the time had come for a treasure-discoverer to unearth another jewel in the fabulous legacy of the lotus-born Master Padma Sambhava. Totally appropriate to this circumstance, a work was discovered that used the mandala, or purified universe, of the *Guhyagarbha (Esoteric Quintessence) Tantra,* one of the most important "old" (that is, translated into Tibetan in the early period of the eighth and ninth centuries) Tantras. This mandala transmuted the ordinary human world into a perfected environment of exalted happiness inhabited by a community of a hundred mild and fierce archetypal Buddha-deities, who represented the elements of human psychophysical existence in their fully evolved form. These deities were forms expressing their complete freedom from any coerced experience, complete happiness in their chosen functions, and complete capability to share their happiness with all others, according to those others' capacity to participate in that sharing. They serve as the templates for the goal of human evolution, and so they are archetypes for the enlightened fruition of all human physical and spiritual energies. This mandala had long been used by adepts for their own creative and transcendent meditations.

The special contribution of this discovered work, then, was the expansion of access to the mandalic world of these contemplative archetypes. The ordinary person who had not received lifelong education at a monastic university and had not had ability, preparation, opportunity, and support to spend years in concentrated practice was able to encounter this hundred-deity mandalic community of her own perfected energies in the time of crisis when she needed it most—at the time of her death and after-death transition. Although the teaching urged her in direct and indirect ways not to wait for that critical juncture, it reached out to her anyway, not requiring initiation or study. It let her know that her intelligence for the understanding of reality, her power of vision, opportunity for independent choice, responsibility for far-reaching beneficence, and readiness for transformation were about to be temporarily boosted ninefold, during the between experience. It offered her immediate access to the highest technology of between-space travel, freely and easily. It allowed her, and family and friends, to have a much better sense of what the psychonauts had been through, what they had faced, and what they had achieved. This, at the very least, enabled her and her associates to increase their faith in the psychonaut lamas, be more open to receiving their help, be more alert on the lookout for their appearance as guides and allies during the difficulties of the between voyage.

Naturally the discovered treasure text was highly appreciated in renaissance Tibet. It was copied and printed from the fifteenth century on, disseminated widely, and widely imitated. Parallel treatises were composed, adding dimensions from lore contained elsewhere in the texts and in the received oral traditions of all four orders. These treatises developed in a wide variety. On the popular level, there are amulet texts, which list protective prayers and diagrams to be printed, tightly wound, and placed into metal amulets to be worn by living or dying persons. There are icon texts, which are themselves icons of Buddha's speech that were used as objects of worship. There are protection mantra texts, which list long and short mantras to be memorized and recited. At the more elite level, there are technical manuals for soul-transmission practices, which instruct adepts in practices for consciously leaving the body. There have been ever more streamlined archetype mandala patterns, refining visualization methods and making them more memorable and efficacious. And there have been ever more explicit contemplative instructions, incorporating new ideas and more sophisticated techniques garnered from the experiences of new generations of adept practitioners.

## THE SECTIONS OF THE BOOK

As might be expected, although the text has become more or less fixed over the centuries, it seems to vary somewhat in different recensions. The *Natural Liberation* collections themselves usually intimate that there are more works in the group than are included in a particular edition. The best organized collection I have so far encountered has the following table of contents, ordered according to the Tibetan alphabet:

Index of works concerning the *Natural Liberation Through Understanding,* from the *Profound Teaching, Natural Liberation Through Contemplating the Mild and Fierce Deities* (1 folio)

**ka.** *The Prayer of the Three Buddha Body Mentor Yoga* from the *Natural Liberation Without Abandoning the Three Poisons* (3 folios)

**kha.** *Prayer of the Reality Between* from the *Natural Liberation Through Understanding* (36 ff)

**ga.** *Way of Arisal of the Fierce Deity Between* (21 ff)

**nga.** *Prayer of Calling for Help from Buddhas and Bodhisattvas* (3 ff)

**ca.** *Root Verses of the Six Betweens* (3 ff)

**cha.** *Prayer for Deliverance from the Straits of the Between* (4 ff)

**ja.** *Orientation for the Existence Between* from the *Great Liberation Through Understanding* (35 ff)

**nya.** *Liberation by Wearing, Natural Liberation of the Body* (24 ff)

**ta.** *The Prayer for Refuge from All Terrors of the Between* (3 ff)

**tha.** *The Dharma Practice, Natural Liberation of the Instincts* (26 ff)

**da.** *The Hundred Homages, Natural Liberation from Sins and Obscurations* (15 ff)

**na.** *The Vast of the Mild and Fierce, The Confession Natural Liberation* (24 ff)

**pa.** *The Natural Liberation Through Naked Vision, Identifying the Intelligence* (15 ff)

**pha.** *Natural Liberation Through Signs, Investigating Death* (25 ff)

**ba.** *Cheating Death, The Natural Liberation from Fear* (11 ff)

**ma.** *The Instruction Teaching the Natural Form of Virtue and Vice in the Existence Between, The Existence Between Natural Liberation* (18 ff)

**tsa.** *Accessory Method of the Instruction Teaching the Natural Form of Virtue and Vice in the Existence Between* (8 ff)

*Total 275 folios, printed in India from the Shahatadara, the Great mNga sde, in the first day of the first month of 1985*

Of these 275 folios, our main text here consists of translations of 150 folios, 108 folios of the main text and 42 folios of preliminary prayers and appended practices. The 108 folios of the main text have been translated twice before, first by the Kazi Dawa-Samdup and W. H. Y. Evans-Wentz team, and later by the Chogyam Trungpa Rinpoche and Francesca Fremantle team. Of the two sections included here in Part Three, *The Dharma Practice, Natural Liberation of the Instincts* is previously untranslated. *The Natural Liberation Through Naked Vision, Identifying the Intelligence* was previously translated by W. H. Y. Evans-Wentz, and again by John M. Reynolds. Since it gives a sustained view of the philosophical underpinnings of the *Book of Natural Liberation,* I retranslated it from the Tibetan using my terminology and interpretation, to fit with the rest of the new translation. Of the remaining sections untranslated here, the "pha" section on the death signs has been translated by Glenn Mullin. The other sections will doubtless be translated in the future, when scholars produce more erudite versions for research.

In the spirit of the original treasure, which was intended by Master Padma Sambhava as a practical help for people in general, I have tried to present a popular, practical version of the *Book of Natural Liberation.* I have arranged the text in the way I thought would be most useful for those who are using it in regard to the actual occasion of death, either when they are approaching their own death or when someone near them is dying. I have placed the all-important prayers in a beginning section (in the order mentioned in the preliminaries section of the reality between), since according to the instructions they must be recited at the outset anyway. Then I present the three betweens—the death-point, reality, and existence betweens—distinguishing by bold typeface those sections that should actually be read aloud in the presence of the dead. The sections of the translation are ordered as follows:

A PRELIMINARY SECTION OF PRAYERS
 *Three Body Mentor Yoga*
 *Help from the Buddhas and Bodhisattvas*
 *Deliverance from the Straits of the Between*
 *Refuge from All Terrors of the Between*
 *Root Verses of the Six Betweens*

THE GUIDEBOOK TO THE BETWEENS
 *Preliminaries*
 *The death-point between*
 *The mild deity reality between*
 *The fierce deity reality between*
 *The existence between*

SUPPLEMENTARY TRANSLATIONS
 *The Dharma Practice, Natural Liberation of the Instincts*
 *The Natural Liberation Through Naked Vision, Identifying the Intelligence*

Both the Tibetan editions I had to work with are somewhat rough and unpolished, as is usual for popular texts. Misprints are frequent, spellings are irregular, and the two texts sometimes differ in their readings in small ways. A useful scholarly enterprise would be to gather a large number of *Book of Natural Liberation* editions and prepare a critical edition. I have not done this, and have not burdened the text with cumbersome footnotes giving variant readings in the editions that I have. The dead and the bereaved are not in the mood for such scholarly niceties. I have used Sanskrit names for deities wherever possible, using a phonetically obvious transliteration system. Their names were originally given in Indian languages, which the Tibetans translated into Tibetan, since the Indo-European diphthongs and consonant clusters were difficult for them to pronounce. English is an Indo-European language and finds the Indian names more congenial.

I have already given an elucidation of the main background concepts I think you will need. I also provide a running commentary to the translation, distinguished from the translation by its smaller print. Unfamiliar terms are footnoted at the first occurrence, and otherwise can be looked up in the glossary.

As I conclude this work, I am struck by the preoccupation with euthanasia among the terminally ill and elderly in America. It is clear that the *Book of Natural Liberation* deplores suicide unless the person has already attained liberation, or is confident he or she can do so in the between. Suicide is the negative evolutionary action of taking life. For a Tantric practitioner, it is deicide, since the body is itself a deity body, and is the abode of numerous micro deities. On the other hand, people are trying to become less passive about their suffering, trying to assert some control over their lives by asserting control over their deaths. They are finally growing up to the fact that authorities have limited knowledge and ability. They are waking up to the fact that the quality of living is more important than the raw quantity of time involved. And they are bravely making their own decisions.

Unfortunately, those who consider themselves terminal in some disease and in pain, who may have used the suicide manual or contemplate doing so, most likely believe that destroying their brains is itself the achievement of "instant liberation" pictured as total oblivion. This will turn out to have been a tragic miscalculation for some of them. There are surely those who are habitually happy and cheerful people, kind and generous and able to let go without much trouble, who will manage to recognize the brighter light and merge with it, in spite of their surprise at not finding oblivion and even without formal preparation. But there will also be those who are more tense and rigid, who try to keep control at all costs, unless they have a guarantee of nothingness, who are very attached to their bodies, their possessions, their identities, their comforts. These people will really suffer in the maelstrom of the between and will have poor chances of coming out well, in a good position on the wheel of possibilities, much less of attaining liberation.

So I hope that at least some of these people, or their loved ones and friends, find this book, this *Great Book of Natural Liberation Through Understanding in the Between,* and try to put it to use, even along the lines of Pascal's wager. I hope the work will be of benefit to them. If it helps even one, it will fulfill the aim of Master Padma Sambhava and his colleagues, and my effort will have been worthwhile.

*May all beings be blessed by the Three Jewels!*
*May the planet be at peace, and the earth stay beautiful!*
*May all beings be happy!*
*May all have good fortune!*

PART
TWO

# THE
# GUIDEBOOK
# FOR THE
# JOURNEY

*The Great Book of Natural Liberation
Through Understanding in the Between*

The whole collection of treasure texts hidden by
Padma Sambhava in Tibet in the eighth century
C.E. is called *The Natural Liberation Through
Contemplating the Buddhas Mild and Fierce.*
Among them, *The Great Book of Natural
Liberation Through Understanding in the Between*
includes the set of texts we are presenting here.

It was composed by Padma Sambhava (the great
adept from Udyana), written down by his consort
Yeshe Tsogyal and hidden as a treasure. It was
discovered and invited out into the world from the
Gampo Dar mountain by the
great Treasure Finder Karma Lingpa.

# CHAPTER 5

# THE
# BETWEEN
# PRAYERS

The following five prayers and verses are the backbone of the entire *Book of Natural Liberation*. They are the core program of the whole process. They are meant to be memorized and then recited at different points while giving the longer instructions. First, the *Three Body Mentor Yoga* provides a meditation on the ideal transformation process envisaged by the *Book of Natural Liberation*. It brings that ideal close by focusing it through the person of the spiritual mentor, a person well known to, and revered by, the practitioner. The other four prayers form a set that is frequently referred to throughout the *Book of Natural Liberation*. The *Prayer for Help* is a straightforward prose appeal to the Three Jewels, the Buddha, the Dharma, and the Sangha, to extend their saving compassion to one who is dying or is in the process of the between. The *Prayer for Deliverance* follows the pattern of experiences in the reality between, praying for all the elements of ordinary existence to transform into agents of liberation. The *Prayer for Refuge* continues entreating the enlightened beings for assistance and protection. The emphasis is not so much on liberation as on refuge throughout future lives. It accords more with the existence between, when it is harder to achieve complete liberation and the concern is more with securing a favorable rebirth. The *Root Verses of the Six Betweens* provide a final summary of the six betweens, their contemplation transforming the entire cycle of time into a vehicle for enlightenment.

If you are using this book for someone who is in the process of dying or has already entered the between, it might be better to read the *Three Body Mentor Yoga* and the *Prayer for Help* to set up a favorable context, and then skip to the *Reality Between* itself, encountering the individual verses of the other prayers set in the context of the general instructions. In this entire translation section, boldface type indicates direct translations that are meant to be read aloud in the performance of the *Natural Liberation* for someone in the dying and between processes. Material set in ordinary type is in two sizes: the larger size indicates direct translations of the treasure text's original instructions and commentary, the smaller size indicates commentary and instructions by the translator.

# THE PRAYER OF
# THE THREE BODY MENTOR YOGA

I include this particular *Natural Liberation* prayer, subtitled *The Natural Liberation Without Abandoning the Three Poisons*, first. It is first in the original collection and it most concisely and beautifully establishes the context you need to use the subsequent Natural Liberations. The importance of the personal mentor relationship—reliance on a person who can represent to you the ultimate reality and power of the cosmos, however you define it—cannot be overstated.

A "mentor yoga" is a visualization meditation invoking the presence of the spiritual teacher who has initiated you into the sacred realm of your chosen form of Buddhahood. Once the presence has been invoked, the mentor is visualized as merging with you indivisibly, so that you become the teacher, the Buddha, the authority. Then you send out your blessing to all beings as the Buddha-mentor has given his blessing to you. Since most of us have not been initiated, we can think of this mentor as Padma Sambhava, the author of the *Book of Natural Liberation*. The Three Bodies of a Buddha are a way to think about the inconceivability of a perfect Buddha, expressing an enlightened being's oneness with ultimate reality, personal beatitude, and emanational creativity for the sake of others. The mentor should be visualized as an embodiment of these three aspects of ultimacy, so that you cultivate the feeling of grace when in the presence of the mentor. The mentor should be visualized in the imaginative space of the mind's eye before you, seated on a royal jewel throne of divine proportions, surrounded by all the Buddhas, deities, angels, and other powerful, wise, and beloved beings. If your personal mentor is a loved one, a priest or holy person of any religion, or a doctor, healer, or shaman, then visualize him or her accordingly.

The three poisons, greed, hate, and delusion, are the three primary addictions that drive the unenlightened, suffering-ridden life cycle. Liberation that occurs without eliminating them is truly natural, the immediate transformation of the Great Perfection teachings.

## OM—AV KAA AAH!

"OM" is the mantric, or magically creative, sound that resonates with transcendent oneness, and so is used at the beginning of mantras to invoke the transcendent or divine into manifestation. "AV KAA AAH" is more unusual. "AV" indicates voidness, the lack of rigid identity in all things and hence their malleability for the creative artistry of great compassion. "KAA" represents the "A" sound of cosmic creativity emerging from the "K" position of beginning, *k* being the first consonant. "AAH" is the mantra of enlightened speech.

To the unborn, nondeveloping, Truth Body Mentor,
In the palace of the perfect, all-pervading Realm of Truth,
With reverent devotion, ardently I pray!
Self-freed without abandoning misknowing delusion,
I freely accept the perfect Truth Body blessing,
As effortless, nonartificial, primal wisdom!

Here you focus on your mentor's oneness with absolute reality, feeling yourself united with that reality through the presence of your mentor. The instant you remember the infinity of the ultimate you feel the overwhelming flood of the grace of your own inseparability from the ultimate, recognizing that it is impossible for anything ever to have not been one with its irresistibly infinite presence. You instantly feel free, and even the mental addiction of delusion feels naturally transformed into the sense of the presence of the absolute, no longer needing to be abandoned. You visualize a deep blue sparkling sapphire HUM at the heart of your mentor. It radiates a sapphire blue light that enters your heart-center and fills it with the buoyant wisdom of freedom. This visualization sequence is associated with receiving the wisdom intuition initiation, practicing the perfection stage, the clear light transparency, the moment of death, the mind, and the Truth Body.

To the deathless, great bliss Beatific Body Mentor
In the palace of bright, pure wisdom's universal bliss,
With reverent devotion, ardently I pray!
Self-freed without abandoning lust and longing,
I freely accept the effortless Beatific Body blessing,
As the natural liberation of inner wisdom's universal bliss!

You focus on your mentor's ceaseless feeling of beatific bliss, noticing his or her smiling, loving look upon you. Instantly you feel flooded with the same joy and bliss of your oneness with the ultimate, articulated as your individual freedom and happiness, freed from any agitation of lust or longing for any supposed happiness outside of yourself. You visualize a bright ruby red AAH at the throat-center of your mentor, radiating brilliant rays of ruby light. These rays shine upon you and enter your own throat-center, blessing your speech with buoyant enlightened wisdom. This visualization is associated with receiving the secret initiation, attaining the magic body, the between, speech, and the Beatific Body.

To the ineffable, self-created Emanation Body Mentor,
In the palace of the flawless perfect lotus,
With reverent devotion, ardently I pray!
Self-freed without abandoning misconceiving hatred,
I freely accept the effortless Emanation Body blessing
As self-evident wisdom's introspective self-illumination!

Here you focus on your mentor's boundlessly creative artistry of emanating active embodiments of enlightenment to interact compassionately with other beings. Instantly you feel partnership in Lotus Clan activity of manifesting distinct embodiments of liberative art, freed from any agitation or irritation at the ugliness and intractability of the forms of life. You visualize a glistening diamond OM at the mentor's crown-center, radiating dazzling rays of white light that fill up your own brain-center. This visualization is associated with receiving the vase initiation, practicing the creation stage, life, the body, and the Emanation Body.

To the impartial great bliss Triple-Body Mentor,
In the palace of authentic clear light introspection,
With reverent devotion, ardently I pray!
Self-freed without abandoning subject-object dualism,
I freely accept the great bliss Triple Body blessing
As original wisdom's Triple Body spontaneity!

Here you focus on the mentor and yourself becoming indivisibly merged as the Absolute, Beatific, and Emanation Bodies of enlightenment in the Great Perfection spontaneity. Instantly you feel complete and perfect within yourself, integrating the infinity of the

Buddhaverse within you, freed from any sense of duality about yourself and any alien, objective universe. You visualize diamond, ruby, and sapphire lights, radiating from the OM AH HUM at the mentor's crown, throat, and heart centers and filling your three centers with white, red, and blue lights and bliss. Then the mentor dissolves into light rays that merge into you, and you and your mentor become one and the same. This visualization is associated with receiving the fourth initiation, the attainment of the integration stage, the practice of the Great Perfection, the enlightened death-between-life indivisible reality, the body-speech-mind indivisible, and the Three Bodies indivisible.

**O compassion on these suffering conscious beings**
**Who wander in the life cycle, darkened with delusions,**
**Not knowing their own minds as the infinite Truth Body—**
**May all of them attain the Body of Truth!**

Now you have yourself become the mentor and so no longer need any further blessing or grace for yourself. You look out upon the infinite field of beings in your mind's eye, seeing them look up to you for help and happiness. You first of all see through them as ultimately one with the infinite transparency of ultimate reality. The deep blue sapphire HUM at your heart center gently explodes with radiant blue light that shines into their hearts, making them, too, feel one with ultimate reality. The happiness they feel from receiving that blessing radiates back to the HUM as more blue light, making it more and more inexhaustibly powerful.

**O compassion on these conscious beings, misguided in desires,**
**Who wander in the life cycle, identifying with lust and clinging,**
**Not knowing their self-awareness as great bliss Beatific Body—**
**May all of them attain the Body of Beatitude!**

Now you, the mentor, look out again upon the infinite field of beings in your mind's eye, seeing them look up to you for help and happiness. You notice their bliss at feeling one with the infinite transparency of ultimate reality. The bright ruby red AAH at your throat center gently explodes with radiant red light that shines into their throats, intensifying their happiness further so they overflow

with the impulse to express their beatitude. That bliss sends forth
infinite poetic expressions of love and joy, which send more ruby
light rays back to the AAH at your throat, making it more and more
inexhaustibly powerful.

**O compassion on these misconceiving beings**
**Who wander in the life cycle, with the dualistic mind of hate,**
**Not knowing their own minds as the born-free Emanation Body—**
**May they all attain the Body of Emanation!**

Now you, the mentor, look out upon the infinite field of beings in
your mind's eye, seeing them look up to you in intensifying bliss.
You notice that their bliss flows toward infinite other beings who
feel excluded from the Great Perfection of reality. The diamond
white OM at your crown center gently explodes with radiant white
light that shines into their crowns, intensifying their bliss further so
they overflow with the impulse to emanate in physical forms that
can interact with infinite alienated beings. Infinite Emanation Bodies stream forth from the network of diamond light rays, interacting
with infinite beings, pleasing and freeing them. Their happiness and
relief flows back as more white light, making your diamond OM
light even more inexhaustibly powerful.

**O compassion on all beings who are not yet Buddhas,**
**Trapped by the presence-habit of addictive and objective veils,**
**Not knowing their own minds as the indivisible Three Bodies—**
**May they all attain the Three Bodies of Buddhahood!**

Now you, the mentor, look out upon the infinite field of beings in
your mind's eye, seeing them look up to you in infinite interpenetrating happiness. You notice that their bliss is integrated with their
sense of oneness with you and all beings in ultimate reality. Their
rays of blessing toward you become as infinitely powerful as your
rays toward them. You feel the infinitely expanding bliss of inter-
penetration with them, which seems a multifocal radiance of blue,
red, and white light rays swirling infinitely around the infinite communion of you all, become OM AH HUM, the body, speech, and
mind of all Enlightened Ones. You celebrate the inconceivability of
the perfect integration of your deep blue ultimate unborn primal

oneness, your deep red all-embracing communicating artistry, and your diamond white interreflecting individuating manifestation.

The "presence-habit" is the deepest level of misknowing conceptualization, which maintains the sense of "being here now" as something or someone finite, apart from the inconceivable Buddhaverse, supporting addictive and objective instincts of self-preservation, and blocking awareness of the primal bliss-wisdom indivisible of the eternal reality of enlightenment.

# THE PRAYER FOR HELP FROM THE BUDDHAS AND BODHISATTVAS

This prayer is the first of the four frequently mentioned as a set throughout the *Natural Liberation* literature. It can be used when you are confronting your own death, the death of another, or just in general when you intensify your spiritual practice by the remembrance of death. The parts to be recited aloud are set in boldface type. The first syllable, OM, is the mantric sound that functions as the invocation of the presence of all the infinite numbers of Buddhas and Bodhisattvas throughout the infinite universes.

**OM**

This is to be performed at the time of one's own death, or whenever else, this prayer for help from the Buddhas and Bodhisattvas. First one should make offerings to the Three Jewels, either physically or imaginatively. Hold incense in your hand, and speak with strong intensity.

Here you call upon the Buddhas and Bodhisattvas as messianic heroes or heroines who live only to liberate all beings from suffering. You are invoking the most advanced Bodhisattvas, who are very highly evolved, close to Buddhahood, and have the same powers of intervention as gods or angels. Some of them, such as Avalokiteshvara, the Lord of Compassion, or Tara, the goddess of miracles, are actually Buddhas already, but have vowed to help beings by appearing as Bodhisattvas.

The Three Jewels are the Buddha, Dharma, and Sangha Jewels, the precious Teacher, Teaching, and Community, which provide refuge from the unenlightened life cycle and its horrors; thus they are considered jewels of the greatest value for suffering beings.

For these prayers referring to a specific person, the reader in a specific situation will have to supply the name of the person and the gender for the pronouns. I will use the feminine, just to vary the usual assumption.

O ten directions' Buddhas and Bodhisattvas, compassionate, all-
knowing, all-seeing, all-loving—you are the refuge of beings! By the
power of your compassion, please come to this place! Please accept
these physical and visualized offerings! You compassionate ones com-
mand inconceivable all-knowing wisdom, miraculous deeds performed with loving compassion, and power to give refuge! O you
compassionate ones, this person named So-and-so is going from this
world to the beyond, leaving this world, making the great migration.
She has no friend. She has great suffering, no refuge, no protector,
and no allies. Her perception of this life is declining. She is going to
another life-realm, entering a thick darkness, falling into a great abyss,
and getting lost in a dense forest. She is driven by the power of evolution, going into a vast wilderness, swept off by a huge ocean. She is
blown away by the wind of evolution, going to a place without firm
ground, entering a vast battleground. She is being seized by a great
devil, terrified by the messengers of Yama. She is going from one
evolutionary existence to another, without any power of her own. The
time has come when she must go, friendless and alone. Therefore,
may you compassionate ones please give refuge to this helpless one
named So-and-so! Protect her! Be her ally! Save her from the great
darkness of the between! Hold her back from the harsh red wind of
evolution! Save her from the great terror of Yama! Deliver her from
the great long straits of the between! O compassionate ones, don't
hold back on your compassion! Help her! Don't let her fall into the
three horrid states! Don't waver from your ancient vows! Extend your
compassion power! O Buddhas and Bodhisattvas, enfold this one
named So-and-so with your compassionate art and power! Look after
her with compassion! Don't abandon her to the power of negative
evolution! I strongly pray that you Three Jewels save her from the
suffering of the between!

You and others should recite this three times with sincere faith. Then
you should use the prayers *Deliverance from the Straits of the Between*
and *Refuge from All Terrors of the Between*.

This *Prayer for Help from the Buddhas and Bodhisattvas* will not be
exhausted until the life cycle is empty. SAMAYA!

The "messengers of Yama" are the wraithlike minions of Yama, the
Indian and Tibetan Lord of Death. The belief is that these fearsome
creatures, often with Indian buffalo heads, come upon your soul at

the moment of death and drag you away into the nether region where Yama resides. There you are judged, your good and evil deeds are weighed, and your next life in the six realms of beings is determined.

The life cycle is called samsara; it is the state of existence of any being who is not completely enlightened. It becomes empty only when all beings have been liberated, when all have become Buddhas. Since the number of beings is infinite, this will take infinitely long, when thought of in a linear way. Since enlightenment is the realization of the infinity of time and the ultimate unreality of all moments of time, the life cycle empties itself in the realization of each enlightened being. It is not to be taken too literally.

"SAMAYA" in Sanskrit literally means "vow." It is often uttered after a text considered esoteric, or one in which strong determination is manifested, as a seal of that determination.

# THE PRAYER FOR DELIVERANCE
# FROM THE STRAITS OF THE BETWEEN

This *Prayer for Deliverance*, the following *Prayer for Refuge*, and the *Root Verses* almost flow together as one prayer. This first prayer summarizes the elements of existence personified as deities: the five Buddha-clans, which represent the five wisdoms, the Scientist deities, and the fierce deities. It calls on them for deliverance, focusing upon the transmutation of the five poisons of ignorance, lust, hate, pride, and envy. The verses follow the sequence of the experiences of the reality between. The verses are recited for the between-being in the text. A person preparing for the transition would do well to memorize them.

Homage to the host of Mentors, Archetypes, and Angels!
Please guide me on the path with your great love!

When I roam the life cycle driven by sheer error,
May the Oral Transmission Mentors lead me on the path
Of unwavering light of learning, thought, and meditation!
And may their consort host of Angels back me on the way,
Deliver me from the dangerous straits of the between,
And carry me to perfect Buddhahood!

When I roam the life cycle driven by strong delusion,
May the Lord Vairochana lead me on the path
Of the clear light of reality-perfection wisdom!
May his Consort Buddha Dhatvishvari back me on the way,
Deliver me from the dangerous straits of the between,
And carry me to perfect Buddhahood!

When I roam the life cycle driven by strong hate,
May the Lord Vajrasattva lead me on the path
Of the clear light of the mirror wisdom!
May his Consort Buddhalochana back me on the way,
Deliver me from the dangerous straits of the between,
And carry me to perfect Buddhahood!

When I roam the life cycle driven by strong pride,
May the Lord Ratnasambhava lead me on the path
Of the clear light of the equalizing wisdom!
May his Consort Buddha Mamaki back me on the way,
Deliver me from the dangerous straits of the between,
And carry me to perfect Buddhahood!

When I roam the life cycle driven by strong passion,
May the Lord Amitabha lead me on the path
Of the clear light of discriminating wisdom!
May his Consort Buddha Pandaravasini back me on the way,
Deliver me from the dangerous straits of the between,
And carry me to perfect Buddhahood!

When I roam the life cycle driven by strong envy,
May the Lord Amoghasiddhi lead me on the path
Of the clear light of the all-accomplishing wisdom!
May his Consort Buddha Samayatara back me on the way,
Deliver me from the dangerous straits of the between,
And carry me to perfect Buddhahood!

The following verse is quoted in the text of the reality between, but
not included in the versions of this prayer I have encountered so
far. It takes the five poisons, five Buddhas and Consorts, and five
wisdoms all together.

When I roam the life cycle driven by the five strong poisons,
May the Lord Victors of the five clans lead me on the path
Of the clear light of the four wisdoms in combination!
May the five Consort Buddhas back me on the way,
And deliver me from the impure lights of the six realms!
Delivering me from the dangerous straits of the between,
May they carry me to the five supreme pure lands!

When I roam the life cycle driven by strong instincts,
May the Hero Scientists lead me on the path
Of the clear light of orgasmic wisdom!
May their best consort Angel host support me from behind,

eliver me from the dangerous straits of the between,
nd carry me to perfect Buddhahood!

*Vidyadhara* in Sanskrit literally means "knowledge-holder," and is
translated here as Hero Scientist. They are the mind-scientists of
ancient India and Tibet. They do not wear white coats and their
laboratories are in the inner realms, accessed through the mastery
of the mind and its faculties. But they have been the quintessential
scientists of that nonmaterialist civilization.

I translate the Tibetan *lhan skyes* (the Sanskrit *sahaja*), which
literally means "produced by connection," as "orgasm," or adjec-
tivally as "orgasmic." It is often translated "innate" or "natural,"
but these terms are too general. It specifically refers to that great
bliss of the melting of self-habits arising from the realization of
selflessness, a bliss whose mundane metaphor is sexual bliss. "Orgasmic" may shock at first, but it is exactly on target for this ordinary life-and-death transcending totalization of orgasmic bliss by
the inconceivable wisdom of selflessness.

When I roam the life cycle driven by strong hallucinations,
May the host of mild and fierce Lords lead me on the path
Of the light that conquers terrifying visions of hate and fear!
May the space-goddess Angel hosts back me on the way,
Deliver me from the dangerous straits of the between,
And carry me to perfect Buddhahood!

Hey! May the space elements not arise as enemies,
And may I behold the realm of the sapphire Buddha!
May the water elements not arise as enemies,
And may I see the realm of the diamond Buddha!
May the earth elements not arise as enemies,
And may I behold the realm of the golden Buddha!
May the fire elements not arise as enemies,
And may I behold the realm of the ruby Buddha!
May the wind elements not arise as enemies,
And may I behold the realm of the emerald Buddha!
May the rainbow elements not arise as enemies,
And may I behold the realm of the rainbow Buddha!
May sounds, lights, and rays not arise as enemies,
And may I behold the magnificent realm of the mild and fierce Lords!

May I know all sounds as my own sounds!
May I know all lights as my own lights!
May I know all rays as my own rays!
May I know the between's reality as mine!
And may I realize the realm of the Three Buddha Bodies!

## THE PRAYER FOR REFUGE
## FROM ALL TERRORS OF THE BETWEEN

This prayer is a general appeal to the various deities one might appeal to for refuge in the death transition. It does not follow closely the pattern of the visions in the reality between, but rather rehearses elements generally involved in the whole process, prepares the between-being for the difficulties of the experience, and confirms the feeling of refuge extending on into future lives in all situations. It should likewise best be memorized by people preparing to guide their own death.

Hey! When the impulse of my lifespan is worn out,
As dear ones cannot help beyond this world
And I must wander alone in the between,
May Buddhas mild and fierce exert the force of their compassion
And clear the dense fog of darkness of misknowledge!

Now that I wander alone, apart from my loved ones,
And all my visions are but empty images,
May the Buddhas exert the force of their compassion
And stop the fear and hate-drawn terrors of the between!

When the five lights of brilliant wisdom dawn,
Fearlessly, bravely, may I know them as myself!
When the forms of the Lords mild and fierce arise,
Bold and fearless, may I recognize the between!

Now when I suffer by the power of negative evolution,
May the Archetype Deities dispel that suffering!
When reality crashes with a thousand thunders,
May they all become OM MANI PADME HUM!

When I'm pulled by evolution without recourse,
May the Lords mild and fierce dispel my suffering!
When I suffer due to evolutionary instincts,
May the clear-light bliss samadhi dawn upon me!

When I'm born by apparition in the existence between,
May evil prophecies of perverse devils not come true!
When I arrive wherever by the power of thought,
May fears created by negative evolution not occur!

When wild beasts of prey roar savagely,
May it become the Dharma sound—OM MANI PADME HUM!
When I am driven by snow, rain, wind, and darkness,
May I find the divine vision of brilliant wisdom!

May all beings, compatible types in the between,
Avoid all rivalry and find rebirth in high estates!
When I am hungry and thirsty from intense addictions,
May I not suffer real hunger, thirst, heat, and cold!

When I behold the coupling of my next life's father and mother,
May I see them as the Lord of Compassion Father-Mother themselves!
Free consciously to choose my birth, then for the sake of others
May I obtain the best body adorned with the signs and marks!

> Here the prayer refers to the practice of visualizing the parental
> couple that all between-beings behold in the process of being reborn
> in mammalian embodiments—as the Lord of Compassion, Avalok-
> iteshvara, and his consort, the female Buddha Tara. The expression
> "Father-Mother" (Tib., *yab yum*) is commonly used in Tantric con-
> texts to refer to a Buddha-deity couple in the sexual union pose.

Having obtained for myself the finest body living,
May all who see or hear me swiftly be delivered!
Not pursuing any negative evolutions
May I follow and develop all my existing merits!

Wherever I am born in every life to come,
May I meet again my Archetype Deity of this life!
Speaking and understanding the moment I am born,
May I have the retention to remember my former lives!

Knowledge great and small, average and various,
May I understand it just by hearing it or seeing it!

May good luck prevail in the land wherein I'm born,
And may all beings be endowed with happiness!

You Victors mild and fierce, as are your bodies,
Your retinues, lifespans, and your pure worlds,
And your superior auspicious signs of greatness—
May I and all others become just like you!

By the vast compassion of the All-Goods mild and fierce,
By the power of the truth of reality-perfection,
And by the blessing of Tantric adepts' single-minded success—
May I accomplish just what I have prayed for!

# THE ROOT VERSES
# OF THE SIX BETWEENS

These *Root Verses* summarize the six betweens, each verse formulating the insights and resolves that are keys to the successful redirection of each being away from the continuing life-cycle between, toward liberation and enlightenment.

Hey! Now when the life between dawns upon me,
I will abandon laziness, as life has no more time,
Unwavering, enter the path of learning, thinking, and meditating,
And taking perceptions and mind as path,
I will realize the Three Bodies of enlightenment!
This once that I have obtained the human body
Is not the time to stay on the path of distractions.

Hey! Now when the dream between dawns upon me,
I will give up corpselike sleeping in delusion,
And mindfully enter unwavering the experience of reality.
Conscious of dreaming, I will enjoy the changes as clear light.
Not sleeping mindlessly like an animal,
I will cherish the practice merging sleep and realization!

Hey! Now when the meditation between dawns upon me,
I will abandon the host of distracting errors,
Focus in extreme-free experience, without releasing or controlling,
And achieve stability in the creation and perfection stages!
Giving up business, now one-pointed in meditation,
I won't surrender to the power of erroneous addictions!

Hey! Now when the death-point between dawns upon me,
I will give up the preoccupations of the all-desiring mind,
Enter unwavering the experience of the clarity of the precepts,
And transmigrate into the birthless space of inner awareness;
About to lose this created body of flesh and blood,
I will realize it to be impermanent illusion!

Hey! Now when the reality between dawns upon me,
I will let go of the hallucinations of instinctive terror,
Enter the recognition of all objects as my mind's own visions,
And understand this as the pattern of perception in the between;
Come to this moment, arrived at this most critical cessation,
I will not fear my own visions of deities mild and fierce!

Hey! Now when the existence between dawns upon me,
I will hold my will with mind one-pointed,
And increase forcefully the impulse of positive evolution;
Blocking the womb door, I will remember to be revulsed.
Now courage and positive perception are essential;
I will give up envy, and contemplate all couples
As my Spiritual Mentor, Father and Mother.

"With mind distracted, never thinking, 'Death is coming,'
To slave away on the pointless business of mundane life,
And then to come out empty—it is a tragic error.
Recognition of necessity is the holy teaching of the gods,
So won't you live this divine truth from now on?"
These are the words of the great adepts.
If you don't put the Mentor's precept in your mind,
Won't you be the one who deceives yourself?

# CHAPTER 6

# THE GUIDEBOOK
# TO THE BETWEENS

## THE PRAYER OF THE REALITY BETWEEN

O Amitabha, boundless light of the Truth Body,
O mild and fierce Beatific Body Lotus Deities,
O Padma Sambhava, incarnate savior of beings—
I bow to the Three Bodies in the Spiritual Mentors!

The Sanskrit name "Amitabha" means "boundless light." He is the
Buddha of the western Buddhaverse known as Sukhavati, and the
Lord of the Lotus Clan of Tantric archetype deities. In this invocation, he is associated with the Truth Body, the aspect of Buddhahood associated with ultimate reality. The Lotus Deities themselves
are associated with the Beatific Body, the subjective, transcendent
wisdom aspect of Buddhahood, and Padma Sambhava represents
the Incarnational Emanation Body. Thus the practitioner salutes at
the outset the spiritual teachers as embodiments of the Three Bodies
of Buddhahood. In this spot, modern practitioners should substitute
an invocation of whatever trinity, duality, or unity they hold most
sacred and helps them feel most comfortable and secure.

This *Great Natural Liberation Through Understanding* is the art that
liberates average practitioners when they go through the between state.

*PRELIMINARIES*

Implementing the practical instructions that teach the art of liberating
beings, those of greatest ability will surely be liberated. If they are not,

hey should practice the *Natural Liberation Through Soul-transmission* in the death-point between.

> "Soul-transmission" (Tibetan, '*pho-ba*) is a contemplative practice through which advanced yogis and yoginis can voluntarily leave their bodies by ejecting their subtlest consciousness out of the top of their heads and transmitting it into a Buddhaverse, or pure land. They learn to do this by receiving initiation into this art, then practicing through long retreats the alignment of consciousness and the subtle neural energies. The *Natural Liberation* mentioned is a version of this practice associated with our text, not usually published because it would be dangerous to practice without initiation.

The practitioners of average ability will surely be liberated by that. If they are not, they should strive to implement this *Great Natural Liberation Through Understanding* during the reality between.

To that end, first you should examine the situation with a systematic death analysis, according to the *Natural Liberation through Death Signs.*

> This *Natural Liberation* is published with our text. It provides a lore of omens, dream interpretation, and medical insight that helps a person foresee the danger of death in specific situations.

When the signs of death are clearly complete, you should employ the *Natural Liberation Through Soul-transmission.* If soul-transmission succeeds, it is unnecessary to read this *Book of Natural Liberation.* If it does not succeed, you should read this *Book of Natural Liberation* clearly and distinctly, sitting beside the body. If the body is gone, then you should sit at the bed or seat of the deceased. You should invoke the power of truth, summon the soul, visualize the deceased as sitting in front of you listening, and read this *Book of Natural Liberation.* During that procedure, it would be very disturbing if the loved ones and relatives were to weep and lament. They should be quieted. If the body is still there, during the time when the outer breath has ceased but the inner breath has not, the dead person's teacher, fellow disciple, or trusted and beloved relative or friend, should read this *Book of Natural Liberation* with lips not quite touching the ear.

## USING THE BOOK OF NATURAL LIBERATION

> It is not necessary, in fact it would be confusing, to read aloud for the deceased the many instructions intended for the readers of the *Book of Natural Liberation.* Thus, you should read aloud the indented sections set in boldface type. The instruction parts of the text tell you how and when to read them.

You should make extensive offerings to the Three Jewels. If you cannot afford it, you should set up whatever symbolic offering you can afford and then visualize limitless offerings. You should then recite three or seven times the prayer *Help from the Buddhas and Bodhisattvas.* Then you should accurately and melodiously recite the prayers *Refuge from All Terrors of the Between* and *Deliverance from the Straits of the Between,* and the *Root Verses of the Six Betweens.* Then you should read seven times or three times, or as the occasion permits, this *Great Book of Natural Liberation Through Understanding in the Between.*

> The "Three Jewels" are the Buddha, his Teaching, and the Holy Community. The text is recommending setting up an altar with an icon or statue of the Buddha and perhaps a copy of a Buddhist book to represent the teaching. Offerings consist of water in little cups, flowers, incense, a candle or other light, and so on. Even without any physical objects, you can visualize a whole arrangement, offering universes full of things of beauty to all enlightened beings. If you or the deceased have a different religion, set up an icon, symbol, or text that represents the sacred, and think of offerings traditional in that religion. If you or the deceased have no religion, think of a favorite environment of the deceased and adorn it symbolically or imaginatively in a way that would please and attract the deceased. The prayers mentioned are included in chapter 5.

## RECOGNITION OF THE CLEAR LIGHT IN THE DEATH-POINT BETWEEN

> The clear light is an indescribable transparency, a light that is omni-directionally illuminating yet beyond the brightness of sun or moon

and also beyond dimness or darkness. The text uses the terminology of "betweens" in a somewhat confusing way. This section is called the *Prayer of the Reality Between*. The "death-point between" is also one of the six main betweens, considered different from the "reality between." The death-point between again is divided into two betweens, one called "reality clear-light" death between and the other unnamed. The first occurs when the deceased's consciousness is still held within the central channel of the deceased's subtle nervous system, while the second occurs just after the consciousness has left the body through any path other than the crown of the head. So I have called these two the "central channel reality clear-light death-point between" and the "out-of-body reality clear-light death-point between." Both of these occur quite soon after the cessation of breathing, the first immediately after. They are extremely crucial times, when you wish to intervene to assist someone to have a successful death-transition, ideally into a state of conscious liberation, or at least into a positive, enlightenment-oriented realm, such as a Buddhaverse or pure land. For at the death point every being, especially a human being, has the ideal opportunity to discover real freedom from addictive habits, delusive perceptions, and misleading conceptions. Therefore, in Tibetan culture it is considered important to help a loved one through the actual process of death, to avoid distracting and frightening places such as hospital emergency rooms, and to arrange circumstances where the assistants can stay with the body at least for some hours.

For the sake of clarity, I have omitted from the translation the Tibetan subject headings, which enumerate topics far ahead in the text to orient the reader.

### The Central Channel Reality Clear Light

"Between" is used in at least three senses here, which causes a slight confusion. It is used in its basic colloquial sense of the whole period between death and rebirth. It is used in its technical sense in "between yoga," in the main set of the six betweens, life, dream, meditation, death-point, reality, and existence betweens, where the last three are subdivisions of the colloquial "between." And it is used in this text in the sense of "phase of a between," where the experience of a particular period in one of the six betweens is itself called a between. Thus, in the death-point between, there are the two clear light betweens; and in the reality between, there are the mild deity between and the fierce deity between, each of these being divided again into several days. I have simplified this by calling the third usage a "between phase," and by occasionally omitting the casual use of the term.

You should use this *Natural Liberation* with all types of persons—some who have good understanding but have not yet recognized the clear light, some who have recognized it but have not developed that recognition with practice, and even some ordinary egocentric individuals who lack any instruction. Once they recognize the objective clear light, they will attain the birthless Body of Truth by the straight upward path without going through any between.

The power of the teaching of this *Natural Liberation* is noted here. The consciousness is so flexible in the between state that the mere understanding of reality can transform the whole structure of delusion and liberation can occur instantaneously.

As for the use of this *Natural Liberation:* it is best if you can bring (to the bedside) the main mentor of the deceased, from whom he has received instructions. If you cannot bring her, then spiritual brothers or sisters with the same commitments will do. If they cannot come, then a spiritual teacher of the same spiritual lineage will do. If he cannot come, then any person who can read this text accurately and distinctly should read it many times. When the deceased is reminded in this way of the mentor's description, there is no doubt that she will recognize the objective clear light and will instantly be liberated.

The Tibetan language rarely uses pronouns during such instructions, since the third person subject is included in the verbal form, without differentiating the gender of the person. While it is true that male spiritual teachers are more numerous in Tibet, there are female mentors, or lamas, as well. And of course death is no respecter of gender, and the deceased is as often female as male. If I simply use the male pronoun all the time in English, it makes the Tibetan seem more sexist than it is. If I use "he or she," "him or her" all the time, it makes the flow of the language clumsy. So I have chosen to alternate male and female pronouns loosely when giving general third-person descriptions.

As for the time to use the *Natural Liberation:* after the outer breath ceases, the neural winds dissolve into the wisdom central channel and the consciousness arises distinctly as the unfabricating clear light. That is when the *Natural Liberation* should be used, before the winds reverse themselves and escape through the right and left channels, and the visions of the between arise invitingly. After the outer breath has ceased, the inner breath remains (within the central channel) just for the time it takes to eat a meal.

Again, as for how to use it: it is best if one can succeed in soul-ejection when the breath is just about to cease. If this does not succeed, you should say this:

Hey! Noble one, you named So-and-so! Now the time has come for you to seek the way. Just as your breath stops, the objective clear light of the first between will dawn as previously described to you by your teacher. Your outer breath stops and you experience reality stark and void like space, your immaculate naked awareness dawning clear and void without horizon or center. At that instant, you yourself must recognize it as yourself, you must stay with that experience. I will describe it again to you at that moment.

The standard instruction for recognizing the clear light is as just given. The *Natural Liberation Through Naked Vision* in chapter 8 is a much fuller description of this type. Awareness is clear and contentless, infinite and stripped of all structures, seeming free of all point of subjectivity or sense of objectivity. The difficulty of recognition comes from the habit-momentum of feeling present as a subjective perspective, hence feeling fear or faint at losing the sense of holding on. That is why the instruction urges the deceased to identify with the infinite transparency, to recognize it as the essential selfless self.

Before his (outer) breath ceases, you should repeat this in his ear many times, in order to plant it firmly in his mind. Then when the outer breath is just at the point of stopping, place him in the lion posture, his right side on the ground, and squeeze the pulsing waves in the blood vessels (of the neck). Press them strongly, cutting off pulsation in the two sleep channels (in the neck). Then the winds will enter the central channel and will not be able to reverse, and his soul will definitely exit up the path of the Brahma-hole.

Clearly, judging the moment exactly right as the breath ceases is a very tricky business, requiring an expert touch and timing, not to be casually attempted by anyone. The "Brahma-hole" is where the soft fontanelle aperture is located on the fore of the crown of the head. The soul embodied in the subtle energy life-drop exits there through understanding the *Natural Liberation,* in the same way it ejects in the practice of soul-ejection.

Then one should again read the description. This moment is called the "first between reality clear light." An unerring realization of the Body of Truth arises in the process of all beings. Further, during the time the inner breath abides after the outer breath stops, the winds are dissolved into the central channel. Ordinary persons call this "loss of consciousness." Its duration is uncertain, depending on the quality of the individual's life and her degree of cultivation of the neural winds and channels. It can abide for a long time in those who have considerable practice, stable quiescence, or highly cultivated channels. For such persons you should read the description repeatedly to increase their determination, until lymph oozes from their sense apertures. For those who are great sinners or have blocked channels, this time will last no longer than a finger snap. For some others it will last the time of eating a meal. Since most philosophical and yogic scriptures state that deceased persons stay unconscious for four and a half days, they will usually remain (in and around their central channels) for that length of time; so you should persist in describing the clear light for them.

As for how to do it: if the deceased has the ability, she should develop her resolve from beforehand. If she cannot do it herself, then her teacher, her disciple, her spiritual brothers or sisters, or like-minded friends should sit nearby her. They should then pronounce the signs of dissolution in order.

Now this mirage you see is the sign of earth dissolving in water. This smoke is the sign of water dissolving into fire. These fireflies are the sign of fire dissolving into wind. This candle flame is the sign of wind dissolving into consciousness. This moonlit sky is the sign of consciousness dissolving into luminance. This sunlit sky is the sign of luminance dissolving into radiance. This dark sky is the sign of radiance dissolving into imminence. This predawn twilight sky is the sign of imminence dissolving into clear light.

> The text only mentions "the signs of mirage and so forth." I have restored the full description of the eight subjective signs of the eight dissolutions because these signs are so important for the deceased to recognize, giving her a sense of orientation in a new and strange realm of unfamiliar experiences.

When those signs are about to culminate, you should remind the deceased of his conception of the spirit of enlightenment. If the deceased is a spiritual teacher, you should gently say:

**Venerable teacher! Please act on your spiritual conception without wavering.**

> I translate the Sanskrit *bodhichitta* as "spirit of enlightenment," and *bodhicittotpada* as "spiritual conception." It is the spiritual attitude that distinguishes a bodhisattva, a messianic hero or heroine who lives to save all others from suffering. It is a messianic resolve to become perfectly enlightened in order to be capable of saving others from suffering and bringing them to happiness. It is, for a bodhisattva, the logical outcome of love and compassion toward beings, combined with the wisdom about their real situation and about the infinite horizon of interconnectedness between self and others. Tibetan psychology considers paradoxically that this selfless attitude is the best guarantee of a good destiny for the self. Hence it is crucial to remind the deceased of his or her spiritual conception at this moment.

If the deceased is a spiritual companion or any other person, call him by name and say the following:

Hey, noble one! Now you have arrived at so-called "death," so you should conduct yourself according to your conception of the spirit of enlightenment. You should conceive your spirit of enlightenment thus: "Alas! I have arrived at the time of death. From now, relying on this death, I will develop my spirit only by contemplating the conception of the spirit of enlightenment of love and compassion. For the sake of the whole space-full of beings, I must attain perfect Buddhahood." And especially you should think, "Now for the sake of all beings, I will recognize the death clear light as the Body of Truth. Within its experience, I will attain the supreme accomplishment of the Great Seal, and I will accomplish the purposes of all beings. If I don't attain that, then in the time of the between, I will recognize it as the between. I will realize that between as the Great Seal Body of Integration, and I will accomplish the purposes of all the infinite space-full of beings by manifesting whatsoever is needed to tame whomsoever." Thus never losing the willpower of that spiritual conception, you should remember the experience of whatever instructions you have previously practiced.

> I render the Sanskrit *mahamudra* as "Great Seal." This expression refers to ultimate reality as the ultimate lover, experiencing voidness as a total mental and physical union between oneself as orgasmic bliss with the impassioned consort of the infinitely expansive intimate wisdom of universal voidness. Like the expression "Great Perfection," it refers to the ultimate as approached by the most advanced adept of Tantric contemplative practice.

This should be clearly enunciated with the lips near the ear. In this way, not allowing even an instant's distraction, you should pray for the deceased to accomplish this practice.

Then, when the outer breath has ceased, you should press the sleep channels (at the neck) forcefully and say the following; first, to a spiritual teacher or spiritual superior:

Venerable teacher! Right now the objective clear light dawns for you. Recognize it! Please incorporate it within your experience.

You should describe it to all others as follows:

Hey, noble one, you named So-and-so, listen here! Now the pure clear light of reality dawns for you. Recognize it! Hey, noble one, this, your present conscious natural clear void awareness, this presence in clear voidness without any objectivity of substance, sign, or color— just this is the reality, the Mother, Buddha All-around Goodness! And this, your conscious awareness natural voidness, not succumbing to a false annihilative voidness, just your own conscious awareness, unceasing, bright, distinct, and vibrant—just this awareness is the Father, Buddha All-around Goodness! Just this presence of the indivisibility of your awareness's naturally insubstantial voidness and the vibrant bright presence of your conscious awareness—just this is the Buddha Body of Truth. Your awareness thus abides in this vast mass of light of clarity-void indivisible. You are free of birth or death—just this is the Buddha Changeless Light. It is enough just to recognize this. Recognizing this your own conscious awareness's purity nature as the Buddha, yourself beholding your own awareness—that is to dwell in the inner realization of all Buddhas.

"All-around Goodness" translates the Sanskrit name Samantabhadra, with its male and female forms. All-around Goodness is the famous divine bodhisattva of the *Flower Garland Sutra,* the Samantabhadra who has developed the interpenetrating samadhi so highly that he can multiply all his good actions infinitely throughout the micro- and macrocosms, for example consciously bowing in miniature subatomic bodies in subatomic universes to subatomic Buddhas at the same moment he bows in the ordinary universe to the Buddha before him. The Buddhas Samantabhadra Father and Mother represent the inconceivable ultimate dimension itself, the Body of Truth, the experience of which is the eternally blissful union of bliss-awareness and transparent reality-voidness. The identification given here resembles the expressions of the Word Initiation, the "Great Fourth Initiation," considered the highest of the esoteric initiations in the Unexcelled Yoga Tantras. The nature of the reality evoked is such that it is not created, not attainable by any effort, because it is never lost, it has been beginninglessly present to enlightened awareness. Thus there is no progression into the realization of its presence. One is instantly liberated by the mere understanding of the identification.

You should repeat this three or seven times, clearly and correctly. With the first repetition, the deceased will remember her spiritual teacher's previous description. With the second repetition, she will recognize her own naked awareness as the clear light. With the third repetition, recognizing her nature, she will become the Body of Truth, free of union and separation, and will definitely be liberated. Thus recognizing the first clear light, the deceased will be liberated.

### The Out-of-Body Reality Clear Light

However, if one doubts and does not recognize the first clear light, again the "second clear light" dawns. As for its timing, it comes a little longer after the outer breath has ceased than it takes to eat a meal. By the good or bad impulses of evolution, the wind is released into either the right or left channel and escapes through one or the other bodily aperture; then consciousness emerges in the clear path of the between. Again, though the time is described as "the time it takes to eat a meal," this depends on the nature of the deceased's channels, and their degree of cultivation.

At this point, the deceased feels his consciousness emerge out of the body, but he does not recognize the situation, worrying instead, "Have I died or not?" He still feels as if connected with his loved ones. He hears their weeping. Before his intense evolutionary hallucinations arise and his full terror of death arrives, you should again use the instructions. There are various versions, those for the perfection-stage practitioner and those for the creation-stage practitioner. For the perfection-stage practitioner, you call him by name three times and then repeat the clear light orientation just given above. If he is a creation-stage practitioner, you should read the meditation literature and the visualization practice of whichever was his Archetype Deity. Then pray as follows:

Remember that you are still at the bedside of the deceased, whose consciousness now has emerged from his body and is floating precariously around the room. This period probably begins around a half an hour after the breath has completely stopped and can continue for several days. In Tibetan culture, therefore, it is considered desirable to keep the body without disposal for several days, though this is impossible in warm climates due to decomposition. The bodies of highly adept lamas are often reported to stay sitting immobile for several days, without decomposing in a normal way. The perfection-stage practitioner has cultivated the energy channels of the subtle nervous system, untangled its knots, and developed a familiarity with subtle interior and out-of-body states. So the clear light is directly identified for him or her. The creation-stage practitioner has developed strong expertise in visualization, and the Archetype Deities and their mandala sacred environments are highly familiar, their forms and structures having subliminally cultivated the winds, channels, and drops of awareness. So for them, the instructions should bring them back to the Archetype Deities with which they feel secure and open.

**Hey, noble one! Meditate on this your Archetype Deity! Don't be distracted! Aim your intense willpower toward your Archetype Deity! Meditate it as apparent but realityless like the moon in water! Don't meditate it as material!**

If the deceased is an ordinary person, orient her as follows:

**Meditate on the Lord of Great Compassion!**

The ordinary person here means one who has no systematic practice of either visualization or transformation into altered states of physical energies or consciousness. However, her participation in a culture is itself a visualization and transformation process, a routinization of imagination and perception. If she is religious, her long-term familiarity with a particular god, goddess, savior, or prophet will make that being into an archetype deity for her. If she is not religious, her familiarity with specific political leaders, celebrities, national symbols, or other persons or places will have turned them into archetypes or mandalas for her. The text invokes the Lord of Great Compassion, the archangelic Bodhisattva Avalokiteshvara, the Savior figure for any participant in Tibetan culture, a powerful deity who looks out for all living creatures, helping them avoid suffering and discover happiness. You may prefer to invoke Jesus here, or Moses, Muhammad, Krishna, or Wakan Tanka, Odin, Zeus, or the Great Mother in any of her myriad forms. Any archetype of sacredness, any compassionate personification or representation of ultimate reality, here serves to make the soul's consciousness feel secure and integrated with the gracious presence of sacred ultimacy. This is necessary for her not to fear any hallucinations or startling happenings, and to move toward positive destinies. It is also considered that the imagined figure of any of these great saviors serves as an icon to focus awareness to make the soul receptive to the active compassion of those beings themselves.

Thus orienting them, there is no doubt that even those who have never recognized the between will recognize it. Further, those who in life had a mentor describe the between to them, but gained only slight familiarity through practice, will not by themselves be able to become lucid in the between. They must have a spiritual teacher, loved one, or friend evoke it for them. And those who are likely to be reborn in the horrid states, who previously gained familiarity with and insight into the path, but then lost their vows or destroyed their basic commitment, for them this is extremely necessary.

The consequences of breaking vows and commitments on the part of one who has achieved some degree of insight into the path are very grave. This is not because of some punitive tendency in the tradition. It rather is due to the fact that one who enters the path to some degree begins to attain a level of freedom from inner instinctual drivenness and becomes more open. Their potential life energy thus becomes more malleable and flexible, as their horizon opens all the way to Buddhahood and evolutionary perfection. If they then get radically turned around toward evil or "the dark side," as it were, their expanded horizon has now come to include extremely negative, hellish states, and they may find themselves in great danger.

If the deceased succeeds in understanding in the first between, it is best. If he has not succeeded, then when reality is evoked in the second between, awareness is awakened and he is liberated. Here, when instructed in the second between, his awareness, previously unsure if he has died or not, suddenly becomes clear; this is called the "impure magic body" state. At that time, if the instruction succeeds, mother and child realities meet and evolution loses its power over him. It is like sunlight conquering the darkness. The path clear light conquers the power of evolution and he is liberated.

The magic body, remember, is the consciously constructed, dream-bodylike, subtle energy body created on the third stage of the perfection stage. Here, due to the power of the teaching, the evolutionarily constructed subtle body of the between-state is transformed by instantaneous clarity of understanding into the third stage impure magic body. This intense acceleration of evolution toward Buddhahood is possible because of the great malleability and transformability of the soul and its subtle embodiment in the between state. The "mother reality" is the objective clear light, the actual transparency of ultimate reality directly experienced beyond the subject-object dichotomy, called "mother" because of her being the matrix of all possibility. The "child reality" is the semblant clear light, transparency still filtered through conceptuality, targeted by an accurate conceptual understanding, retaining still an instinctive sense of subjectivity and objectivity. It is the level of clear light experience that fits with the impure magic body presence. When it develops into the mother clear light, the magic body becomes purified, the supreme union between father magic body and mother clear light becoming the unexcelled Integration, the Great Seal, the Great Perfection—the evolutionary consummation that is Buddhahood.

Once more, what is called the "second between" dawns suddenly before the mental body; and the consciousness wanders within the range of hearing. At that time, if this instruction is given, its aim will be achieved. At this moment, the evolutionary hallucinations have not dawned, and he is capable of any sort of transformation. Thus even if he failed to recognize the objective clear light, still he can recognize the second between clear light and so can reach liberation.

## THE MILD DEITY REALITY BETWEEN

Each between phase and day begins with the suggestion that one carry on with the reading of the *Book of Natural Liberation* in case the deceased is still not liberated. Each previous section has ended with statements about how surely the deceased will be liberated by the understanding of the preceding instruction. An expert lama or spiritual mentor, one with direct clairvoyance, is considered easily able to monitor the progress of the soul of the deceased. The rest of us should probably keep going, preferring to err on the side of overdoing than failing to provide an opportunity for the deceased.

If the deceased is still not liberated, it is then called the "third between phase." The reality between dawns. This becomes the third between, in which the evolutionary hallucinations dawn. Therefore it is crucial to read this great orientation to the reality between at that time, with its very great power and benefits. At that time, her loved ones will weep and wail, her share of food is no longer served, her clothes are stripped off, her bed is broken. She can see them, but they cannot see her. She can hear them calling her, but they cannot hear when she calls them. So she must depart, her heart sinking in despair. Perceptions arise of sounds, lights, and rays, and she feels faint with fear, terror, and panic. Then you must use this great description of the reality between. You should call the deceased by name, and clearly and distinctly say as follows:

Hey, noble one! Listen unwavering with intense concentration! There are six kinds of between: the natural life between, the dream between, the contemplation between, the death-point between, the reality between, and the emergent existence between.

Hey, noble one, three betweens will dawn for you; the death-point between, the reality between, and the existence between will dawn. Until yesterday, in the death-point between, the reality clear light dawned. But you did not recognize it, so you had to wander here. Now the reality between and the existence between will dawn for you. As I describe them, you must recognize them without fail.

Hey, noble one! Now you have arrived at what is called "death." You are going from this world to the beyond. You are not alone; it happens to everyone. You must not indulge in attachment and insistence on this life. Though you are attached and you insist, you have no power to stay, you will not avoid wandering in the life cycle. Do not lust! Do not cling! Be mindful of the Three Jewels!

Hey, noble child! Whatever terrifying visions of the reality between may dawn upon you, you should not forget the following words. You must proceed remembering in your mind the meaning of these words. Therein lies the key of recognition.

Hey! Now when the reality between dawns upon me,
I will let go of the hallucinations of instinctive terror,
Enter the recognition of all objects as my mind's own visions,
And understand this as the pattern of perception in the between;
Come to this moment, arrived at this most critical cessation,
I will not fear my own visions of deities mild and fierce!

This verse comes from the *Root Verses of the Six Betweens*. The deceased here has entered into the dreamlike world of the between, and is not yet used to the ghostly senses of the between. To his or her heightened sensitivity, sights and sounds can have a startling intensity. Further, the underlying instincts can emerge from the subconscious easily and quickly, and can color any experience with intense moods, either of terror or joy. Our instincts are so patterned after fear of harm and the expectation of pain that we tend easily to paranoia. This fearful state in the between can itself create distressing manifestations. Should we give ourselves to such terrors, we would become more and more tied up in knots of defensiveness, would close down our sensitivity more and more, and would inevitably descend into the sea of patterns of negativity. Therefore, the verse serves to remind us of the urgent necessity not to give in to fear but to see through it and remain open and at ease.

You should proceed clearly saying this verse aloud and remembering its meaning. Do not forget this, as it is the key to recognizing whatever terrifying visions dawn as certainly being your own perceptions.

Hey, noble one! At this time when your mind and body are parting ways, pure reality manifests in subtle, dazzling visions, vividly experienced, naturally frightening and worrisome, shimmering like a mirage on the plains in autumn. Do not fear them. Do not be terrified! Do not panic! You have what is called an "instinctual mental body," not a material, flesh and blood body. Thus whatever sounds, lights, and rays may come at you, they cannot hurt you. You cannot die. It is enough just for you to recognize them as your own perceptions. Understand that this is the between.

Hey, noble one! If you don't recognize them as your own perceptions in this way—whatever other meditations and achievements you may have experienced in the human world, if you did not meet this particular instruction—the lights will frighten you, the sounds will panic you, the rays will terrify you. If you don't know the key of this instruction, you will not recognize the sounds, lights, and rays, and you will wander in the life cycle.

## THE FIRST DAY

The text does not place this label here, beginning to label in this way only below when it inserts "The Second Day." I have added it for clarity, and to keep you oriented in terms of your use of the book in actual cases. Below it tells the deceased he has been unconscious for four and a half days, precisely one hundred and eight hours. The precise time does not matter so much, as you can fruitfully read these between instructions on the days immediately after death, and you can continue for up to forty-nine days.

In the day-sequences that follow, you reach into the mandala or sacred environment of the universe as structured by the Buddha wisdoms. You invoke those five wisdoms personified by the five Lords of the Buddha-clans, Vairochana and so on (see figure 10, page 69). Each one emanates with qualities and attributes that align with the elements and processes of the ordinary universe of suffering, representing their transmutation into the Buddhaverse, or pureland reality, where love, compassion, bliss, and wisdom are the dominant energies of life. Similarly, each manifestation parallels the appearances of the six realms of worldly migration, heavens, hells, and worlds of titans, humans, animals, and pretans. This is in order to help souls not to seek embodiment in those ordinary, driven life-states, but rather to bring them into a more ideal, enlightenment-oriented environment where they can proceed more swiftly toward liberation. In reading the sequences, just try to imagine the general colors, lights, and overall qualities of each archetype. Do not worry about trying to fix every detail in exact order, or it can become distracting. Those who feel uncomfortable with the Buddhist imagery should substitute in its place the figures or symbols that give them comfort. For one artist's vision of the look of these five deities, and all of them in tableau together, see color insert, plates 5, 6, 7, and 8.

Hey, noble one! Having fainted for four and a half days, you are now proceeding. You have woken up with the worry, "What is happening to me?" Recognize that you are in the between! Now, since the life cycle is in suspension, all things dawn as lights and deities. All space dawns full of azure light. Now, from the central Buddha-land, All-pervading Drop, the Lord Vairochana appears before you, white bodied, sitting on a lion throne, holding in his hand an eight-spoked wheel, united with his consort Akasha Dhatvishvari. The natural purity of the consciousness aggregate, the blue light of the Reality Perfection wisdom, a clear and vivid color blue, frighteningly intense, shines piercingly from the heart center of this Vairochana couple, dazzling your eyes unbearably. Simultaneously the soft white light of the gods shines upon you and penetrates you in parallel with the bright blue light. At that time, influenced by negative evolution, you panic and are terrified of that bright blue light of Reality Perfection wisdom and you flee from it. And you feel a liking for the soft white light of the gods, and you approach it. But you must not panic at that blue light, the clear, piercing, brilliant, frightening supreme wisdom clear light! Do not fear it! It is the light ray of the Transcendent Lord, the Reality Perfection wisdom. Feel attracted to it with faith and reverence! Make it the answer to your prayer, thinking, "It is the light ray of the compassion of Lord Vairochana—I must take refuge in it!" It is the way Lord Vairochana comes to escort you through the straits of the between. It is the light ray of the compassion of Vairochana. Don't be enticed by the soft white light of the gods. Don't be attached to it! Don't long for it! If you cling to it, you will wander into the realm of the gods, and you will continue to cycle through the six realms of driven existence. It is an obstacle to cessation, the path of freedom. So don't look upon it, but be devoted to the brilliant penetrating blue light, aim your intense willpower toward Vairochana, and repeat after me the following prayer:

When I roam the life cycle driven by strong delusion,
May the Lord Vairochana lead me on the path
Of the clear light of reality-perfection wisdom!
May his Consort Buddha Dhatvishvari back me on the way,

Deliver me from the dangerous straits of the between,
And carry me to perfect Buddhahood!

Thus praying with fierce devotion, you dissolve in rainbow light
into the heart of the Vairochana couple, whence you will enter the
central pure land Ghanavyuha, Dense Array, and become a Buddha
by way of the Body of Perfect Beatitude!

The cosmology invoked here is that the Five Buddha mandala is
connected to the ordinary universe as a set of Buddha-lands, universes built up out of enlightenment energies, with one in the center
and one in each of the four directions. The verse recited comes from
*The Prayer for Deliverance from the Straits of the Between.* If you
substitute a Jesus figure accompanied by a host of angels, it would
still be good to preserve the sense of centrality; the type of wisdom
involved; the fact that this archetype should be the transmutation
of the consciousness process and the addiction of delusion; the need
at this point to turn the attraction towards the heavens into the
aspiration to enter a Buddha-land; and the colors of the lights.

## THE SECOND DAY

It might happen that, even though you provide this orientation, because
of his faults of anger, sins, and blocks, the deceased fears the light ray
and flees; though he prays, he still errs. Then on the second day, the
Vajrasattva Deity host and the negative evolutionary impulses leading
to hell approach to escort him in their different directions. Here, calling
upon the deceased by name, you should orient him as follows:

Hey, noble one! Listen without wavering! On this second day,
the white light that is the purity of the element water dawns before
you. At this time, from the blue eastern pure land of Abhirati, Intense
Delight, the blue Lord Vajrasattva Akshobhya arises before you seated
on an elephant, carrying a five-pronged vajra scepter, in union with
his consort Buddhalochana, attended by the male Bodhisattvas Kshitigarbha and Maitreya and the female Bodhisattvas Lasya and
Pushpa—a group of six Archetype Deities. The white light of the
Mirror wisdom, purity of the form aggregate, white and piercing,

bright and clear, shines from the heart of the Vajrasattva couple before you, penetrating, unbearable to your eyes. At the same time the soft smoky light of the hells shines before you in parallel with the wisdom light. At that time, under the influence of hate you panic, terrified by that brilliant white light, and you flee from it. You feel a liking for that soft smoky light of the hells and you approach it. But now you must fearlessly recognize that brilliant white, piercing, dazzling clear light as wisdom. Be gladdened by it with faith and reverence! Pray, and increase your love for it, thinking, "It is the light of the compassion of Lord Vajrasattva! I take refuge in it!" It is Lord Vajrasattva's shining upon you to escort you through the terrors of the between. It is the tractor-beam of the light of the compassion of Vajrasattva— have faith in it! Don't be enticed by that soft smoky light of hell! Hey! That is the path of destruction from the sins you have accumulated by your strong hatred! If you cling to it, you will fall into the hells; you will be stuck in the mire of unbearable ordeals of suffering, without any escape. It is an obstacle to the path of liberation. Don't look upon it, and abandon all hate! Don't cling to it! Don't long for it! Have faith in that dazzlingly bright white light! Aim your intense willpower toward Lord Vajrasattva and make the following prayer:

Alas! When I roam the life cycle driven by strong hate,
May the Lord Vajrasattva lead me on the path
Of the clear light of the mirror wisdom!
May his Consort Buddhalochana back me on the way,
Deliver me from the dangerous straits of the between,
And carry me to perfect Buddhahood!

By praying in this way with intense faith, you will dissolve into rainbow light in the heart of Lord Vajrasattva, and you will go to his eastern pure land Abhirati and attain Buddhahood in the Body of Perfect Beatitude.

## THE THIRD DAY

Even though they are so oriented, some people of persistent pride and sinfulness will fear the tractor beam of the light rays of compassion and will flee from it. Then on the third day, the Lord Ratnasambhava Deity host and the light path of the human realm come to escort them. Here, calling upon the deceased by name, you should orient her as follows:

Hey, noble one! Listen without wavering! On this third day, the yellow light that is the purity of the element earth dawns. At this time, from the yellow southern Buddha-land of Shrimat, the yellow Lord Ratnasambhava appears seated on a fine horse, carrying a precious wish-granting gem, in union with his consort Mamaki, attended by the male Bodhisattvas Akashagarbha and Samantabhadra and the female Bodhisattvas Mala and Dhupa—a group of six Buddha deities in a background of rainbows, rays, and lights. The yellow light of the Equalizing wisdom, the purity of the sensation aggregate, yellow and piercing, dazzling and clear, adorned with glistening drops and droplets, shines from the heart of the Ratnasambhava couple before you, penetrating your heart center, unbearable to see with your eyes. At the same time, the soft blue light of the human realm shines before you, penetrating your heart in parallel with the wisdom light. At that time, under the influence of pride, you panic and are terrified by that brilliant, energetic yellow light, and you flee it. You feel a liking for that soft blue light of the human realms and you approach it. But at that time you must fearlessly recognize that brilliant yellow, piercing, dazzling clear light as wisdom. Upon it place your mind, relaxing your awareness in the experience of nothing more to do. Or again be gladdened by it with faith and reverence! If you can recognize it as the natural energy of your own awareness, without even having to feel faith or make prayers, you will dissolve indivisibly with all the images and light rays and you will become a Buddha. If you do not recognize it as the natural energy of your own awareness, then pray and increase your love for it, thinking, "It is the light ray of the compassion of Lord Ratnasambhava! I take refuge in it!" It is the tractor beam of the light rays of the compassion of Lord Ratnasambhava—have faith in it! Don't be enticed by that soft blue light of the human realms—for that is the path of destruction from the sins you have accumulated by your fierce pride! If you cling to it, you will fall into the human realms; you will experience the suffering of birth, sickness, old age, and death, and you will find no time for liberation from the life cycle. It is an obstacle blocking the path of liberation. Don't look upon it, and abandon all pride! Abandon its instinct! Don't cling to it! Don't long for it! Have faith in that dazzlingly bright yellow light! Aim your one-pointed willpower toward the Lord Ratnasambhava and make the following prayer:

Hey! When I roam the life cycle driven by strong pride,
May the Lord Ratnasambhava lead me on the path
Of the clear light of the equalizing wisdom!
May his Consort Buddha Mamaki back me on the way,
Deliver me from the dangerous straits of the between,
And carry me to perfect Buddhahood!

By praying in this way with intense faith, you will dissolve into rainbow light in the heart of the Lord Ratnasambhava couple, and you will go to the southern pure land Shrimat and attain Buddhahood in the Body of Perfect Beatitude.

If the deceased recognizes the equalizing wisdom in this way, there is no doubt that even the weakest minded will be liberated.

## THE FOURTH DAY

However, even if you orient them many times thus, ill-fated persons such as those who were very sinful and those who have lost their vows still do not succeed in recognizing their reality. Disturbed by passions and sins, they fear the sounds and lights and flee from them. So again on the fourth day the Lord Amitabha Deity host and the dull light path of the passion- and avarice-created pretan realm come to escort them in their directions. Here, calling upon the deceased by name, you should orient him as follows:

Hey, noble one! Listen without wavering! On this fourth day, the red light that is the purity of the element fire dawns. At this time, from the red western world of Sukhavati, the red Lord Amitabha appears before you seated on a peacock throne, carrying a lotus, in union with his consort Pandaravasini, attended by the male Bodhisattvas Avalokiteshvara and Manjushri and the female Bodhisattvas Gita and Aloka—a group of six Buddha deities in a background of rainbows and lights. The red light of the Discriminating wisdom, purity of the conceptual aggregate, red and piercing, dazzling and clear, adorned with drops and droplets, shines from the heart of the Amitabha couple, precisely penetrating your heart center, unbearable to see with your eyes. Do not fear it! At the same time a soft yellow light of the pretan

1. PADMA SAMBHAVA IN HIS COPPER MOUNTAIN PARADISE
*Tibetan tangka, 19th century, Horch Collection, Rose Art Museum, Brandeis University.*

The Indian great adept and first guru of Tibet, Padma Sambhava, here depicted at home in his palace atop the Copper Mountain, a hidden paradise in jungles somewhere to the southwest of India. To his left and right are his two consorts, the Tibetan princess Yeshe Tsogyal and the Indian princess Mandarava. Above his head are the four-armed Avalokiteshvara Bodhisattva and the red Amitabha Buddha. He is the author of the *Natural Liberation*.

2. AVALOKITESHVARA AS THE THOUSAND-ARMED LORD OF COMPASSION
*Tibetan tangka, 15th century, Robert Hatfield Ellsworth Private Collection.*
The *Natural Liberation* often refers to "the Lord of Compassion," meaning this great Bodhisattva. Avalokiteshvara is praised by the Buddha in many scriptures as the living quintessence of the compassion of all Buddhas. His ten heads and thousand arms symbolize his ability to see the sufferings of all beings and reach out to them his saving hand, whether in the sea of troubles of ordinary life or in the crisis of the between.

3. THE BUDDHA AKSHOBHYA IN THE EASTERN PURE LAND, ABHIRATI
*Tibetan tangka, 15th century, Los Angeles County Museum of Art.*
The Buddha of the eastern direction sits in his Buddha-land, flanked by two
Bodhisattva attendants, surrounded by the many Buddhas, Bodhisattvas, deities,
and ordinary beings who have been reborn in this special world, which is
constructed by Akshobhya's great compassion for all beings.

4. WHEEL OF LIFE

*Tibetan tangka, 19th century, Tibet House, New York City, gift of Ms. Jacqueline Dunnington.*

The wheel is held in the mouth, hands, and feet of a form of Yama, Lord of Death. The rim of the wheel has symbols for the twelve causal links of dependent origination, the Buddhist scheme of world-origination. Inside, the wheel is divided into six spaces; the uppermost is desire-realm heaven, then moving clockwise are the realms of the anti-gods, the animals, the hells (on the bottom), the pretans, and the humans. In the center are a pig, a cock, and a snake, symbolizing the three poisons—delusion, greed, and hate.

5. Fierce Chemchok Heruka and the Between Deities
*Tibetan tangka, 19th century, The Newark Museum.*
This remarkable work presents in one painting all the major deities that appear
in the between as described in the *Natural Liberation*. At the top center sits
the ultimate Buddha, Samantabhadra, dark blue, in union with his consort,
Samantabhadri, who is white. Below him sits Vairochana with his consort, surrounded by the five Scientist adept deities with their consorts. In four circles
around them sit the four Buddhas of the directions with their consorts and
male and female Bodhisattva attendants, blue Vajrasattva, yellow
Ratnasambhava, red Amitabha, and green Amoghasiddhi (clockwise from eight
o'clock). Outside of them are arranged the six Buddhas of the six realms of
existence, with four fierce knowledge-guarding deity couples between them.
The upper left-hand corner has the four-armed Avalokiteshvara, the upper right
the peaceful white Tara, his female colleague. In the center stands the fierce
Heruka Buddha Chemchok, with his consort, surrounded by five fierce Buddha
couples, eight Gauri human-headed goddesses, sixteen animal-headed fierce
goddesses, and four circles with twenty-four animal-headed fierce protectress-
es. A tiny Padma Sambhava outlined in gold sits in the dark blue sky above the
central figure on his right, and a vibrant green Tara sits below him at his left.

6. CHEMCHOK HERUKA
Detail of center of tangka in plate 5.

7. Peaceful Deities All Together
Upper detail of tangka in plate 5.

8. FIERCE DEITIES ALL TOGETHER
Lower detail of tangka in plate 5.

realm shines before you, penetrating your heart in parallel with the wisdom light. Do not indulge in it! Abandon clinging and longing! At that time, under the influence of fierce passion, you panic and are terrified by that brilliant, energetic red light, and you want to flee it. You feel a liking for that soft yellow light of the pretan realms and you approach it.

But at that time you must fearlessly recognize that brilliant red, piercing, dazzling clear light as wisdom. Upon it place your mind, relaxing your awareness in the experience of nothing more to do. Or again be gladdened by it with faith and reverence! If you can recognize it as the natural energy of your own awareness, without feeling faith, without making prayers, you will dissolve indivisibly with all the images and light rays and you will become a Buddha. If you do not recognize it as the natural energy of your own awareness, then pray and hold your aspiration for it, thinking, "It is the light ray of the compassion of Lord Amitabha! I take refuge in it!" It is the tractor beam of the light rays of the compassion of Lord Amitabha—have faith in it! Don't flee it! If you flee it, it still will not leave you! Don't fear it! Don't be enticed by that soft yellow light of the pretan realms! It is the path of the instincts of the sins you have accumulated by your fierce attachment! If you cling to it, you will fall into the pretan realms; you will experience the intolerable suffering of hunger and thirst, and it will be an obstacle blocking the path of liberation. Without clinging to it, abandon your instinct for it! Don't long for it! Have faith in that dazzlingly bright red light! Aim your one-pointed will toward the Lord Amitabha couple and make the following prayer:

Hey! When I roam the life cycle driven by strong passion,
May the Lord Amitabha lead me on the path
Of the clear light of the discriminating wisdom!
May his Consort Buddha Pandaravasini back me on the way,
Deliver me from the dangerous straits of the between,
And carry me to perfect Buddhahood!

By praying in this way with intense faith, you will dissolve into rainbow light in the heart of the Lord Amitabha couple, and you will go to the western pure land Sukhavati and attain Buddhahood in the Body of Perfect Beatitude.

It is impossible for the deceased not to be liberated by this.

*THE FIFTH DAY*

However, even so oriented, by influence of extremely long association with animal instincts, not abandoning instincts, under the influence of envy and negative evolutionary actions, the deceased may still feel anxiety and fear the sounds and lights, and may still not be picked up by the tractor beam of the light rays of compassion. Then, on the fifth day the Lord Amoghasiddhi Deity host's compassion light rays and the addictive envy light path of the titan realm come to escort him. Here, calling upon the deceased by name, you should orient him as follows:

Hey, noble one! Listen without wavering! On this fifth day, the green light that is the purity of the element wind dawns. At this time, from the green northern Buddha-land of Prakuta, the green Lord Amoghasiddhi appears seated on an eagle throne, carrying a vajra cross, in union with his consort Samayatara, attended by the male Bodhisattvas Vajrapani and Sarvanivaranaviskambhin and the female Bodhisattvas Gandha and Nartya—a group of six Buddha deities in a background of rainbows and lights. The green light of the All-accomplishing wisdom, purity of the creation aggregate, green, piercing, dazzling and clear, adorned with glistening drops and droplets, shines from the heart of the Amoghasiddhi couple, precisely penetrating your heart center, unbearable to see with your eyes. Not fearing it, knowing it as the natural force of the wisdom of your own awareness, enter the experience of the great, unoccupied equanimity, free of attraction to the familiar and aversion to the alien! At the same time a soft, envy-made red light of the titan realm shines upon you together with the wisdom light-ray. Meditate upon it with attraction and aversion in balance. If you are of inferior mind, do not indulge in it! At that time, under the influence of fierce jealousy, you panic and are terrified by that brilliant, piercing green light, and you flee it in alarm. You enjoy and are attached to that soft red light of the titan realm and you approach it. But at that time you must fearlessly recognize that brilliant green, piercing, dazzling clear light as wisdom. Upon it relax your awareness in the experience of transcendence with nothing to do. Or again pray and increase your love for it, thinking, "It is the light ray of the compassion of Lord Amoghasiddhi! I take refuge in it!" It is the All-accomplishing wisdom, the light ray of the tractor beam of the compassion of Lord Amoghasiddhi—have faith in it! Don't flee it! If you flee it, it still will not leave you! Don't fear it! Don't be enticed by that soft red light of the titan realms! It is the path of destruction from the negative evolutionary actions you have committed through your powerful jealousy! If you cling to it, you will fall into the titan realms; you will experience the intolerable suffering of interminable fighting, and it will be an obstacle blocking the path of liberation. Without clinging to it, abandon your instinct for it! Don't long for it! Have faith in that dazzling bright green light! Aim your one-pointed willpower toward the Lord Amoghasiddhi couple and make the following prayer:

Hey! When I roam the life cycle driven by strong envy,
May the Lord Amoghasiddhi lead me on the path
Of the clear light of the all-accomplishing wisdom!
May his Consort Buddha Samayatara back me on the way,
Deliver me from the dangerous straits of the between,
And carry me to perfect Buddhahood!

By praying in this way with intense faith, you will dissolve into rainbow light in the heart of the Lord Amoghasiddhi couple, and you will go to the northern pure land Prakuta and attain Buddhahood in the Body of Perfect Beatitude!

When you thus repeatedly orient the deceased, however feeble his affinity, if he does not recognize one wisdom, he will recognize another. It is impossible not to be liberated.

*THE SIXTH DAY*

However, even though you orient the deceased repeatedly in this way, still through long association with the myriad instincts and little previous experience with the purified perception of wisdom, even though he is clearly oriented, he is pulled beyond these recognitions by the force of negative evolution. Not held by the tractor beam of the light rays of compassion, he panics and is terrified by the lights and rays, and he wanders downward. Then, on the sixth day, the five Buddha couples with their retinues all appear together simultaneously. Here, calling upon the deceased by name, you should orient him as follows:

Hey, noble one! Listen without wavering! Up until yesterday, the visions of the five Buddha-clans appeared to you one by one. Though they were clearly described, under the influence of negative evolution you were panicked, and still up to now you are left behind here. If you had already recognized the natural shining of one of the wisdoms of the five clans as your own visions, it would have caused you to dissolve into rainbow light in the body of one of the five Buddha-clans and to attain Buddhahood in the Body of Beatitude. As it is, you did not recognize the light and you are still wandering here. Now, behold without distraction! Now the vision of all the five clans and the vision of the joining of the four wisdoms have come to escort you in their direction. Recognize them!

Hey, noble child! The purity of the four elements is dawning as the four lights. In the center the Vairochana Buddha couple as described above appears from the pure land All-pervading Drop. In the east the Vajrasattva Buddha couple with retinue appears from the pure land Abhirati. In the south the Ratnasambhava Buddha couple with retinue as described above appears from the pure land Shrimat. In the west the Amitabha Buddha couple with retinue as described above appears from the lotus-heaped pure land Sukhavati. In the north the Amoghasiddhi Buddha couple with retinue as described above appears from the pure land Prakuta, in a rainbow light background.

Hey, noble child! Outside of those five Buddha-clan couples appear the fierce door guardians Vijaya, Yamantaka, Hayagriva, and Amertakundali; the fierce door guardian goddesses Ankusha, Pasha, Sphota, and Ghanta; and these six Lord Buddhas: Indra Shatakratu, the Buddha of the gods; Vemachitra, the Buddha of the titans; Shakyamuni, the Buddha of the humans; Simha, the Buddha of the animals; Jvalamukha, the Buddha of the pretans; and Dharmaraja, the Buddha of the hells. Also appearing is the All-around-goodness Samantabhadra Father-Mother, the general ancestor of all Buddhas. Altogether the host of the forty-two deities of the Beatific Body emerges from your own heart center and appears to you—recognize it as your own pure vision!

Hey, noble one! Those pure lands are not anywhere else—they abide in your own heart within its center and four directions. They now emerge from out of your heart and appear to you! Those images do not come from anywhere else! They are primordially created as the natural manifestation of your own awareness—so you should know how to recognize them!

Hey, noble one! Those deities, not great, not small, symmetrical, each with ornamentation, color, posture, throne, and gesture; those deities each pervaded by five mantras, each of the five circled by a five-colored rainbow aura; with male Bodhisattvas of each clan upholding the male part and female Bodhisattvas of each clan upholding the female part, with all the mandalas arising simultaneously whole—they are your Archetype Deities, so you should recognize them!

Hey, noble one! From the hearts of those five Buddha-clan couples four combined wisdom light rays dawn in your heart center, each extremely subtle and clear, like sun rays woven together in a rope.

Now first, from Vairochana's heart center, a cloth of the frighteningly brilliant white light rays of the reality-perfection wisdom dawns connecting to your heart center. Within that light-ray cloth, white drops glisten with their rays, like mirrors facing toward you, very clear, brilliant, and awesomely penetrating, with each drop itself naturally adorned with five other drops. Thus that light-ray cloth is adorned with drops and droplets without limit or center.

> In this vision the reality-perfection wisdom's light is white, whereas earlier it was blue. Likewise, Vajrasattva-Akshobhya's light has switched from white to blue. The interchangeability of these two is a fascinating question. Reality perfection wisdom is sometimes the transmutation of hate, mirror wisdom sometimes that of delusion, usually associated with the consciousness process and the matter process, respectively. And sometimes they are reversed.

From the heart of Vajrasattva, the mirror wisdom, a cloth of blue light rays shines brilliantly upon you connecting to your heart center, on which shining blue drops like turquoise bowls facing down toward you, adorned by other drops and droplets, all shine upon you.

From the heart of Ratnasambhava, a cloth of the equalizing wisdom yellow light rays shines brilliantly upon you, on which golden drops like golden bowls adorned by other golden drops and droplets face down and dawn upon you.

From the heart center of Amitabha, the discriminating wisdom red light cloth shines brilliantly upon you, on which radiant red drops like coral bowls facing down to you, endowed with the deep luster of wisdom, very bright and penetrating, each adorned by five natural red drops—all these shine upon you adorned by drops and droplets without center or limit. These also shine upon you connecting to your heart center.

Hey, noble one! These all arise from the natural exercise of your own awareness. They do not come from anywhere else. So do not be attached to them! Do not be terrified of them! Relax in the experience of nonconceptualization. Within that experience all the deities and light rays will dissolve into you and you will become a Buddha!

Hey, noble one! Since the exercise of the wisdom of your awareness is not perfected, the all-accomplishing wisdom's green light does not shine.

Hey, noble one! These are called the vision of the four wisdoms in combination, the inner passageway of Vajrasattva. At that time, you should remember the orientation previously given by your spiritual teacher! If you remember that orientation, you will trust those visions, you will recognize reality like the child meeting the mother, or like the greeting of a long familiar person; and you will cease all reifying notions. Recognizing your visions as your own creations, you will trust your being held on the changeless path of pure reality, and you will achieve the samadhi of continuity. Your awareness will dissolve into the body of great effortlessness, and you will become a Buddha in the Beatific Body, never to be reversed.

Hey, noble one! Along with the wisdom lights, there also arise the impure, misleading visions of the six species; namely, the soft white light of the gods, the soft red light of the titans, the soft blue light of the humans, the soft green light of the animals, the soft yellow light of the pretans, and the soft smoky light of the hells. These six arise entwined in parallel with the pure wisdom lights. Therefore, don't seize or cling to any of those lights. Relax in the experience of nonperception! If you fear the wisdom lights and cling to the impure six-species life-cycle lights, you will assume a body of a being of the six species. You will not reach the time of liberation from the great ocean of suffering of the life cycle. You will experience only trouble.

Hey, noble one! If you lack the orientation given in the instruction of the spiritual teacher, and you fear and are terrified by the above images and pure wisdom lights, you will come to cling to the impure life-cycle lights. Do not do so! Have faith in those dazzling, piercing pure wisdom lights! Trust in them, thinking, "These light rays of the wisdom of the compassion of the Blissful Lords of the five clans have come to me to hold me with compassion—I must take refuge in them!" Not clinging, not longing for the misleading lights of the six species, aim your will one-pointedly toward the five Buddha-clan couples, and make the following prayer:

Hey! When I roam the life cycle driven by the five strong poisons,
May the Lord Victors of the five clans lead me on the path
Of the clear light of the four wisdoms in combination!
May the supreme five Consort Buddhas back me on the way,
And deliver me from the impure lights of the six realms!
Delivering me from the dangerous straits of the between,
May they carry me to the five supreme pure lands!

Thus having prayed, in the best case the deceased recognizes these visions as her own creations, dissolves into nonduality, and becomes a Buddha. In the medium case, she recognizes them through intense faith and becomes liberated. In the worst case, by the power of sincere prayer, she blocks the doors of rebirth among the six species, she realizes the import of the four wisdoms in combination, and she becomes a Buddha by the inner passageway of Vajrasattva. Thus being oriented clearly and in detail, most beings most often will recognize reality and be liberated.

### THE SEVENTH DAY

However, some sinful people with absolutely no Dharma instinct, dwelling in the most highly uncivilized countries, and some who have abandoned their spiritual vows, will be misled by evolution. Though fully oriented, they will not recognize the Truth Realm, and will wander further downward. On the seventh day, from the Pure Land of Buddha-angels, the Scientist Deity host, along with the delusion-created light path of the animal realm, will come to escort them. Here, calling upon the deceased by name, you should orient him as follows:

Hey, noble one! Listen without wavering! On the seventh day a five-colored, rainbow-striped light will dawn to purify your instincts by immersion in reality. At that time, from the pure land of the angels, the Scientist Deity host will come to escort you. In the center of a mandala wreathed in rainbows and lights, the unexcelled Scientist of evolutionary development, Padmanarteshvara, will arise, his body lustrous with the five colors, his consort the Red Angel wound round his body, performing the dance of chopper and blood-filled skull bowl, striking the gazing posture toward the sky.

> These Scientists are great adepts, such as the famous group of eighty-four from classical India, who have passed from the human realm to special paradises associated with hidden valleys of the Himalayan regions, the "pure lands of the dakini angels." They are associated with speech and, though human in embodiment, have many attributes of fierce deities. They hold in their left hands the skull bowl filled with demon blood and other bodily substances transmuted alchemically into elixir of immortality. In their right hands they hold the scepter-handled chopper-knife that symbolizes critical wisdom and cuts into pieces the bones and flesh of ordinary life in order to make it into elixir, just as critical wisdom dissects all appearances of intrinsic substantiality to reveal the elixir of liberating voidness.

From the east of that mandala the Stage-contemplating Scientist will arise, white, his expression smiling, his consort the White Angel wound round his body, performing the chopper and skull-bowl dance and the gesture of gazing into space. From the south of that mandala the Lifespan-master Scientist will arise, yellow with beautiful signs, his consort the Yellow Angel wound round his body, performing the chopper and skull-bowl dance and the gesture of gazing into space. From the west of that mandala the Great Seal Scientist will arise, red with a smiling expression, his consort the Red Angel wound round his body, performing the chopper and skull-bowl dance and the gesture of gazing into space. From the north of that mandala the Effortlessness Scientist will arise, green and smiling fiercely, his consort the Green Angel wound round his body, performing the chopper and skull-bowl dance and the gesture of gazing into space.

Ranged outside of those scientists, the infinite Angel host arises in order to escort the vow-holding devotee, and to punish the breakers of vows; they are the eight death-ground Angels, the four classes of Angels, the three holy place Angels, the ten holy place Angels, the twenty-four holy land Angels, and the Heroes, the Heroines, and the warrior deities, along with all their defenders, the Dharma-protectors. All wear the six human bone ornaments, carry drums, thigh-bone trumpets, skull drums, human skin victory standards, human skin parasols and pennants, singed flesh incense, and play infinite different kinds of music. They fill the entire universe, rocking, dancing, and shaking, all their musical sounds vibrating as if to split your head open, and performing various dances.

The Scientist and Angel Host is composed of the heroic male and female seekers of enlightenment who have embarked upon the profound odyssey of exploring the underworld of the unconscious with all its terrors and intensities. They adorn themselves with all sorts of gruesome ornaments, making jewelry from human bones and intestines of unburnt corpses, musical instruments from thigh bones and skulls and skins of animals and humans, and they smear themselves with ashes from funeral pyres. They often hold court in cemetaries or burning grounds, showing their transcendence of death and terror by using as ornament and equipment that which terrifies ordinary people. If understood, they afford security and assistance to the practitioner or traveler in the between.

Hey, noble one! Spontaneously purifying instincts in reality, the five-colored wisdom light striped like colored threads wound together dazzles, shimmers, and shines steadily, clear and brilliant, startlingly piercing; from the hearts of the five Scientist Lords it blinds your eyes and penetrates into your heart center. At the same time the soft green light of the animal realm dawns together with the wisdom light. At that time, under the influence of your instincts, you fear the five-colored light and flee from it, enticed by the soft green light of the animal realm. Therefore, don't be afraid of that energetic, piercing, five-colored light! Don't be terrified! Recognize it as wisdom! From within the light comes the thousand rolling thunders of the natural sound of teaching. The sound is fierce, reverberating, rumbling, stirring, like fierce mantras of intense sound. Don't fear it! Don't flee it! Don't be terrified of it! Recognize it as the exercise of your own awareness, your own perception. Do not be attached to that soft green light of the animal realms. Do not long for it! If you cling to it, you will fall into the delusion-dominated realm of the animals, and you will suffer infinite miseries of stupefaction, dumbness, and slavery, without any time of escape. So do not cling to it! Have faith in that penetrating, bright, five-colored light! Aim your will one-pointedly toward the Lord Scientist Master Deity host! Aim your will with the thought:

This Scientist Deity host with its Heroes and Angels has come to escort me to the pure angelic heaven! O, you must know how beings such as me have accumulated no stores of merit and wisdom. We have not been taken up by the grip of the light rays of compassion of such a five-clan Deity host of the Blissful Buddhas of the three times. Alas! Such am I! Now, you the Scientist Deity host, from now on do not neglect me no matter what! Hold me with the tractor beam of your compassion! Right now draw me to the pure heaven of the Buddha Angels!

Then you should make the following prayer:


Hey! May the Scientist Deity host look upon me!
Please lead me on the path with your great love!
When I roam the life cycle driven by strong instincts,
May the Hero Scientists lead me on the path
Of the clear light of orgasmic wisdom!
May their consort Angel host back me on my way,
Deliver me from the dangerous straits of the between,
And carry me to perfect Buddhahood!


When you make this prayer with intense faith, you will dissolve into rainbow light at the heart center of the Scientist Deity host and without a doubt will be reborn in the perfect Angel heaven realm.


When any spiritual friend is oriented in this manner, he invariably recognizes the realm of truth and is liberated. Even though his instincts may be negative, he will surely be liberated. Here *The Great Book of Natural Liberation Through Understanding in the Between* concludes the orientation to the clear light in the death-point between and the description of the reality between of the mild deities.

SAMAYA GYA GYA GYA

## THE FIERCE DEITY REALITY BETWEEN

The fierce deities are actually the same five archetype Buddhas—Vairochana, Akshobhya, Ratnasambhava, Amitabha, and Amoghasiddhi—appearing in their terrific, or Heruka, forms. *Heruka* is a Sanskrit term for a powerful, aggressive hero figure, perhaps cognate with "Hercules." The Archetype Deity Buddhas adopt these forms to engage with the subconscious mind of a person in the between. By this time in the between, a person who has not been able to accept the mild Buddhas' invitations to liberation or life in the Buddha-lands is about to lose conscious control and fall under the compulsion of subconscious drives of lust and aggression. This is why he begins to feel panic and terror. In this strait, the Buddhas adopt a ferocious approach, forcefully breaking into the person's awareness and offering him a powerful escort through a realm that has suddenly become frightening. The Heruka Buddhas in the next days are of various wisdom colors, have three faces, six arms, and four legs.

If you are unfamiliar with such fierce deities, or have strong affiliation with another religion, you should investigate the fierce angels of that tradition (all religions have such figures). In Christianity there are the cherubim and seraphim, which you can invoke on these days.

*THE EIGHTH DAY*

Now the fierce deity reality between arises. The previous mild deity between had seven stages of passage through its dangerous straits. Being oriented to those in order, if the deceased did not recognize the clear light on one stage, she recognized it on another. Limitless numbers of beings attain liberation thereby. Though many are liberated, beings are numberless, negative evolution has great power, sins and obscurations are naturally dense, and instincts are long engrained. This vast machine of the cycle of life is neither exhausted nor increased. Thus, even if one has instructed them with great precision, there is a great stream of beings who are still not liberated and continue to wander downward.

Thus, after the mild deity host and the scientist and angel escorts have made their appearances, through the transformation of the mild deity host, the blazing, fierce, fifty-eight-deity Heruka host will arise. Now, they will be different, as this is the fierce between. The deceased comes under the influence of panic, fear, and terror. It becomes much harder to orient her. Her awareness loses all self-control, and she faints with dizziness. However, if she can even slightly recognize the clear light, she can be easily liberated. Why? Because when the visions of panic, fear, and terror dawn, her awareness has no time for distraction, it is forced to focus one-pointedly. On this occasion, if one does not encounter this kind of instruction, even an ocean of knowledge will be of no help. Even the abbots, masters of monastic discipline, and the great teachers of philosophy will err on this occasion; they will not recognize the clear light. They will wander on in the life cycle. And even more so in the case of ordinary persons; fleeing in panic, fear, and terror, they fall into the abyss of the horrid states and suffer untold misery.

The least of the least of the Tantric yoga practitioners, when they see the Heruka deity host, recognize them at once as their archetype deities, like meeting old friends, and they feel faith toward them. Merging nondually with them they become Buddhas. Further, those who in the human realm practiced the visualizations of these Heruka deities, made offerings and praises, or at least made paintings of the deities or saw sculptures of them and so forth, just by that, they will recognize the arisal of these deities and be liberated. And this is the key point. Again, in the human realm, those discipline master abbots and teachers of philosophy, however expert they may be, when they die, they leave no signs such as body jewels, relics, and rainbow lights. While alive, the Tantras did not appeal to their minds, they disparaged them and cultivated no familiarity with the Tantric deity hosts. Thus when those deities dawn in the between, they do not recognize them. Suddenly seeing what they have never seen before, they think they are enemies. They feel anger toward them, and thereby they fall into the horrid states. Therefore, no matter how holy a discipline master or philosopher seems to be, his lack of interior practice of Tantra may be the reason why he leaves no jewels, no relics, no rainbow lights, and so on. The least of the least of Tantric practitioners, even though superficially their acts may be coarse, they may be inexpert, they may indulge in inappropriate and inelegant behavior, and they may not have been able to practice the Tantric teachings thoroughly, still, as long as they have developed no wrong views toward Tantra, as long as they have no doubts, just by having faith in the Tantras they will attain liberation on this occasion. Even if their behavior was unseemly in society, signs will emerge at the time of death, such as bone jewels, relics, images, and rainbow lights. And that is because this Tantra has extremely great blessings.

From the average Tantric practitioner up, those who have meditated on the creation and perfection stages, who have repeated the essence mantras and so on, they have no need to wander down to this reality between. The moment their breath ceases, the scientists, heroes, angels, and retinues will surely come to invite them to the pure angelic heaven. The signs of that will be a clear sky, a profusion of rainbows and lights, a rain of flowers, the smell of incense, the sound of music in the sky, rays, and the presence of bone jewels, relics, and images.

> The spiritual energy of the Tantras is believed to be so great that merely a positive association with the teachings generates a special sanctity in the practitioner. When such yogis or yoginis are cremated after death, it is commonly reported in Tibet that strange, pearllike gems are found in the ashes, and sometimes images of Buddhas, bodhisattvas, or Archetype Deities.

Therefore, the discipline master, the philosopher, the Tantric practitioner who broke his vows, and all ordinary people, have no method better than this *Natural Liberation*. But the great meditators who have practiced the Great Perfection, the Great Seal, and so forth, will attain the Truth Body by recognizing the clear light of the death-point between, and without exception do not need to read this *Book of Natural Liberation*. Again, by recognizing the clear light of the death-point between, one attains the Truth Body. If one recognizes the clear light in the reality between when the visions of the mild and fierce deities arise, one attains the Beatific Body. If one recognizes the light in the existence between, one attains the Emanation Body and is reborn in the higher estates. Encountering this teaching, one gains the benefit of the evolutionary momentum of experiencing one's last life.

> Since enlightened Buddhas have boundless lives in response to the needs of beings, this does not mean that after liberation, one will never live again. It only means that one is not compelled to live an unenlightened life of suffering, driven by confusion and addictive emotions.

Therefore, this *Natural Liberation* is the teaching for attaining Buddhahood without meditation. It is the teaching for attaining liberation just by initial understanding. It is the teaching that leads great sinners to the secret path. It is the teaching that makes an immediate difference. It is the profound teaching that leads to perfect Buddhahood instantly. It is impossible for a being who has found it to descend into the horrid states. You should read this and the *Liberation by Wearing*. To combine these two is like filling a golden offering mandala with chips of turquoise.

> The *Liberation by Wearing, the Natural Liberation of the Body,* is included in the original text in 21 folios. It repeats the mantric formulae of the hundred deities of the *Natural Liberation* system. The mantras are to be written and bound up in an amulet, which the corpse then wears, assuring that the person will not be carried down into any horrid state.

Thus having shown the great necessity of the *Natural Liberation*, now we give the orientation to the arisal of the fierce deity between. You should call the deceased by name three times and then say the following:

> As above, you pronounce the following instructions at the side of the corpse, if there is one, or in a place familiar to the deceased, or even in your own study, visualizing the deceased as present.

Hey, noble one! Listen without wavering! The peaceful between already dawned, but you did not recognize the light. So now you still must wander here. Now on this eighth day, the Heruka Fierce Deity host will arise. Do not waver! Recognize them! Hey, noble one! The great, glorious Buddha Heruka appears, wine maroon in color, with three faces, six arms, and four legs stretched out, his front face maroon, his right face white, his left face red, his entire body blazing with light rays. His eyes glare, fiercely terrifying, his eyebrows flash like lightning, his fangs gleam like new copper. He roars with laughter, "A la la," and "Ha ha ha," and he makes loud hissing noises like "shu-uu." His bright orange hair blazes upward, adorned with skull crown and sun and moon discs. His body is adorned with black snakes and a freshly severed head garland. His first right hand holds a wheel, the middle an ax, and the third a sword; his first left hand holds a bell, the middle a plowshare, and the third a skull bowl. His Consort Buddha Krodhishvari enfolds his body, her right arm embracing his neck, her left hand offering him sips of blood from her skull bowl. She clucks her tongue menacingly and roars just like thunder. Both are ablaze with wisdom flames, shooting out from their blazing vajra hairs. They stand in the warrior's posture on a throne supported by garudas. Thus they arise manifestly before you, having emerged from within your own brain! Do not fear them! Do not be terrified! Do not hate them! Recognize them as an image of your own awareness! He is your own Archetype Deity, so do not panic! In fact, they are really Lord Vairochana Father and Mother, so do not be afraid! The very moment you recognize them, you will be liberated!

This Buddha Heruka archetype deity is adorned in the usual fierce deity way. His skull crown symbolizes his conquest of the five poisons of lust, hate, delusion, pride, and envy. His severed-head garland symbolizes his overcoming of all his own mental addictions and negative attitudes. His union with Krodhishvari (literally, "Goddess of Ferocity") symbolizes the union of compassion with wisdom. His drinking of the blood from the skull bowl symbolizes the ability of ultimate reality wisdom to transmute the life-blood of the demon of ignorance into the elixir of perfect freedom with its blissful peacefulness and compassionate dynamism. Alternatively, blood is a symbol of the female, of transcendent wisdom, and the male Heruka's drinking it symbolizes that wisdom is the source of the energy of compassion. The Heruka's snake necklace, hair ribbon, bracelets, anklets, and belt symbolize his subjugation of the serpent powers of the earth. The hand implements symbolize various realizations and concentrations he can manifest to help beings break free of delusions and shatter bonds. "Vajra" means thunderbolt, diamond, lightning, a substance of the strongest force in the universe, which is the force of wisdom become love. The flames emitted by these deities, their hair and eyebrows, are vajralike in intensity, like controlled lightning, like white-hot welding heat, like contained supernova explosions. Vajra is the highest symbol of compassion as the ultimate power. Sometimes it can be a five- or nine-pronged scepter, with the same symbolism. The eaglelike garudas supporting their pedestal symbolize the power of far-seeing wisdom to conquer any negativity. Once one has identified with such a terrific presence and merged within it, it provides a secure vehicle to traverse any conceivable evolutionary difficulty.

When you recite this, the deceased will recognize them as his Archetype Deity, dissolve indivisibly into them, and become a Buddha in the Beatific Body.

## THE NINTH DAY

If the deceased feels overcome by fear and hate, and flees without recognizing them, then on the ninth day, the Heruka of the Vajra Buddha-clan will come to escort her. After calling the deceased by name, you should orient her as follows:

Hey, noble one! Listen without wavering! Now on the ninth day the Lord Vajra Heruka of the Vajra-clan will arise before you, emerging from within your brain. He is dark blue, with three faces, six arms, and four legs stretched out. His front face is dark blue, his right face white, his left face red. His first right hand holds a vajra, the middle a skull bowl, and the third an ax; his first left hand holds a bell, the middle a skull bowl, and the third a plowshare. His Consort Buddha Vajra Krodhishvari enfolds his body, her right arm embracing his neck, her left hand offering him sips of blood from her skull bowl. Thus they arise manifestly before you, having emerged from within your own brain! Do not fear them! Do not be terrified! Do not hate them! Recognize them as an image of your own awareness! They are your own Archetype Deity, so do not panic! In fact, they are really Lord Vajrasattva Father and Mother, so have faith in them! The very moment you recognize them, you will be liberated!

When you recite this, the deceased will recognize them as her Archetype Deity, dissolve inseparably into them, and become a Buddha in the Beatific Body.

## THE TENTH DAY

If those with heavy obscurations feel overcome by fear and hate, and flee without recognizing them, then on the tenth day, the Heruka of the Jewel Buddha-clan will come to escort them. After calling the deceased by name, you should orient him as follows:

Hey, noble one! Listen without wavering! Now on the tenth day the Jewel-clan Heruka, Lord Ratna Heruka, will manifest to you, emerging from within your brain. He is dark yellow, with three faces, six arms, and four legs stretched out, his front face dark yellow, his right face white, his left face red. His first right hand holds a jewel, the middle a khatvanga staff, and the third a club; his first left hand holds a bell, the middle a skull bowl, and the third a trident. His Consort Buddha Ratna Krodhishvari enfolds his body, her right arm embracing his neck, her left hand offering him sips of blood from her skull bowl. Thus they arise manifestly before you, having emerged from within the southern part of your own brain! Do not fear them! Do not be terrified! Do not hate them! Recognize them as an image of your own awareness! They are your own Archetype Deity, so do not panic! In fact, they are really Lord Ratnasambhava Father and Mother, so have faith in them! The very moment you recognize them, you will be liberated!

A khatvanga staff is a symbol of a Buddha's mastery of the central channel of the yogic inner nervous system. It has an eight-sided shaft, a half-vajra scepter on the bottom, and the top is built up of a vase of immortality, three shrunken heads that symbolize triumph over lust, hate, and delusion, and a trident blade above them.

When you recite this, the deceased will recognize them as his archetype deity, dissolve inseparably into them, and become a Buddha in the Beatific Body.

## THE ELEVENTH DAY

If, when encountering these deities, the deceased is led astray by negative instincts, feels fear and hate, and flees without recognizing them as her archetype deity, mistaking them to be the Lord of Death, then on the eleventh day, the Heruka of the Lotus Buddha-clan will come to escort her. After calling the deceased by name, you should orient her as follows:

Hey, noble one! Listen without wavering! Now on the eleventh day, the Lotus-clan Heruka, Lord Padma Heruka, will manifest to you, emerging from within your brain. He is dark red, with three faces, six arms, and four legs stretched out, his front face dark red, his right face white, his left face blue. His first right hand holds a lotus, the middle a khatvanga staff, and the third a rod; his first left hand holds a bell, the middle a skull bowl filled with blood, and the third a small drum. His Consort Buddha Padma Krodhishvari enfolds his body, her right arm embracing his neck, her left hand offering him sips of blood from her skull bowl. Thus they arise manifestly before you, standing in sexual union, having emerged from within your own brain! Do not fear them! Do not be terrified! Do not hate them! Feel delight! Recognize them as an image of your own awareness! They are your own Archetype Deity, so do not panic! In fact, they are really Lord Amitabha Father and Mother, so have faith in them! The very moment you recognize them, you will be liberated!

When you recite this, the deceased will recognize them as her Archetype Deity, dissolve inseparably into them, and become a Buddha in the Beatific Body.

*THE TWELFTH DAY*

If, when they are encountered, the deceased is led astray by negative instincts, feels fear and hate, and flees without recognizing them as his Archetype Deity, mistaking them to be the Lord of Death, then on the twelfth day, the Heruka of the Karma Buddha-clan deity host, and the Gauri goddesses, the Pishachi ghouls, and the Ishvari goddesses will come to escort him. If they are not recognized he will be terrified. So, after calling the deceased by name, he should be oriented toward them as follows:

> The Gauri goddesses, Pishachi ghouls, and Ishvari goddesses are various types of fierce female deities, who will be described below in the text itself. Encountering them is like encountering extremely deeply repressed elements of your own psyche, terrifying because they are denied. At this juncture in the between, when there is no avoiding the encounter with the grim side of reality, the deceased has no time to insist on a nice self-image. So meeting these fierce female beings, these primal powers of nature, is extremely important, and it is essential that you overcome your initial revulsion.

Hey, noble one! Listen without wavering! Now on this the twelfth day, the Lord Karma Heruka of the Karma-clan will manifest before you, emerging from within your own brain. He is dark green, with three faces, six arms, and four legs stretched out, his front face dark green, his right face white, his left face red. His first right hand holds a sword, the middle a khatvanga staff, and the third a rod; his first left hand holds a bell, the middle a skull bowl, and the third a plowshare. His Consort Buddha Karma Krodhishvari enfolds his body, her right arm embracing his neck, her left hand offering him sips of blood from her skull bowl. Thus they arise manifestly before you, standing in sexual embrace, having emerged from the north of your own brain! Do not fear them! Do not be terrified! Do not hate them! Recognize them as an image of your own awareness! They are your own Archetype Deity, so do not panic! In fact, they are really Lord Amoghasiddhi Father and Mother, so have faith in them, feel deep reverence for them! The very moment you recognize them, you will be liberated!

When you recite this, the deceased will recognize them as his Archetype Deity, dissolve inseparably into them, and become a Buddha.

Thus through the instructions of the spiritual teacher, when you recognize these deities as your own visions, the creations of your own awareness, then you will be liberated, just as you become free from fear when you recognize that a frightening lion is only stuffed. If you did not know that a certain lion was stuffed, you would feel fear and hate when encountering it; but when someone tells you what it really is, you are relieved, and lose all fear. So, when you see the host of Heruka deities, with their huge bodies and powerful limbs, arising to fill all space, you will surely feel fear and hate. But as soon as you receive this orientation, you can recognize them as your own visions or as your Archetype Deities. The clear light you have previously meditated on and the clear light that now arises can merge like mother and child, and you are instantly liberated in the natural clarity of your own awareness, like meeting an old friend, since in such awareness whatever arises is naturally liberated. If you have not received this orientation, even if you are a good person, you will turn away from these fierce deities and wander further in the life cycle.

Then the eight fierce Gauri goddesses and the eight Pishachi ghouls with their animal heads will emerge from within her brain and appear to her. After calling the deceased by name, you should orient her as follows:

Hey, noble one! Listen without wavering! The eight Gauri goddesses will emerge from within your brain and appear to you! Do not fear them! From the east of your brain appears to your east a white Gauri, her right hand holding a corpse as a club and her left hand holding a blood-filled skull bowl. Do not fear her! From the south, a yellow Chauri, aiming a bow and arrow; from the west, a red Pramoha, holding a crocodile victory standard; from the north, a black Vetali, holding a vajra and a blood-filled skull bowl; from the southeast, an orange Pukkasi, her right hand holding intestines, her left hand feeding them into her mouth; from the southwest, a dark green Ghasmari, her left hand holding a blood-filled skull bowl and her right hand holding a vajra, with which she stirs the blood and feeds it into her mouth; from the northwest, a pale yellow Chandali holding a body and head across her shoulders, her right hand holding a heart and her left hand feeding herself with the corpse; from the northeast, a dark blue Shmashani, feeding on a headless body; all these eight holy-ground Gauri goddesses emerge from within your brain and appear to you surrounding the five Herukas! Do not fear them!

These Gauri goddesses have humanlike heads and faces, except that they have three eyes, with one vertical eye in the middle of their forehead. They have two arms and two legs. They appear with the most fearsome aspect imaginable—you have not visualized them correctly if they do not inspire terror. They are said to come from the holy grounds in the various quarters of the earth, as they are awesome guardians associated with the sacred burial places and power spots of the land.

Hey, noble one! Listen without wavering! After that, the eight Pishachi ghouls of the holy lands will appear to you! From the east, a dark maroon, lion-headed Simhasya, crossing her arms over her chest, holding a corpse in her mouth, and tossing her mane; from the south, a red, tiger-headed Vyaghrasya, crossing her arms downward, staring hypnotically and gnashing her fangs; from the west, a black, jackal-headed Shrgalasya, with a razor in her right hand, holding and feeding on intestines in her left hand; from the north, a dark blue, wolf-headed Shvanasya, lifting a corpse up to her mouth with her two hands and staring hypnotically; from the southeast, a light yellow, vulture-headed Grdhrasya, carrying a corpse over her shoulder and holding a skeleton in her hand; from the southwest, a dark red, hawk-headed Kankhasya, carrying a corpse over her shoulder; from the northwest, a black, crow-headed Kakasya, with a sword in her right hand, eating lungs and hearts; from the northeast, a dark blue, owl-headed Ulukasya, eating flesh and holding a vajra in her right hand and a sword in her left hand; all these holy-land Pishachi ghouls emerge from within your brain and appear to you surrounding the five Herukas! Do not fear them! Recognize whatever arises as the creativity of your own visionary awareness!

> These ghouls have animal heads, as described, and two arms and two legs. They are cannibalistic and revolting.

Hey, noble one! Listen without wavering! The four Door-guardian goddesses will emerge from your own brain and appear to you, so recognize them! From the east of your brain, a white, horse-headed Ankusha, with an iron hook in her right hand, and a blood-filled skull bowl in her left hand, will appear to your east. From the south, a yellow, pig-headed Pasha holding a noose; from the west, a red, lion-headed Shernkhala, holding an iron chain; from the north, a green, serpent-headed Ghanta holding a bell; these four Door-guardian goddesses will emerge from your brain and appear to you! Recognize them as being your own Archetype Deities!

Hey, noble one! Outside of these thirty fierce Heruka deities, the twenty-eight Ishvari goddesses with their various heads and their various implements will emerge from within your brain and appear to you. Do not fear them, but recognize them as the creativity of your own visionary awareness! At this time when you have arrived at the crucial moment of cessation, remember the instructions of your spiritual teacher!

> The thirty fierce Heruka deities are the ten Heruka Fathers and Mothers, the eight Gauris, the eight Pishachis, and the four Door-guardian goddesses. The Ishvari goddesses below are also called "Yoginis," indicating that they are deities of the subtle realms of the interior experience of advanced adepts. They are also goddesses

of the Indian pantheon, many of them being female forms of well-known deities, such as Brahma, Indra, Kumara, and so forth. A person from another culture would want to include fierce angels from his own culture, thinking of them as icons of these spiritual beings alive within his own psyche. Their animal heads also indicate that they represent the powers of the natural world. Making your peace with them thus puts you into a balanced state in relation to your culturally induced sense of the divine realm as well as to the living presences in your natural environment.

Hey, noble one! From the east, the dark maroon, yak-headed Rakshasi holding a vajra; the orange, serpent-headed Brahmi holding a lotus; the dark green, leopard-headed Maheshvari holding a trident; the blue, mongoose-headed Lobha holding a wheel; the red, mule-headed Kumari holding a javelin; the white, bear-headed Indrani holding an intestine-noose; these six eastern Yoginis emerge from your own brain and appear before you! Do not fear them!

Hey, noble one! From the south, the yellow, bat-headed Vajra holding a razor; the red, crocodile-headed Shanti holding a vase; the red, scorpion-headed Amerta holding a lotus; the white, hawk-headed Chandra holding a vajra; the dark green, box-headed Gada holding a club; the yellow-black, tiger-headed Rakshasi holding skull-bowl blood; these six southern Yoginis emerge from your own brain and appear before you! Do not fear them!

From the west, the dark green, vulture-headed Bhakshasi holding a club; the red, horse-headed Rati holding a human torso; the white, garuda-headed Mahabali holding a club; the red, dog-headed Rakshasi holding a vajra razor; the red, hoopoe-headed Kama aiming a bow and arrow; the red-green, deer-headed Vasuraksha holding a vase; these six western Yoginis emerge from within your brain and appear before you! Do not fear them!

Hey, noble one! From the north, the blue, wolf-headed Vayavi holding a banner; the red, ibex-headed Narini holding an impaling stake; the black, boar-headed Varahi holding a tusk-noose; the red, crow-headed Rati holding a child's skin; the green-black, elephant-headed Mahanasi holding a fresh corpse and drinking blood from a skull bowl; the blue, serpent-headed Varuni holding a serpent-noose; these six northern Yoginis will emerge from within your brain and appear before you! Do not fear them!

Hey, noble one! The four outer Door-guardian Yoginis will emerge from within your brain and appear before you! From the east, the white, cuckoo-headed Vajra holding an iron hook; from the south, the yellow, goat-headed Vajra holding a noose; from the west, the red, lion-headed Vajra holding an iron chain; from the north, the green-black, serpent-headed Vajra holding a bell; these four Door Yoginis will emerge from within your brain and appear before you! All these twenty-eight goddesses arise naturally from the creativity of the self-originating bodies of the fierce Herukas—so you should recognize them as Buddha-wisdom!

Hey, noble one! The Truth Body arises from the voidness side as the peaceful deities! Recognize it! The Beatific Body arises from the clarity side as the fierce deities! Recognize it! At this time when the fifty-eight-deity Heruka host emerges from within your brain and appears before you, if you know that whatever arises is arisen from the natural energy of your own awareness, you will immediately become nondual with the Heruka Body and become a Buddha!

The concept of clarity-voidness indivisible is precisely parallel to the inconceivable nonduality of the ultimate Truth Body and the relative Beatific Body of the Buddhas. Voidness is not a dark nothingness, the purely negative zone we might think of when we allow our mind to imagine something corresponding to the unimaginable absolute. Voidness is the voidness of the intrinsic reality of everything, including voidness itself. It is precisely that form of the absolute that does not pose as any sort of pseudo-relative absolute— it does not get in the way of the infinite network of relativities. Therefore it *is* the creativity of clarity, of light, of infinite distinctness. And that distinctness is capable of relationality because it is free of intrinsic realities. Creativity and freedom, clarity and voidness are nondual. The void side of the nonduality is aligned with the Truth Body, the presence in enlightenment of the absolute as a body, an experiential, infinite, calm presence. And the clear side of the nonduality is aligned with the Beatific Body, the presence in enlightenment of the relative awareness of the absolute through self-releasing ecstasy as a body, and experiential, infinite, orgasmic ecstasy. The Truth Body presence is imaged forth to human consciousness in the form of the calm Archetype Deities. The Beatific Body ecstasy is imaged forth in the form of the fierce archetype deities. And both these aspects of perfect enlightenment are completely inseparable from your own natural intelligence and sensitivity. If you recognize them as your own essential nature, then freedom is yours, and the enlightenment of Buddhahood.

Hey, noble one! If you do not recognize that, you will cling to superficial reality, feel fear and hate, and flee these deities. You will go down again into excessive misery! If you do not recognize them, you will perceive the whole Heruka Deity host as if they were Yamas, Lords of Death, and you will fear the Heruka deities. You will hate them! You will panic! You will faint! Your own visions having become devils, you will wander in the life cycle!

You have met Yama before as the Lord of Death, the lord of the underworld who acts as judge of the good and bad deeds of the deceased, and assigns them their destiny. His minions are those who come for the soul of the dying, and so to perceive Yama is to meet death perceived as an alien, hostile being who threatens one with the ultimate power of life and death and destiny in the beyond. So the deceased who refuses to acknowledge the power and glory of her own consciousness, who cannot incorporate all the repressed imagery of her unconscious, perceives the fierce deities as alien, hostile beings, mortal enemies, and thereby gives herself over to terror and hatred. Thus, to help the dying effectively, it is not enough to prepare the departing person for mild and peaceful images. If the Indian and Tibetan imagery seems too strange and exotic, then local imagery of fierce cherubim or seraphim, of animal totems or shamanic nature spirits—whatever it takes—will be required to prepare the dying person for the wild and intense imagery her own mind will naturally generate.

Hey, noble one! These mild and fierce deities at most will be as big as space, at medium will be as large as Sumeru, the planetary axis, at the least will be as large as eighteen times the height of your own body—so do not be afraid of them! All visible existence will arise as lights and deities! And all visions arising as lights and deities must be recognized as the natural energy of your own awareness. When your own energy dissolves nondually into these natural lights and deities, you will become a Buddha!

O my child! What you see and perceive, whatever terrifying visions occur, recognize them as your own visions! Recognize the clear light as the natural energy of your own awareness! If you so recognize, there is no doubt you will become a Buddha right away! The so-called "instantaneous perfect Buddhahood" will have come to pass! Remember this in your mind!

Hey, noble one! If now you do not recognize the light, and if you cling to terror, all the mild deities will arise as black Mahakala guardians! All the fierce deities will arise as Yama Dharmaraja deities! Your own visions having become devils, you will wander in the life cycle!

Even the mild deities will appear as demonic guardians, grisly and frightening in aspect, just as the fierce deities will appear as death gods.

Hey, noble one! If you do not recognize your own visions, though you become expert in all scriptures of sutra and Tantra, though you practice the Dharma for an eon, you will not become a Buddha! If you recognize your own visions, with one key, one word, you will become a Buddha! If you do not recognize your own visions, then the moment you die, reality arises in the between in the image of Yama Dharmaraja the Lord of Death! The Yama Dharmaraja deities will arise at most filling all of space, at medium like huge mountains, filling the whole world. Their fanglike teeth protruding over their lips, their eyes like glass, their hair bound up on top of their heads, with protruding bellies, with thin necks, they carry punishment boards and shout, "Beat him!" and "Kill him!" They lick up your brains, they sever your head from your body, and they extract your heart and vital organs. Thus they arise, filling the world.

Thus the Yama death-gods appear as the crystallizations of the dying person's vivid guilt and anxious sense of remorse not only for bad deeds committed, but also for all the negative and evil impulses that he has repressed.

Hey, noble one! When it happens that such a vision arises, do not be afraid! Do not feel terror! You have a mental body made of instincts; even if it is killed or dismembered, it cannot die! Since in fact you are a natural form of voidness, anger at being injured is unnecessary! The Yama Lords of Death are but arisen from the natural energy of your own awareness and really lack all substantiality. Voidness cannot injure voidness!

Except insofar as they arise from the natural creativity of your own awareness, you must firmly decide that all that you see—the mild and fierce deities, the Herukas, the animal-headed angels, the rainbow lights, and the Yama deities—none is substantially, objectively existent! Once you understand that, then all the fears and terrors become liberated on the spot, you dissolve into nonduality and become a Buddha! If you so recognize them, you must feel intense faith, thinking, "They are my Archetype Deities! They have come to escort me through the straits of the between! I take refuge in them!"

Be mindful of the Three Jewels! Remember whoever is your Archetype Deity! Call him or her by name! Pray to him or her, "I am wandering lost in the between—be my savior! Hold me with your compassion, O precious deity!" Call on your spiritual teacher by name, praying, "I am wandering lost in the between—be my savior! For compassion's sake, do not let me go!" Feel faith in the Heruka Deity host, and pray to them:

When I wander in the life cycle driven by powerful instincts,
May the host of mild and fierce Lords lead me on the path
Of the clear light that conquers terror-visions of hate and fear!
May the fierce Ishvari goddess hosts back me on the way,
Deliver me from the dangerous straits of the between,
And carry me to perfect Buddhahood!

Now that I wander alone, apart from my loved ones,
And all my visions are but empty images,
May the Buddhas exert the force of their compassion
And stop the fear- and hate-drawn terrors of the between!

When the five lights of brilliant wisdom dawn,
Fearless, bravely, may I know them as myself!
When the forms of the Lords mild and fierce arise,
Bold and fearless, may I recognize the between!
Now when I suffer by the power of negative evolution,
May the Archetype Deities dispel that suffering!
When reality crashes with a thousand thunders,
May they all become OM MANI PADME HUM!

When I'm pulled by evolution without recourse,
May the Compassionate Lord provide me refuge!
When I suffer due to evolutionary instincts,
May the clear light bliss samadhi dawn upon me!

May the five main elements not arise as enemies!
May I behold the pure lands of the five Buddha-clans!

Thus you should pray with intense reverence and faith! It is
extremely important, since your fear and terror will thus disappear
and you will surely become a Buddha in the Beatific Body! Do not
waver!

You should read these instructions three or seven times. Thereby, however great the sins, however negative the evolutionary momentum, it is
impossible for the deceased not to become liberated! Yet, however these
are employed, if there is no recognition of the light, it will be necessary
to wander in the third between, the existence between. So the orientation for it is taught in detail below.

People in general, whether slightly or greatly experienced, feel confusion and panic at the point of death. There is no recourse for them
other than this *Great Book of Natural Liberation Through Understanding
in the Between*. Those highly familiar with clear light reality come to
the path of reality immediately on the parting of matter and mind.
Those who have recognized the light of reality in their awareness while
still alive and have true realization have the greatest strength when the
clear light dawns in the death-point between. So practice while living
is very important! Further, those who while living have meditated on
the creation and perfection stages of Tantric deities have very great
strength when the mild and fierce visions dawn in the reality between.
So it is very important during your life to cultivate your mind with this
*Book of Natural Liberation*. You should practice this! You should read
it! You should recite it! You should understand it! You should memorize
it accurately! You should rehearse it three times a day without fail! You
should become very clear about its words and meaning! You should not
forget them even if chased by a hundred murderers!

This is the *Great Natural Liberation Through Understanding in the
Between*. Even if a person who has committed the five unpardonable
sins were just to hear it, he would surely be liberated. Therefore read it
in the middle of the great marketplace and spread it widely. Even if you
hear it just once like this and do not yet understand its meaning, since
the intellect becomes nine times clearer in the between, you will remember it at that time without forgetting even a single word. Therefore,
you should proclaim it in the hearing of all while they are still living.

You should read it at the pillow of every sick person. You should read it beside every corpse. You should spread it extensively.

Whoever encounters this has a very positive destiny. It is very hard for anyone to encounter this who does not have great stores of merit and wisdom, and who has not cleared away their emotional and intellectual obscurations. All will be liberated who understand this, as long as they do not adopt any misguided views. Therefore, this teaching should be cherished as extremely precious. It is the quintessence of all teachings.

# ORIENTATION
# TO THE EXISTENCE BETWEEN

With deep reverence I bow to the Deity host
Of Spiritual Mentors, Archetypes, and Angels!
I pray you to free me in the between!

From the *Book of Natural Liberation,* the reality between has already been taught. Now, for the existence between, the prayer is to be performed as follows:

> The existence between is the between that ensues when a person has failed to accept the invitation of the five wisdoms in either calm or terrific forms to leave the ordinary life cycle and enter into the boundless lifestyle of enlightenment. It is called "existence" because the appetite for ordinary existence has determined that, almost inevitably, there will be one. It is still possible for liberation to be attained, and the guide still urges that possibility. But there also is a note of concern for the quality of the coming life. If a further ordinary existence is inevitable, then at least it should be a good one with favorable circumstances, in a pleasant environment, with good opportunities for study and practice of the Dharma teachings and, thereby, evolutionary advancement.

## BASIC INTRODUCTION

You may have already given the reality-between orientation many times, and persons with great experience and positive evolutionary momentum may have already recognized the light. Still, people with only slight experience and heavy sins, being caught by terror and negative evolution, will find it difficult to recognize the light. So from the tenth day on, you should also perform this prayer of the existence between. You should make offerings to the Three Jewels. You should recite the prayer *Help from the Buddhas and Bodhisattvas.* Then, calling the deceased by name three or seven times, you should say the following:

**Hey, noble one! Listen well, and keep this in your mind! In hell, heaven, and the between, the body is born by apparition. But when**

the perceptions of the mild and fierce deities arose in the reality between, you did not recognize them. So after five and a half days, you fainted with terror. Upon awakening, your awareness became more clear, and you immediately arose in a likeness of your former body. As it says in the Tantra:

> Having the fleshly form of the preceding and emerging lives, senses all complete, moving unobstructed, with evolutionary magic powers, one sees similar species with pure clairvoyance.

> The Tantra is not identified, but can be presumed to be one of the *Guhyagarbha* tantras. The quotation is treated as if it had authority; the following sections are presented as commentary on the passage. It is obviously a *locus classicus* of description of the between-state embodiment.

Here "preceding" means that you arise as if in a flesh-and-blood body determined by the instincts of your preceding life. If you are radiant and have traces of the auspicious bodily signs and marks of a mythic hero, it is because your imagination can transform your body; thus, that perceived in the between is called a "mental body."

> The body in the between is made of subtle energy, like a holographic image. Thus, the imagination functions concretely to hold it together. If one has a stabilized and focused imagination, one can reshape the body just by a thought. Thus, if one's instincts during life have been shaped by deep identification with a mythic archetype, one can easily transform into such a hero in the between-state. This is the purpose of the creation stage visualization practices, using various Archetype Deities. It is to focus and train the imagination so that it can perform a vital, life-shaping function in this between-state context.

At that time, if you are to be born as a god, you will have visions of the heavens. If you are to be born as a titan, a human, an animal, a pretan, or a hell-being, you will have visions of whichever realm you will be born in. "Preceding" here means that for up to four and a half days you experience yourself as having a fleshly body of your previous life with its habitual instincts. "Emerging" means that you begin to have visions of the place where you are heading for rebirth. So much for "preceding and emerging."

Therefore, do not follow after every vision that happens. Don't be attached to it! Don't adhere to it! If you are stubborn and attached to all of them, you will roam in suffering through the six realms. Up until yesterday, the visions of the reality between dawned for you, but you did not recognize them. So you have had to wander here now. So now, if, without wavering, you can develop recognition, the spiritual teacher's orientation can open your awareness of the clear light, the naked, pure, vibrant void. Enter into it, relax into the experience of nonholding, nondoing! Without having to enter a womb, you will be liberated.

If you do not recognize the light, then meditate that your spiritual teacher or Archetype Deity is present on the crown of your head, and devote yourself totally with a strong force of faith. It is so important! Do it without wavering, again and again!

So you should say. If the deceased recognizes the light at this point, she will not wander in the six realms, and will be liberated.

*POWERS AND PROBLEMS*
*OF A BETWEEN-BEING*

If the power of negative evolution still makes recognition of the light difficult, you should again speak as follows:

Hey, noble one! Listen without your mind wandering! "Senses all complete, moving unobstructed" means that even if in life you were blind, deaf, crippled, and so on, now in the between, your eyes clearly discern forms, your ears hear sounds, and so forth. Your senses become flawlessly clear and complete; so, "senses all complete." Recognize this as a sign that you have died and are wandering in the between! Remember your personal instructions!

Hey, noble one! What is "unobstructed" is your mental body; your awareness is free from embodiment and you lack a solid body. So now you can move hither and thither everywhere, through walls, houses, land, rocks, and earth, even through Meru, the axial mountain; except through a mother's womb and the Vajra Throne at Bodhgaya. This is a sign that you are wandering in the existence between, so remember the instructions of your spiritual teacher! Pray to the Lord of Great Compassion!

The between-being cannot pass through a mother's womb because that is the place where he or she will take rebirth—a being that can go through mountains cannot get through that delicate membrane. The Vajra throne at Bodhgaya is the place where Supreme Emanation Body Buddhas attain enlightenment in this world, and the place is believed to have a special physical density as well as a special sanctity. So no between-being can pass through it.

Hey, noble one! "With evolutionary magic powers" means that you, who have no special abilities or meditational magic powers whatsoever, now have magic powers arising as the result of your evolution. In a split second, you can circle this four-continent planet with its axial mountain. You now have the power just to think about any place you wish and you will arrive there in that very instant. You can reach anywhere and return just as a normal man stretches out and pulls back his arm. But these various magic powers are not so miraculous; if you don't specially need them, ignore them! You should not worry about whether or not you can manifest this or that, which you may think of. The fact is you have the ability to manifest anything without any obstruction. You should recognize this as a sign of the existence between! You should pray to your spiritual teacher!

The person in the between-state naturally has all these supernormal abilities. However, they should not become a diversion, a distraction from the main issue of the between, the opportunity to attain liberation from the compulsive lifestyle by confronting the nature of reality; or at least, the opportunity to obtain a new life favorable to such an attainment, avoiding any horrid states or lives shorn of liberty and opportunity.

Hey, noble one! "One sees similar species with pure clairvoyance" means that beings of the same species in the between can see each other. Thus if some beings are of the same species, all going to be reborn as gods, they will see each other. Likewise, other beings of the same species, to be reborn in whichever of the six realms, will see each other. So you should not be attached to such encounters! Meditate on the Lord of Great Compassion!

"With pure clairvoyance" refers also to the vision of those whose pure clairvoyance has been developed by the practice of contemplation, as well as to the vision of those whose divine power of merit has developed it. But such yogis or deities cannot always see between-beings. They see them only when they will to see them, and not when they do not, or when their contemplation is distracted.

> If a clairvoyant were forced to perceive all between-beings around, she would have no time to see anything else. Infinite numbers of beings of all species are dying and traversing the between all the time, and their subtle embodiments can effortlessly penetrate solid objects, or coexist in the same coarse space with other things. Therefore, they are everywhere evident to one with clairvoyant abilities, whether natural or developed. What many cultures refer to as "ghosts" clearly fit the description of the between-state wanderer (which is why the pretan, who has become reborn in that horrid form, should not be translated "hungry ghost"). Indeed, the hero in the recent film *Ghost* is presented as having many of the characteristics of the between-being.

Hey, noble one! As you have such a ghostly body, you encounter relatives and familiar places as if in a dream. When you meet these relatives, though you communicate with them, they do not answer. When you see your relatives and dear ones crying, you will think, "Now I have died, what can I do?" You feel a searing pain, like a fish flopping in hot sand. But however greatly you suffer, tormenting yourself at this time does not help. If you have a spiritual teacher, pray to your spiritual teacher. Or else pray to the compassionate Archetype Deity. Don't be attached to your loved ones—it is useless. Pray to the Compassionate Ones, and do not suffer or be terrified!

Hey, noble one! Driven by the swift wind of evolution, your mind is helpless and unstable, riding the horse of breath like a feather blown on the wind, spinning and fluttering. You tell the mourners, "Don't cry! Here I am!" They take no notice, and you realize you have died, and you feel great anguish. Now do not indulge in your pain! There is a constant twilight, gray as the predawn autumn sky, neither day nor night. That kind of between can last for one, two, three, four, five, six, or seven weeks—up to forty-nine days. Though it is said that for most people the suffering of the existence between lasts twenty-one days, this is not always certain due to people's different evolutionary histories.

This disclaimer of precision in timing comes as something of a relief. The time in the death-point between has been mentioned above as seeming to be four and a half days of unconsciousness to the ordinary person, though developed practitioners can prolong it indefinitely. Then there are twelve days mentioned in the reality between. If you add the twenty-one days of the existence between, you have a total of thirty-seven and a half days. Then there is the traditional number of forty-nine days, mentioned in various Buddhist sources. The bottom line is that waking-reality time-lines cannot convey with precision the experience of the between.

Now begins the experience of the existence between. The fierce deity apparitions in the reality between were interventions by the compassionate deities into a level of the person's consciousness where primal impulses were lodged. Powerful emotions were stirred up in those areas of being. Now, the person's conviction about the substantiality of reality and attachment to the ordinary, delusion-driven lifestyle have been so persistent that a further birth in the realm of ordinary existence appears imminent. It is only natural then, that this threshold is attended by psychic simulations of the most dramatic and terrifying sort of experiences.

Hey, noble one! At this time the great red wind of evolution will drive you from behind, fiercely, unbearably, terrifyingly. Don't be afraid of it! It is your own hallucination! A frightening thick darkness draws you from the front, irresistibly. You are terrified by harsh cries, such as "Strike!" "Kill!" Don't be afraid of them! Heavy sinners will see cannibal ogres brandishing many weapons, shouting war cries, "Kill! Kill!" and "Strike! Strike!" You will see ferocious wild animals. You will be hunted by troops in blizzards, storms, and fogs. You will hear sounds of avalanches, flood waters, forest fires, and hurricanes. In panic you will escape by any means, only to stop short on the brink of falling down a yawning triple abyss, red, black, and white, bottomless and horrifying.

Hey, noble one! It is not really an abyss. It is lust, hate, and delusion. You should recognize this as the moment of the existence between! Call upon the Lord of Great Compassion, and pray intensely, "O Lord of Great Compassion! Spiritual teacher! Three Jewels! I am named So-and-so—please don't abandon me to the horrid states! Don't forget me!"

Those who have gathered merit, virtuous and sincere in Dharma practice, are entertained with various delights and enjoy various excellent pleasures. And those dominated by delusion, who have neither strong virtue nor strong vice, have neither happiness nor suffering, but feel only stupefaction and indifference.

O noble one, whatever happens along those lines, don't crave! Don't long for pleasures or joys! Offer them all to the jewel of the spiritual teacher! Abandon attachment to them! Even without any visions of pleasure or pain, with only feelings of indifference, set the mind on the experience of the Great Seal, free of both concentration and distraction! That is most important.

Hey, noble one! At that time, structures such as bridges, temples, cathedrals, huts, and stupas will seem to shelter you for a moment—but don't cling to them at length. Since your mind lacks a body, it cannot settle down. You feel cold, you become angry and distraught, and your awareness seems erratic, volatile, and unsteady. Then you will have the thought, "Now I have died—what can I do!" Your heart will feel cold and weak. You will feel fierce and boundless suffering. The fact is you must travel and cannot be attached to any one place. So don't worry about it, and let your mind come to rest.

From now on you have no food except for what is dedicated for you. There is no certainty about your friends. These are signs of your mental body wandering in the existence between. Your present joys and sorrows are determined by your evolution. When you see your lands, friends, loved ones, and your own corpse, and you think, "Now I have died, what can be done?" at that time, your mental body feels greatly stressed.

> The guide here implicitly accepts the magical efficacy of food ritually dedicated to a deceased person, that a portion of food set out for the recently deceased can provide the between-state embodiment a sense of nourishment. The guide reminds the deceased that her body is mental, made by pure imagery. Her sensation of feeling hungry, weak, and distressed is purely mental.

You think, "How nice it would be to have a new body!" Then you will have visions of looking everywhere for a body. Even if you try up to nine times to enter your old corpse, due to the length of the reality between, in the winter it will have frozen, in the summer it will have rotted. Otherwise, your loved ones will have burned it or buried it or given it to birds and beasts, so it affords no place to inhabit. You will feel sick at heart, and will have visions of being squeezed between boulders, stones, and dirt. This kind of suffering is in the nature of the existence between. Even if you find a body, there will be nothing other than such suffering. So give up longing for a body! Focus yourself undistractedly in the experience of creative nonaction!

Having been oriented in this way, she can attain liberation in this between.

## ENCOUNTERING THE LORD OF DEATH

If by the force of negative evolution she does not recognize the light of reality in spite of being so oriented, you should again call the deceased by name and say the following:

> Hey, noble one! You named So-and-so, listen to me! This suffering of yours comes from your own evolutionary acts; there is no one else to blame. It is your own evolution, so pray strongly to the Three Jewels. They can protect you. If you don't pray to them, don't know how to meditate on the Great Seal, and don't meditate on an Archetype Deity, then your native angel will count out a white stone for each virtue you accumulated, and your native demon will count out a black stone for every sin.

> This refers to the popular belief in Buddhist societies, probably from ancient tradition, that each person has a personal angel and a personal demon who are born together with him, who push for good and evil, respectively, and count out his good and evil deeds. These then turn informers after death, and count out the person's tally of good and evil acts before the tribunal of Yama, Lord of Death.

> Then you will be very worried, angry, and terrified. Trembling, you will lie, saying, "I committed no sins!" But then Yama, the Judge

of the Dead, will say, "I will look into the mirror of evolution!" When he looks into the mirror of evolution, all your sins and virtues will clearly and distinctly appear therein. Your lies will not help. Yama will tie a rope around your neck and lead you away. He will cut off your head, rip out your heart, pull out your guts, lick your brains, drink your blood, eat your flesh, and gnaw your bones. But since you cannot die, even though your body is cut to pieces, you revive again. Being cut up again and again, you will suffer immense pain.

So when the white stones are being counted, don't be afraid, don't panic, do not lie! Don't fear Yama! Your body is mental, so even if it is killed and cut up, you cannot die. In fact, your form is the void itself, so you have nothing to fear. The Yama-deities are your own hallucinations and themselves are forms of the void. Your own instinctual mental body is void. Voidness cannot harm voidness. Signlessness cannot harm signlessness. You should recognize that there is nothing other than your own hallucination. There is no external, substantially existent Yama, angel, demon, or bull-headed ogre, and so on. You must recognize all this as the between!

Two levels of reassurance are contained here. First is the relative or circumstantial reassurance, that the dreamlike, mental body of the between has no coarse flesh, blood, or nerves, and therefore cannot be hurt as substantially as can a coarse reality body. The second is more profound, and provides reassurance on the ultimate level. In the nondual reality wherein form or matter is voidness, and voidness is form or matter, all things are what they are only because the routinized imagination perceives them to be so. All experiences are like a dream, none of them are intrinsically substantial, and so a liberated person can reshape his environment and experience as easily as a dreamer can imagine himself out of a nightmare. All that is necessary is for the dreamer to become conscious that he is in a dream, and either reshape the dream into a better state or else simply awaken.

### Meditate on the samadhi of the Great Seal!

Here meditation in the ultimate nonduality of form and voidness, in the form of bliss-void indivisible, is recommended, just for good measure.

If you don't know how to meditate, examine carefully whatever terrifies you and see the voidness that is its lack of objective status. That is the Natural Body of Truth. And that voidness is not merely an annihilation. Your triumphant, distinct awareness of the terror of the void is itself the blissful mind of the Body of Beatitude. Voidness and clarity are indistinguishable; the actuality of the void is clarity, the actuality of clarity is voidness. Your awareness of voidness-clarity indivisible is stripped naked, and now you abide in the unfabricated experience. That is the Wisdom Body of Truth. And that spontaneously and unobstructedly arises anywhere. And that is the Body of Compassionate Emanation.

> This is a brief instruction in the most advanced form of understanding and meditation, the Great Perfection or Great Seal. In normal reality, it would be pointless to instruct a person gripped with terror in such an exalted awareness. For the between-being, however, the guide feels it worthwhile to bring this up, since the between-consciousness is so radically mutable and transformable, and there is always the chance that the between-being can instantly shift straight into the utter actuality of her own reality. As for the Four Bodies of Buddhahood, it is developed from the Three Bodies by dividing the Truth Body into subjective, wisdom, and objective, natural, aspects.

Hey, noble one! Behold this without wavering! Recognize it! You will definitely become a Buddha, the perfection of the Four Bodies. Do not be distracted! This is the borderline between a Buddha and an ordinary being. Now is the time described as, "One instant alienated, one instant perfectly enlightened."

Until yesterday you were given to distraction, you did not recognize what arose as the between, and you were gripped by so much terror. If you again surrender to distraction, the cord of compassion will be cut and you will go into the abodes that lack all freedom; so be careful!

> This is the first time there has been a mention of "cutting of the cord of compassion." The guide here is trying to stir up the consciousness of the between-being, which so far has still refused to awaken from involvement in the ordinary life-impulse. Perhaps unconsciously he is relying on the compassion of the enlightened be-

ings, thinking that they will save him whatever he does. So the guide is indicating that the connection with the enlightened beings can be experientially severed by persistent delusion on the between-being's part.

If you orient them in this way, even those who did not recognize before will now recognize the light of reality and will be liberated. If the deceased had lived as a negative person, and does not know how to reflect in such a way, you should say again:

Hey, noble one! If you don't know to meditate thus, then remember and pray to the Buddha, the Dharma, the Sangha, and the Compassionate Lords. Contemplate all the terrors and visions as the Compassionate Lord or your own Archetype Deity. Remember your esoteric initiation name and the spiritual teacher who gave you the initiations you received in the human realm; proclaim them to Yama, the Lord of Truth! You won't be injured even if you fall off cliffs, so abandon fear and hate!

When you pronounce this orientation, those still unliberated will become liberated.


*DETACHMENT FROM THE PREVIOUS LIFE*

As it is still possible the deceased will not recognize the light and will not be liberated, and because persistence is important, call the deceased by name again and say as follows:

The present visions will propel you into the hardship of the changing states of pleasure and pain, as if flung by a catapult. So do not become absorbed in any visions of love or hate! Even when you are about to be born in the higher estates, when the visions of the higher estates arise, should the relatives you have left behind begin to make sacrifices with the slaughter of living beings, to dedicate them to the Lord of Death, you will have many impure visions and begin to feel fierce anger.

In some religions, people sacrifice animals out of the conviction that the life of the animal can be offered to a dread deity as a substitute for the life of a loved one, usually living and perhaps threatened by illness or other danger. It may also be considered in some societies that the offering of an animal life to a protective deity can influence positively the destiny of a deceased loved one. Buddhism has always abhorred such practices, considering them to accomplish the opposite of the desired effect. They harm the animal sacrificed, of course, award to the sacrificer the negative effect of the sin of killing, and cause even more harm to the supposed beneficiary, by stirring up their own negative emotions. In Tibet, some of the followers of some forms of the Bon religion, or else certain tribespeople on the frontiers who still follow animistic practices, might perform or commission such an animal sacrifice.

Conditioned by that, you will be reborn in hell. So no matter what actions are committed among the surviving, do not become angry, but contemplate love! Or, if you yourself have great attachment to the wealth and possessions you left behind, or if you know that others are using your possessions, you will feel attached to them and angry at the people who are using them. Conditioned by that, even though you might have attained the high estates, you will be reborn in hell or in the pretan realm. Therefore, even if you are attached to your old possessions, you have no power to own them anymore. They are of no use to you at all. Abandon fondness and attachment for your possessions left behind! Totally throw them away! Be decisive! Whoever uses your things, don't be stingy! Let go of them in your mind! Generate a one-pointed will to offer them to the spiritual teacher and the Three Jewels, and abide in the experience of detachment and unconcern!

When death rites, such as exorcistic food-offering rites, or other rites that purify the dangers of the horrid states, are performed for your sake, and, with your subtle evolutionary clairvoyance, you perceive the performers being inaccurate, sleepy, or distracted, breaking their vows and commitments, and acting carelessly, and you notice their lack of faith, distorted views, fearful negative actions, and impure practices, then you think, "Alas! These people are betraying me. They are surely letting me down!" You become depressed, you become disgusted. You lose your positive attitude and all respect and you become cynical and disillusioned. Conditioned by that you will be reborn in the horrid states, and thus their actions, rather than helping you, will harm you greatly. So whatever your surviving relatives perform in the way of incorrect religious rites, you must think, "Well, my perception is certainly imperfect! How can any impurity adhere to the Buddha's Teaching? I see these as a result of my own negative attitude, like seeing the mirror's faults as if in my own form. The bodies of these performers are the Sangha, their speech is the Holy Dharma, their minds are the actual Buddha—so I must take refuge in them!" So you must respect them and project your most positive attitude upon them. Then whatever your dear ones do for you will definitely help you. Such keeping of a positive attitude is very important, so do it without forgetting!

Again, even if you are heading for rebirth in the three horrid states, when the visions of the horrid states arise, when you see the pure virtue, unsullied with sins, performed by your surviving relatives, and when you see the perfect physical, verbal, and mental practices of your spiritual teachers and mentors, then, when you are compelled to rebirth, your feeling of great delight has the invaluable benefit of lifting you up into the higher estates just as you were about to be reborn in the horrid states. So be very careful, as it is so important for you to construct a positive attitude of reverence and faith and not allow any place for impure negativity of perception.

Hey, noble one! In short, since your present between-consciousness is highly unstable, volatile, and mobile, and virtuous or vicious perception is very powerful, don't think at all about any unvirtuous evolution, and remember your own virtuous practice. If you have no virtuous practice, then adopt a positive perception and feel faith and reverence. Pray to your Archetype Deity and to the Lord of Compassion! With intense willpower, perform this prayer!

Now that I wander alone, without my loved ones,
And all my visions are but empty images,
May the Buddhas exert the force of their compassion
And stop the fear-and hate-drawn terrors of the between!

Now, when I suffer by the power of negative evolution,
May my Archetype Deities dispel my suffering!
When reality crashes with a thousand thunders,
May they all become OM MANI PADME HUM!

When I'm pulled by evolution without recourse,
May the Lords mild and fierce dispel my suffering!

When I suffer due to evolutionary instincts,
May clear light bliss samadhi arise for me!


Thus perform this fervent prayer! It will surely guide you on the path. It is crucial that you decide it is sure not to let you down!


When you say this, the deceased should become aware, recognize the light, and attain liberation.


## AVOIDING THE DULL LIGHTS TO BLOCK REBIRTH

Even though you say this many times, it may still be hard for recognition to arise, due to the power of strong negative evolution. There is great benefit in further repetition. Calling the deceased by name, you should say as follows:


Hey, noble one! If you have not recognized the clear light by remembering what we have already said, from now your sense of your body from the preceding life will become vague, and your sense of your body of the emerging life will become more distinct. Then you will feel sad and think, "I am suffering so—now I will seek whatever body comes along!" Then you will move toward whatever appears, gradually and uncertainly, and the six lights of the six realms will dawn. The realm toward which evolution impels your rebirth will dawn most clearly.

Hey, noble one! Listen to me! What are the six lights? The dull white light of the gods will dawn; and also the red light of the titans, the blue light of the humans, the green light of the animals, the yellow light of the pretans, and the dull smoky light of the hells—all these will dawn. These are the six lights. So your body's color will become that of the light of the realm of rebirth.

Hey, noble one! At that time the essence of the instruction is very important. Contemplate the particular light that arises as the Lord of Great Compassion! When the light arises, hold the thought, "It is the Lord of Great Compassion." This is the extremely profound key of instruction. This is crucial to block rebirth.

One of the six dull lights emerges in the deceased's awareness at this point, to indicate the realm of his rebirth. The trick here is not to accept that light as leading to that realm, but to align that light itself with the Bodhisattva Avalokiteshvara, the Lord of Great Compassion (Jesus for the Christian, Krishna for the Hindu, the Prophet for the Moslem, the most beloved figure for the secularist).

**Again, meditate long and carefully that, whoever your Archetype Deity is, he or she appears like a magic illusion, lacking intrinsic reality. It is called the "pure Magic Body." Then, contemplate that Archetype Deity as dissolving from the edges inward, and enter the experience of not holding rigidly to the insubstantial, the clear light of voidness. Again contemplate that as the Archetype Deity! Again contemplate it as clear light! Thus meditating deity and clear light in alternation, then let your own awareness dissolve from the edges; where space pervades, let awareness pervade. Where awareness pervades, let the Truth Body pervade. Enter comfortably into the experience of the ceaseless nonproliferation of the Truth Body.**

Having aligned the dull light of one of the realms with the Lord of Compassion, here the deceased is instructed in something more advanced, in contemplating the nonduality of the supreme integration of magic body and clear light. He contemplates the form of the archetype deity as magic illusion, as a dream apparition. He then dissolves the image into transparency and contemplates that as the deity. He then alternates contemplating the deity as magic body and as transparency, oscillating toward contemplating their nonduality. He then contemplates his subjective awareness of deity-transparency integration as itself dissolving, contemplating the nonduality of insentient space and awareness, voidness and clarity. He then rests in the inconceivable integration of the Truth Body as the integration of voidness and awareness, magic body and clear light. The Truth Body does not proliferate or fabricate anything because it already *is* everything—it is the actual reality of everything in every possible state. Again, Padma Sambhava guides even the most ordinary between-being in the highest possible meditation, showing that he takes most seriously the concept that a person's between-awareness is nine times more intelligent than his ordinary coarse awareness of the previous life.

From within that experience, rebirth is prevented and enlightenment is attained.

## BLOCKING THE DOOR OF THE WOMB

Those whose practice was weak and inexpert will still not recognize the light. They will err and wander to the door of a womb. Since for them the instruction about blocking the door of the womb is very important, call the deceased by name and say as follows:

Hey, noble one! If you have not understood from the above, at this time, by power of evolution the vision will arise of your proceeding upward, on the level, or downward with head hanging. Now meditate on the Lord of Great Compassion! Remember him! Then, as already explained, you will have visions of hurricanes, blizzards, hailstorms, dense fogs, and being chased by many men, and you will seem to escape. Those without merit will seem to escape to a miserable place, but those with merit will seem to escape to a happy place. At that time, noble one, all the signs will arise showing the continent and place where you will be reborn. For this time there are many profound keys of instruction, so listen carefully! Even though you did not recognize freedom from the previous keys of orientation, here even those of the weakest practice can recognize freedom through the following keys, so listen!

Now, here, the method of blocking the womb door is very effective and important. There are two methods of blocking that door; blocking the entering person and blocking the womb door entered. First, the instruction for blocking the enterer.

"Blocking the womb door" refers to using the *Natural Liberation* art—relaxed focusing on the presence of the archetype or patron deity as indivisible from the natural transparency of all things—as a way of intervening in the mechanical processes of assuming rebirth.

Hey, noble one! You named So-and-so! Clearly visualize your Archetype Deity appearing like magic without intrinsic reality like the moon in water. If you are unsure about your Archetype Deity, then vividly envision Avalokiteshvara, thinking, "He is the Lord of Great Compassion!" Then dissolve the Archetype from the edges and contemplate the void clear light transparency of ultimate nonperception. That is the profound key. Using it, the Buddhas said, the womb will not be entered; so meditate in that way!

But if this still does not block the way and you are just about to enter a womb, there is the profound instruction to block the door of the womb about to be entered. So listen! Repeat after me the following from *The Root Verses of the Six Betweens!*

Hey! Now when the existence between dawns upon me,
I will hold my will with mind one-pointed,
And increase forcefully the impulse of positive evolution;
Blocking the womb door, I will remember to be revulsed.
Now courage and positive perception are essential;
I will give up envy, and contemplate all couples
As my Spiritual Mentor, Father and Mother.

Repeat this loud and clear and stir your memory. It is important to meditate on its meaning and put it into practice. As for its meaning, "Now when the existence between dawns upon me" means that you are now wandering within the existence between. A sign of that is that when you look in water you will not see your reflection. You have no shadow. You have no substantial flesh-and-blood body. These are signs that your mental body is wandering in the existence between. Now you must hold one-pointed in your mind the unwavering willpower. This one-pointed will is of chief importance. It is like reins to guide a horse. You can achieve whatever your will intends, so don't open your mind to negative evolution, but remember the teachings, instructions, initiations, authorizations, and inspirations you received in the human realm, such as this *Great Book of Natural Liberation Through Understanding in the Between,* and intensify the result of all good evolutionary actions. This is very important. Don't forget it! Don't be distracted! This is the exact time that determines whether you go up or you go down. Now is the time when indulgence in laziness definitely will bring on suffering. Now is the time when one-pointed positive willpower definitely brings on happiness. Hold one-pointed goodwill in your mind! Sustain forcefully the result of good action!

Now is the time to block the door of the womb! As the root

verse says, blocking the womb door, remember to be revulsed! Now courage and positive perception are essential! That time is now. You should block the door of the womb. There are five methods to block the womb door; fix them well in your mind.

Hey, noble one! At this time you will have visions of couples making love. When you see them, don't enter between them, but stay mindful. Visualize the males and females as the Teacher, Father and Mother, prostrate to them, and make them visualized offerings! Feel intense reverence and devotion! Aim a strong will to request them to teach the Dharma, and the womb door will definitely be blocked.

If that does not block it, and you are about to enter the womb, then visualize them as Mentor Father-Mother, Archetype Deity Father and Mother, or Compassion Lord Father and Mother. Offer them visualized offerings! Form the powerful intention to receive spiritual attainments from them, and that will block the womb door.

If that does not block it, and you are again about to enter a womb, then third there is the instruction for reversing lust and hate. There are four modes of birth; egg birth, womb birth, magic birth, and warm-moisture birth. Egg birth and womb birth are alike. As before, you begin to see males and females engaged in love-making. If you enter the womb under the influence of lust and hate, whether you are reborn as horse, bird, dog, or human, if you are going to be male, you arise appearing to be male; you feel strong hate toward the father, and attraction and lust toward the mother. If you are going to be female, you appear as a female; you feel strong envy and jealousy toward the mother, you feel strong longing and lust for the father. Conditioned by that, you enter the path of the womb. You experience orgasmic bliss in the center of the union between white and red drops, and within the experience of that bliss you faint and lose consciousness. Your body develops through the embryonic stages of "custard," "gelatin," and so forth. Eventually you will be born outside the mother's womb. Once your eyes are open, you realize you have been born a puppy. Having been a human, now you are a dog. In the dog's kennel, you suffer. Or in the pig's sty, or in the anthill, or in the wormhole, or in the herds of cows or goats or sheep—born there you cannot return to the human state. Being extremely stupid, in the state of delusion you suffer various miseries. In this way you will cycle through the hells and the pretan realms, and will be tortured by limitless suffering. There is nothing more powerful, nothing more terrible than this. Alas! Alas! Those lacking the holy spiritual teacher's instruction fall down this deep abyss into the life cycle. They are tormented uninterruptedly by unbearable sufferings. So listen to what I say! Hold my personal instruction in your mind!

Now I will teach you an instruction to close the womb door by reversing lust and hate. Listen to it and remember it! As the verse says:

Blocking the door of the womb, I will remember to be revulsed.
Now courage and positive perception are essential;
I will give up envy and contemplate all couples
As my Spiritual Mentor, Father and Mother.

As before, you will have strong feelings of envy; if reborn as a male, you will lust for the mother and hate the father, if reborn as a female you will lust for the father and hate the mother. For that time, there is this profound instruction.

Hey, noble one! When such lust and hate arise, meditate like this. "Alas! Such a creature of negative evolution as myself will wander in the life cycle under the influence of lust and hate. If I still persist in lust and hate, I will know no end to my wanderings. I am in danger of being sunk forever in the ocean of miseries. Now I must give up lust and hate entirely. Alas! I must hold intensely the one-pointed will never to entertain lust and hate." The Tantras state that this meditation itself will close the door of the womb.

Hey, noble one! Don't waver! Hold your will one pointed in your mind! Even though you have done that, if the womb door did not close and you are about to enter the womb, you should block the womb door by the instruction of truthless magical illusion. Meditate as follows: "Male and female, father and mother, the thunderstorm, the hurricane, the thunder, terrifying visions, all phenomena are naturally like magical illusions. However they arise, they are truthless. All things are untrue and false. Like mirages. Impermanent. Noneternal. Why be attached to them? Why fear and hate them? It is to see nothing as something. All of these are but visions of my mind. The mind itself is as originally nonexistent as a magical illusion. So where—out there—do they come from? Since I never understood this in the past, I held the nonexistent to exist. I held the untrue to be true. I held illusion as truth. So for this long time I wandered in the life cycle. If I still now do not recognize the illusoriness of things, I will wander even longer in the life cycle, and I will be stuck in the quicksand of various miseries. So now I will recognize all these things as like a dream, a magical illusion, an echo, a fairy city, a mirage, a reflection, an optical illusion, the moon in water, lacking even a moment's truth-status, definitely untrue, and false."

"Truth-status" is the state of something's existing by virtue of its intrinsic reality. If things were not empty, if they existed by virtue of a fixed, absolute, real core, then that core would be discovered by truth-seeking scientific awareness and those things would be acknowledged as possessing "truth-status." The involuntary habit of all beings is to assume that things do have such status. When we see a thing, it seems to us to exist in its own right, as an independently established thing-in-itself. This habitual perception is called our "truth-habit." It is equivalent to our misknowledge, the root of all our delusionary existence. The Buddha's key liberative insight is that all things lack such truth-status, and that therefore our truth-habits are misguided. Our experience of this is called wisdom, and is the antidote for our delusionary grasping at life. Freedom from truth-habits does not mean that our consciousness is annihilated, only that it is less grasping, less dominating, allowing things to be the relative, fleeting, dreamlike, fluid things that they are, and not insisting that they conform rigidly to our set of preconceived categories. This is the most advanced teaching of all. Though it is not complicated, it is emotionally challenging, as releasing the habitual perception of truth-status in things can be frightening, can feel like succumbing to annihilation. Yet Padma Sambhava again uses these advanced teachings for between-beings, considering their extreme malleability, their ninefold intelligence, and their unique opportunity.

Thus, holding these thoughts one-pointedly in mind, the truth-habit erodes, and, as the resulting freedom is impressed in your continuum, the deeper self-habit is reversed. As you thus deeply understand cosmic unreality, the womb door will definitely be blocked.

Yet even doing that, if the truth-habit does not erode, the womb door is not blocked, and you are about to enter the womb, again there is a profound instruction.

Hey, noble one! Even doing that, if the womb door is not blocked, now, fifth, you should block the womb door by meditating on the clear light. This is how to contemplate. "Hey! All things are my own mind. That mind is voidness, free of creation and destruction." Thinking thus, do not artificially compose your mind. Like water being poured in water, let the mind flow into its own reality condition; release it into its own nature. Letting it relax easily and openly will decisively and definitely block the womb door for all four forms of rebirth. Thus meditate again and again until the womb door is blocked.

Up to here, you have given many authentic and profound instructions for blocking the womb door. Using them, it should be impossible for any person, whether bright, mediocre, or dull, not to become liberated. Why is that? The deceased's between-consciousness has a mundane form of clairvoyance, so whatever you say, it can understand, experience, and embody. Even if persons were deaf and blind in life, in the between their faculties are complete and they can understand whatever you say. They have hypermindfulness, being constantly overwhelmed by terror and panic, so they always listen to what you say. Their consciousness is without coarse embodiment, so wherever they aim their will, they reach immediately; they are easy to direct. Since their intelligence is nine times more clear, even if persons were stupid in life, in the between, by the power of evolution, their intellect is extremely clear, and they have the quality of knowing how to meditate on whatever they understand. These are the key reasons why it is useful to perform prayers and rites of teaching for the deceased. They can be very important for them. And it is very important to make the effort to read this *Book of Natural Liberation* during the nine days after death. If the deceased is not liberated by means of one orientation, he or she will be liberated by another. That is why there are many different orientations.

### CHOOSING A GOOD WOMB

Still, there are many beings who, due to slight familiarity with virtue, great, primal familiarity with nonvirtue, and powerful sins and dense obscurations, though they are confronted by such concerns and hear the previous orientations, have not become liberated. If the womb door was not already blocked, you should teach them from now on the instructions on how to choose a womb. First, recite the prayer *Help from the Buddhas and Bodhisattvas;* take refuge in the Three Jewels, and conceive the spirit of enlightenment. Then call the deceased three times by name, and say the following:

Hey, noble one! You, the deceased named So-and-so, listen to me! All the previous instructions for orientation have been given to you and still you do not understand. Now, since the womb door is not blocked, it is time to assume a body. You have many different authentic and profound instructions for the choosing of a womb. Hold them in your mind! Listen well with strong intent, and hold them in your mind!

The instructions on choosing a womb are full of allusions to the ancient Buddhist cosmology, in which the planet consists of four main continents radiating outward from an axial mountain, with eight subcontinents, all sitting within a huge surrounding ocean, ringed by numerous iron mountain ranges. The pretan and hell realms are far beneath the base of the mountain, and the many realms of the heavens radiate upward from the upper slopes of the mountain. This picture can be related to modern, round-planet cosmology, by thinking of the earth's axis as the axial mountain, and the continents around the globe radiating outward from it. We can think of Videha, the eastern continent of the ancient cosmology, as Oceania, including Japan, the Philippines, Indonesia, Micronesia, Polynesia, down to New Zealand and Australia; Jambudvipa, the southern continent, corresponds to Asia in general, though it some-times refers to the Indian subcontinent alone; western Godaniya to the Middle East, Europe, and Africa; and northern Kuru to the ancient Americas, around the planet from India, at that time places of peace, long life, and comfortable prosperity, but little opportunity to attain ultimate liberation.

Hey, noble one! Now signs and marks will arise about which continent you will be reborn in—recognize them! Now you should explore where to be reborn, you should choose a continent. If you are reborn in eastern Videha, you will see lakes and waters adorned with male and female geese. Think of renunciation and do not go there. If you are born there, your situation will be comfortable; but you should not go there as the Dharma is not available there. If you are going to be reborn in the southern Jambudvipa, you will see beautiful and comfortable houses. If you can go there do so. If you are to be reborn in western Godaniya, you will see lakes adorned with male and female horses. Turn back and do not go there. Although it is very enjoyable, the Dharma has not spread there, so do not go there. If you are going to be reborn in northern Kuru, you see lakes adorned with cattle or with evergreen trees. Recognize these as signs of being reborn there. Do not go there! Though you will have long life and much fortune there, the Dharma is not available there. Do not go there!

If you are to be reborn as a god, you will see delightful, divine, multistoried mansions made of various jewels. It is alright to dwell there, so you may enter there. If you are to be reborn as a titan, you will see a pleasant grove and spinning wheels of fire; remember renunciation, and by all means do not go there! If you are to be reborn among the animals you will see caves, ant holes, and grass huts, as if through a fog. Do not go there! If you are to be reborn as a pretan, you will see charred stumps, black spots, dark ravines, darkness, and shadows. If you go there, reborn as a pretan, you will experience various sufferings of hunger and thirst. So don't go there! Remember renunciation! Be fiercely courageous! If you are to be reborn in the hells, you will hear the songs of negative evolution, or you will feel a helpless need to go there, and you will have visions of an island of darkness, a black house or a red house, black pits, and black roads. If you go there, you will be stuck in the hells. You will experience unbearable pains of heat and cold. You will never escape. You must take every care not to get caught there! By any means, never enter there at all! "Block the womb door and remember renunciation!" Now is the time when that is essential.

> Padma Sambhava seems almost to have given up getting the between-being released from the ordinary life cycle into clear light transparency, and is resigned to his being reborn. When he orders the deceased, "Don't go there!" about one of the unpleasant or horrid states, he is calling for a final act of will and courage, a summoning of the power of renunciation, to recoil from the prospect of such a terrifying rebirth. He is quite aware, however, that a between-being still caught in the currents of habitual drives and evolutionary momentum from former acts will not easily be able to reverse course at this point, not without heroic effort.

Hey, noble one! Though you might wish not to go on, helplessly you are chased by the butchers of evolution. You find yourself powerless to stop, you must go on. Ahead of you are butchers and killers to drag you along. You will feel as if you are fleeing from overwhelming darkness, hurricanes, tempests, harsh noises, snow and rain, hailstorms, thunderstorms, and violent blizzards. Escaping in panic, you will seek a refuge, and you will feel safe in the previously mentioned beautiful houses, in rock caves, in earthen caverns, in forest thickets, within the round blossoms of lotuses and so forth. Hiding in such places, you will think, "I must not leave here now!" And feeling so anxious about losing your place, you will become very attached to it. Feeling so anxious about meeting the terrors of the between if you go out, hating those terrors, you hide within and assume no matter what kind of inferior body, and you will come to experience various sufferings. All that is the sign that demons and ogres are troubling you. There is a profound, crucial instruction for you at this time. Listen to it and hold it in your mind!

At that time when you are helplessly chased by butchers and are overwhelmed by terror, instantaneously visualize all at once the Lord Chemchok Heruka, or Hayagriva, or Vajrapani, and so forth, whoever is your Archetype Deity; gigantic in size, with bulging limbs, terrifying, furious, able to crush all demons to dust. By his blessing and compassion, you will free yourself from those butchers, and you will gain the power to choose a good womb. This is the authentic profound key of the instruction; so hold it in your mind!

Chemchok Heruka is the most powerful archetype deity in the old Tantras of Padma Sambhava's time. His most elaborate form has many heads, arms, and legs, and represents enlightenment in its adamantine triumph over evil in all directions. Hayagriva is the fierce, dark red form of the Lord of Compassion, Avalokiteshvara, usually distinguished by a small green horse's head emerging from the crown of his head. Vajrapani is a deep blue fierce Bodhisattva, considered the incarnation of the power of all Buddhas, with many different forms used in the contemplations of different practitioners. Here these most powerful Archetype Deities are invoked to provide a shock intervention, to slow the course of a between-being's rebirth; not at this time to attain liberation, but to find a brief respite to change course and choose a better rebirth. For a person with no experience of an Archetype Deity, this is a moment to invoke the most powerful seraphim or cherubim that they can imagine, anything fierce and of overwhelming power, that still can be thought of as a benevolent protector by the person.

Hey, noble one! Further, the deities of the contemplation realms are reborn by the power of their samadhi. The majority of the demonic types such as the pretans, by changing their self-images while in the between, manifest various magical transformations in bodies of pretans, demons, and ogres, and then become mental bodies just like them. The pretans of the underworld, the pretans of the sky realms, and the eighty thousand types of demons adopt their bodies just by changing their self-concepts. At such a time, if you remember the import of voidness, the Great Seal, it is best. If you cannot, you should practice meditation on magical illusion. If you cannot do that, free of any kind of attachment to anything, you should meditate on the greatly compassionate Archetype Deity, and attain enlightenment in the Beatific Body in the between.

> The "contemplation realms" are the four formless heavens: infinite space, infinite consciousness, absolute nothingness, and beyond consciousness and unconsciousness. A being is born as a deity of those realms just by focused concentration in the samadhis by those names. Even lowly creatures such as pretans and various types of demons attain embodiment just by changing their self-images. Padma Sambhava here exhorts the deceased to take responsibility for the power of her imagination, to realize that she can be whatever she wants just by willing it to be so with enough determination and undistracted focus. And he reminds those who have archetype deity Tantric practices to invoke those practices at this crucial juncture.

Hey, noble one! Thus, if it becomes necessary by the power of evolution to enter the womb, you should now rely on the instruction for choosing the womb. Listen! Do not go to just any womb door that presents itself. If, due to the demonic butchers, you lose the power not to go, then meditate on Hayagriva. Since now you have subtle clairvoyance, you will be able to understand the nature of all places, so choose your place of rebirth wisely. There are two instructions, one for transmitting your soul into the pure Buddha-lands, and one for choosing a womb door in the impure life cycle. You should now practice the following.

If you are the most intelligent type of person, to perform the soul-transmission to the angel realms you should formulate the following controlling intention: "Alas! I am sad that I have stayed here in this swamp of the life cycle for so long, beginninglessly for bound-less, countless eons! Alas! During all the lifetimes of so many Buddhas, I have still not been liberated! I am revulsed and nauseated by this interminable life cycle. I am terrified of it. I totally repudiate it. I must now remember the methods of escaping it. I must now take miracu-lous rebirth in the blossom of a lotus in the presence of the Buddha Amitabha in the western pure-land universe, Sukhavati the Blissful!" It is essential here to make great effort to aim all your willpower in this way toward the western pure universe of Sukhavati. Whichever pure universe you have faith in—whether it is Amitabha's Sukhavati; Abhirati, the delightful land of Akshobhya; Ghanavyuha, the pure land of Vairochana; Alakavati, the earthly paradise of Vaishravana; Potalaka, the earthly paradise of Avalokiteshvara, or the lotus light palace of Padma Sambhava in Udyana, if you aim your concentrated willpower at any one of these pure lands and hold it one-pointedly without distraction, you will be reborn immediately in that pure land. Further, if you wish to be reborn in the presence of the Dharma Lord Maitreya in the Tushita heaven, just aim your will, thinking, "Now that I am in this between, it is time to visit the Dharma Lord Maitreya in his Tushita realm, I will go there!" You will be miraculously reborn in the heart of a lotus in the presence of Maitreya.

The pure land universes, Buddha-lands, or Buddhaverses, are uni-verses existing in far-away dimensions, though with the miraculous power of travel of the between-being with her mental body, and by the grace of the compassion of the Buddhas and Bodhisattvas, a between-being can travel to them with the speed of thought. Suk-havati, Abhirati, and Ghanavyuha are Buddhaverses of the celestial variety. Sukhavati is the most famous of these, with several impor-tant sutras giving elaborate descriptions. Beings are born there in lotus buds, instead of wombs. Beings have angelic bodies therein, without sexual differentiation, and they draw pure energy from the atmosphere, with no need to eat or excrete. The land is made of jewel substances and is of the highest beauty. There is no danger and no unhappiness. The Buddha is always present to everyone within the land, and all are able to meditate with the greatest facility. Thus, the environment is ideally suited to the spiritual evolution of its inhabitants, from the point of view of their development of wis-dom. On the other hand, our own universe is said to be the Bud-dhaverse of Shakyamuni Buddha, called Saha. In the *Vimalakirti Sutra,* it is said to be even more conducive to spiritual evolution than a celestial Buddhaverse, because of the immediacy of suffering as well as the presence of teaching. Beings in our world can develop compassion as rapidly as wisdom, for compassion, being sensitivity to the suffering of others, requires proximity to that suffering in order to develop.

There are also enlightenment-sustained paradises on earth, maintained by the field of compassion of a particular Bodhisattva, deity, archetype, or adept. Vaishravana is a deity who became devoted to Buddhism during Shakyamuni's time on earth; his realm, Alakavati, is near the North Pole, and is famous for its treasures (Vaishravana is perhaps the "Santa Claus" of popular Buddhist myth). Potalaka is on the west coast of southern India, hidden on top of a sacred mountain, and home to the Bodhisattvas Avalokiteshvara and Tara, as well as others in their retinue. Udyana is somewhere in the Afghan mountains, and is the magic residence of the retinue of Padma Sambhava—later replaced in Tibetan myth by the Zangdog Pelri (Copper Mountain Paradise), somewhere in the southeast of India. Finally, Maitreya, the next Buddha to descend to earth in the future, dwells in Sudharma, a famous teaching paradise within a heaven called Tushita, which itself is a "normal," desire-realm heaven with pleasure gods sporting about.

Buddhist practitioners sometimes go to one of these celestial or earthly pure lands to take a rest from the ordinary life realms. At other times, they do not choose to visit them, because they do not want to lose time in their evolutionary quest for full enlightenment, when they will be able to create a Buddhaverse of their own for the sake of others. A day in one such paradise might represent years in the ordinary realms. And Bodhisattvas cannot bear to abandon other beings to their sufferings for such long periods of time.

**Again, if you cannot, or do not want to, proceed to any pure land, and must enter a womb, there is this instruction for choosing a womb in the impure life cycle. Listen to it! Choose your continent for rebirth as explained already. Using your clairvoyance, enter a womb in a place where the Dharma has spread. Caution is required, for even if you were to be reborn magically in a heap of dung, you would get the notion that the impure mass smelled delicious and you would be reborn in it by the force of your attraction. Therefore you should not adhere to whatever appearance occurs, and you must discount any signs that trigger attachment or aversion. Then choose a good womb. And here the willed intention is important; so you must create it as follows: "Hey! For the sake of all beings, I will be reborn as a world-ruling emperor, or of the priestly class, sheltering all beings like a great shade tree, or as the child of a holy man, an adept, or of**

a clan with an impeccable Dharma lineage, or in a family where the parents have great faith. I must succeed in this coming life, by adopting a body that has great merit, to enable me to accomplish the aims of all beings!" Aiming your will in this way you should enter the womb. At that time, the womb you have entered should appear to you as if magically transformed into a divine palace. You should pray to the Buddhas and the Bodhisattvas of the ten directions, the Archetype Deities, and especially to the Lord of Great Compassion. And you should visualize that they are all anointing you in consecration as you enter the womb.

> The womb should be visualized as a mandala palace, an ideal environment for the development of an enlightenment-oriented body. In fact, all mandala palaces, or measureless mansions, are consciously constructed as womb environments for Archetype Deities. So, here the mentally highly acute and creative between-being is being instructed to structure his womb in the optimal manner for his growth. His entry therein should be experienced as if it were a royal consecration.

In thus choosing the womb door, there is always danger of erring. Under the influence of evolution, you might see an excellent womb door as bad. You might see a bad womb door as excellent. So here the key instruction for choosing is important; do as follows: Even if a womb door appears to be excellent, do not become attached to it. Even if it appears bad, do not become averse to it. Enter it within the experience of the universal loving equanimity, free of lust and hate and compulsive choosing between good and bad. This is the authentic profound key instruction.

> The idea is for the between-being to enter her womb without coming under the heavy influence of the emotional addictions, lust, hate, or delusion. This is important in order to remain alert to the true nature of the place, and not make the worse than fatal error of taking rebirth in a horrid life form.

## TAKING REFUGE
## IN THE THREE JEWELS

Here, except for a few persons with deep experience, it is hard to be free of the disease of negative instincts. So if the deceased cannot avoid attachment and aversion, even the dumbest, most sinful, most bestial person can eliminate negative instincts by taking refuge in the Three Jewels: the Buddha, the Dharma, and the Community. So once again, you should call the deceased by name and say the following words up to seven times:

Hey, noble one! If you cannot abandon lust and hate, and know how to choose a womb door, then, no matter what visions come to you, say the name of the Three Jewels, and go to them for refuge! Pray to the Lord of Great Compassion! Go forward with your head held high! Recognize that you are in the between! Abandon possessive love toward your dear ones left behind, your son, your daughter, your friends! They cannot help you now. Now go to the blue light of the human realm and the white light of the divine! Go to the beautiful jewel house and the pleasure garden!

After saying this seven times, pray to the Buddhas and Bodhisattvas, and read seven times the *Prayer for Refuge from All Terrors,* the *Root Verses of the Six Betweens,* and the *Prayer for Deliverance from the Straits of the Between.* Then read loudly and precisely the *Liberation by Wearing, the Natural Liberation of the Body.* Also read the *Dharma Practice, Natural Liberation of the Instincts.*

The *Prayer for Refuge from All Terrors,* the *Root Verses of the Six Betweens,* and the *Prayer for Deliverance from the Straits of the Between* are all included at the beginning of Part II, in chapter 5, "The Between Prayers." The *Dharma Practice, Natural Liberation of the Instincts* is included as chapter 7, the first of the supplementary translations. The *Liberation by Wearing, Natural Liberation of the Body* is not translated here. As mentioned before, it contains mantras to be put into amulets and placed on the body of the deceased, or to be read aloud.

If you perform these practices properly, the yogi or yogini with high realization will succeed in the death-point soul-transmission, will not need to wander in the between, and will be liberated on the great straight upward path. Some less developed but practiced persons will recognize the reality clear light after the death-point between and will attain enlightenment on the straight upward path. Others still less developed, during the progressive sets of seven days when the visions of the mild and fierce deities arise in the reality between, will be liberated by one manifestation or another, according to their specific evolutionary destinies and intellectual propensities. Being offered these practices suitable for many different stages, they will recognize the one fitting for them and will be liberated.

However, those with weak evolutionary destinies or with negative evolutionary momentum of sins and obscurations may yet wander downward into the existence between. Since there are different levels of orientation like the rungs of a ladder, if one does not help them recognize the clear light, another will; and they will become liberated. Again among these, some with very weak destinies may not recognize the clear light and may lose themselves to terror and panic. Even in their case, as there are various different instructions about blocking the womb door and choosing the womb door, if one does not help them recognize the clear light, another will. They can hold on to their guiding intentions and will attain the boundless good qualities of the higher stages. Finally, even the lowest, most bestial type of person can rebound from the horrid states through the excellence of taking refuge in the Three Jewels. They can attain the precious human embodiment endowed with liberty and opportunity. In their next life they can encounter spiritual teachers and friends, they can receive spiritual instructions, and they, too, will be liberated.

If this teaching is available during the existence between, this instruction can magnify the continuing impact of good evolution, like extending an irrigation ditch with a water trough. It is impossible for even the most sinful persons not to be liberated by this teaching. Why? In the occasion of the between, both the compassion of the whole host of mild and fierce Buddha deities and the negative presence of the devils and demons are constantly escorting the soul of the deceased. Therefore, understanding this teaching at this time can completely change his perception and lead him to liberation. Further, as the mental body of the between-person has no flesh-and-blood embodiment, transformation is easy. In the between, the soul can wander far, wherever he wants, and his evolutionary subtle clairvoyance can see and hear everything. Held by memory, the soul's awareness can transform in an instant. The very nature of the between is highly advantageous for spiritual development. It is like an acceleration machine. The mental continuum of a person in the ordinary lifetime is like a huge tree trunk that cannot be moved by a hundred men; when it is in the between, it is as if floated in water— it can be brought where you wish in an instant. Or it is like turning a horse with a rein.

Therefore, friends should go to all who die and not disturb the corpse, but read this Teaching and pray until blood and lymph run from the nostrils. Out of devotion to this Teaching, animals should not be sacrificed in dedication to the deceased. Near the corpse, no one, neither friend nor relative, should be allowed to weep, wail, and lament. You should generate as much virtue as possible.

Further, all teachings associated with this *Great Book of Natural Liberation Through Understanding in the Between* should also be read, after completing the guiding instructions, as they are also extremely excellent. This teaching should constantly be recited. You should cultivate it, both word and meaning. Then when you know that the time of your death is certain from recognizing the signs of death, if your health allows, you should read it aloud yourself and think about it. If your condition does not allow, you should have your friends read the text and pray. There is no doubt you will effectively be liberated.

This is the Teaching that does not require meditation and extensive practice. It is the profound instruction that liberates by regarding, liberates by hearing, and liberates by reading. This profound instruction guides even the great sinner on the secret path, if you don't forget its words and meanings even when being chased by seven hounds. Even if the Buddhas of the past, present, and future were to search for instructions to attain perfect enlightenment at the point of death, they would come up with nothing better than this.

This completes the instruction on the between, this means of liberating embodied beings, this profound quintessence, the *Great Book of Natural Liberation Through Understanding in the Between.*

## HAA THVA THVA GYA GYAH

We have reached the end of this journey, hopefully having helped the departed to achieve liberation, or, as is more likely if the departed did not practice for this between-transition during her lifetime, to attain a favorable rebirth. In either case, according to the worldview of the *Book of Natural Liberation,* we can count on further interaction with our friend or loved one. If she has attained liberation, she will voluntarily reincarnate to help us and other "mother beings" find our way through our crises and achieve the joy of freedom, wisdom, and compassionate interconnection. If she has attained a favorable rebirth, it will be in the same kind of circumstances we already enjoy or will enjoy in our next lives, and we will continue to work on developing the best in our relationship, whether we recognize each other or not.

Having brought our minds into focus on the art of traveling in the between, we should renew our resolve to prepare ourselves for the time when we will need it for ourselves. We should set a time with like-minded "Dharma friends" to reread it once every month or two, mentally extending our assistance to those who have died during that time, whether known or unknown. We should learn more about the *Three Body Mentor Yoga* and the *Natural Liberation Through Naked Vision, Identifying the Intelligence.* We should memorize the prayers if possible, or at least become very familiar with them. We should contemplatively read over the *Dharma Practice, Natural Liberation of the Instincts,* investigating the look and feel of the Buddha-clans, and developing a sense of familiarity, even family-feeling, with the archetype Buddha-deities, mild and fierce. We should read more broadly in the Buddhist literature, especially the *Jataka* (former lives of the Buddha tales), the descriptions of Buddha-lands, and the biographies of enlightened saints. If we belong to a religion other than Buddhism, we should investigate the iconography of its Deity, angels, and mentor saints, not believing attenuated traditions that may think there are no such intercessionary beings in that religion. We should cultivate a feeling of familiarity with the Great Mother, or with Abraham, Moses, Jesus, Muhammad, Confucius, Lao Tzu, Rama, Krishna, Shiva, or whichever of their saintly followers. If we don't believe in anything nonmaterial, we should feel friendly with all posited divine or superhuman beings, just to help us not be afraid in case we remain conscious and meet someone after we should have entered peacefully into oblivion.

Above all, we should heed the *Book of Natural Liberation* and try not to become morbid when we consider or encounter death. If our loved one dies, we should channel our grief into helpful activity, remaining joyous and cheerful, not indulging in weeping and wailing either just because we feel like it (which feeling is after all a culturally determined, conventional reaction), to convince others (including the departed) that we care, to assuage our own sense of guilt at surviving, or to avoid facing our new aloneness. We can accept the testimony of the *Book of Natural Liberation* that we will only frighten and annoy the soul of the departed and distract her from optimally navigating the between. She is the most important guest at a death and funeral, she is in the most momentous transition point of her life cycle, and positive or negative influences will affect her for years and lives to come. So in dealing with death let us honor the spirit of the *Book of Natural Liberation* at least by trying to do the right thing by having a good time! May all enjoy happiness and the best of luck!

PART
THREE

# SUPPLEMENTARY
# TRANSLATIONS

# THE DHARMA
# PRACTICE, NATURAL
# LIBERATION
# OF THE INSTINCTS

This supplementary translation and the succeeding one in chapter 8 (*The Natural Liberation Through Naked Vision*) are included for the person who wants to make a long-term, systematic effort to prepare for the between-state practice.

The Dharma Practice is a contemplative visualization of the entire assembly of the hundred mild and fierce deities located within the contemplator's body. It is to be repeated frequently, with an attempt to visualize each deity, its appearance, its ornaments, its posture, and so forth. Slowly, over time, the deities will become more and more familiar. If one wants to make more substantial progress in this practice, one should seek a qualified teacher and receive initiation and further instruction. I also consider the practice to serve as a model for a practitioner of any other religious tradition to invoke the deities, angels, and symbols of that tradition, to arrange them in a similar pattern in relation to the subtle patterns of the individual body, and to develop a deeper and more vivid familiarity in that way.

This practice is a systematic visualization, an imaginative contemplation that aims to cultivate a positive inclination toward the mild and fierce deities of the *Natural Liberation* teachings. The idea is that the negative instincts toward lust, hate, delusion, and so on should be contemplatively replaced by the positive instincts of generosity, love, and wisdom, intensified by being personified by the archetype deities. A person who is concerned about eventually dying, and who wants to prepare herself to use the *Book of Natural Liberation* with the greatest effect, should use this visualization regularly. Of course, ideally a teacher should be sought, initiation should be received, and more detailed instructions about how to do this contemplation should be secured. Not expecting the reader to have accomplished those steps, I include this practice here to give some sense of how further to prepare to use the *Book of Natural Liberation*. The text is very dense with allusions to deities and their appearances and accoutrements. If I stopped to comment on the symbolic meaning of all of them, this practice would fill another entire book. I include it to provide an overview. Precise grasp of all details will come only from your own further research.

The mild All-good and fierce Chemchok Deity hosts,
And the host of the union of the holy hundred clans—
Reverently saluting them, being liberated in the between,
May all beings abide in the reality of the Three Bodies!

May those fortunate in evolution who have holy teachers
Contemplate and recite always without forgetting
This brilliant Dharma practice, the union of the mild and fierce!

## THE TEN BRANCHES
## OF ACCUMULATING MERIT

All Tibetan contemplation practices begin with some version of these ten branches, which are 1) refuge, 2) evocation, 3) invitation, 4) salutation, 5) offerings, 6) confession, 7) congratulation, 8) requesting teachings, 9) requesting continuing presence, and 10) dedication. All of these are deeds that can be physically performed during entire lifetimes of practitioners. In these contemplations, the practitioner rehearses them imaginatively in order to inculcate the pattern of the acts within the mindstream. They are rehearsed in the visualized presence of all the deities in a vast field of refuge in space, often in the pattern of jewel fruits growing on a giant wish-granting gem tree, known as the "refuge field."

Visualize in the space before you the refuge field,
The Three Jewels and the Hundred Clan Deities
And say the following words:

*REFUGE*

OM AH HUM
To the fabulous mild and fierce blissful Victors,
The precious Three Jewels and Archetype Deities,
Along with oceans of Angels and the oath-bound host,
In the fabulous realms in the limits of space—
Never abandoning till my total enlightenment,
I reverently go for refuge!

> OM AH HUM are seed mantras that represent, respectively, the
> body, speech, and mind of all enlightened beings. The deities here
> invoked are all familiar, except the "oath-bound host," who are
> mainly mundane deities who once dominated particular tribes or
> regions and who have been tamed by a Buddha or great adept at
> some time in the past, then bound on oath to serve as protectors of
> practitioners of the Teachings of wisdom and compassion.

*EVOCATION*

From the vast and fabulous deep of the reality realm,
Emanating bodies of wisdom, art, and compassion,
May the fabulous mild and fierce deities of three times
Please come here for the sake of all beings!

*INVITATION*

In this pure wisdom sphere of apparent possibility,
On thrones of jewel lions and so forth,
On suns and moons of flawless art and wisdom,
Please sit with uncontaminated great pleasure!

> The deities are invited to be seated on jewel thrones, on cushions
> of sun and moon discs of radiant energy.

## SALUTATION

In the secret vulva of the All-good Lady,
The undissipated bliss of the All-good Lord,
Playfully creates the mild and fierce deity host,
Fathers and Mothers with their Children—
I bow down to all of them!

> As a way of praising the enlightened deities, the enlightened universe
> here is envisioned as contained within the drop of seed of the divine
> Father, All-good Buddha, standing in perfect balance in the vulva
> of the divine Mother, the All-good Mother Buddha, radiating its
> creativity in the forms of all the hundred deities of the mild and
> fierce hosts.

## OFFERINGS

To the Victor ocean of mild and fierce blissful Lords,
Immeasurable outer, inner, and secret offerings,
Actually arrayed and mentally emanated,
I offer for the sake of all—please accept them!

> Here you imagine the whole universe in front of the deities in the
> space before you, filled with huge clouds of offerings, sweet waters,
> perfumes, incenses, luscious foods, jewels, cloths, lights, elixirs, and
> every conceivable beautiful thing. The inner and secret offerings are
> constituted by your own self-habits of body and mind, offered up
> to the enlightened beings.

## CONFESSION OF SINS

Beginninglessly influenced by the three poisons,
My physical, verbal, and mental sins, along with their instincts,
All gathering causes of cycling in the horrid states,
Repentantly regretting, I heartily confess!

> Repentance about and separation from your sins are considered
> important methods of diminishing their evolutionary impact. The

point is not to wallow in guilt, but to face up to and then get free
of mistaken deeds on all levels.


## CONGRATULATIONS

In the great bliss world apparent throughout the Truth Realm,
All altruistic deeds, merits, spirit of enlightenment,
Successes of merit and wisdom—
I congratulate with great joy!


> Congratulation is the opposite of jealousy. It is the most effective
> way to vicariously participate in the meritorious successes of others.


## REQUESTING TEACHINGS

May the Teachers, as numerous as atoms in all universes,
Stir from their samadhis for beings' sake,
And please turn the holy wheels of Dharma,
Filling the Realm with teachings to the ends of space!


## REQUEST NOT TO DEPART INTO NIRVANA

Until the cyclic world is free,
Accomplishing magnificently the aims of beings,
May all the boundless Buddha Teachers
Please remain without going into Nirvana!


## DEDICATION

By all my virtues of three times,
May all beings filling all space
Become vessels of the unexcelled Mahayana,
And swiftly reach the state of the fabulous Buddhas mild and fierce!

## ENLIGHTENING,
## PROTECTING, AND PURIFYING

## OM AH HUM BODHICHITTA MAHASUKHAJNANA DHARATU AH

This mantra introduces the following visualization of the enlightened universe by pronouncing ritually: "By the body, speech, and mind of all Buddhas (OM AH HUM), may one uphold (DHARATU) the great bliss intuition (MAHASUKHAJNANA) that is the spirit of enlightenment (BODHICHITTA)—let it be creative (AH)!" The mantra also accompanies the melting of the refuge field into light and that light then melting into you.

## OM RULU RULU HUM BHYO HUM

This mantra invokes the fierce female Dharma protector Shri Devi, who sets up a protection perimeter around the site of your contemplation. You then feel safe to dissolve your ordinary identity into voidness, and arise out of voidness in Archetype Deity forms. The first practice is another preliminary, the Vajrasattva purification, wherein you visualize yourself as the Archetype Deity Vajrasattva, and you recite the cleansing mantra, known as the "Hundred-syllable Mantra."

### *VAJRASATTVA PURIFICATION*

From the uncreated pure Truth realm universe,
In the palace of the ceaseless clear pure drop,
On a jewel throne, on lotus, sun, and moon cushions,
My mind, out of nonartificial freedom spontaneity,
Arises as Vajrasattva, self-aware bright void;
One face clear white, two arms, smiling,
Right hand holding at heart the conscious void vajra-scepter,
Left holding at hip the appearance void ghanta-bell;
My crown the blissful, five-clan, perfect Buddhas,
Adorned with the Beatific Body silks and jewels.
I sit in sporting pose, right leg extended, left drawn in.

At my heart, a vajra HUM syllable shines,
Surrounded by the turning hundred letters.

OM VAJRASATTVA SAMAYA—MANUPALAYA—
VAJRASATTVENOPATISHTA—DRDHO ME BHAVA—
SUTOSHYO ME BHAVA—SUPOSHYO ME BHAVA—
ANURAKTO ME BHAVA—SARVASIDDHI ME
PRAYACCHA—SARVAKARMA SUCHAME—CHITTAM
SHRIYAM KURU HUM—HA HA HA HA HO—BHAGAVAN—
SARVATATHAGATA—VAJRA MAME MUNCHA—
VAJRIBHAVA—MAHASAMAYASATTVA—AH (HUM)

Radiating and reabsorbing [light rays while reciting], I accomplish my
own and other beings' aims, and purify obscurations. I must repeat as
much as possible without distraction this quintessence of the holy
hundred Buddha-clans, to purify emotional and intellectual
obscurations.

> The mantra is too long to translate in full here. It has meaning on
> many levels, from being a simple request to purify your sins and
> obscurations to being the evocation of the seed-quintessence of the
> hundred deities of the mandala. You recite it at least twenty-one
> times each session, visualizing the shining letters turning in an en-
> ergy wheel at your heart center, radiating purifying rainbow rays to
> all beings and then absorbing even brighter rays back into the letters
> from the joy beings feel as they feel more purified.

## THE ACTUAL VISUALIZATION

After thus purifying sins and obscurations, you should invoke and contemplate the mild and fierce hundred-clan deity host in the body mandala, pronouncing the between-prayer as follows.

### SELF-CREATION

Then, myself as Vajrasattva, in the palace of my spiritual jewel heart,
vivid in the five-light-ray drop with its five energy-essences, in the mandala of clear brilliance having five wisdoms, on lotus, sun, and moon

cushions on lion, elephant, horse, peacock, and eagle thrones, shine the thirty-six mild Buddhas in void, bright, ceaseless, rainbow light-ray bodies.

> Remaining stable in the visualization of yourself as Vajrasattva, you now visualize the mild and fierce deities as radiantly present within the universe of your own body. Your "spiritual heart" means the infinitely expanded space within your central channel back near the spine, at the height of the breasts, not the physical heart on the left side. As Vajrasattva, you visualize your body as made of light, not of coarse flesh, blood, and bone.

### THE MILD DEITY INTERIOR MANDALA

> Before visualizing the five Buddhas with their consort Buddhas in the center and four directions of the heart (east lies in front, south to your right, west toward your back, and north to your left), you visualize the primal Buddha and consort "in the deep space of the center." The All-good Buddha Father-Mother is not one of the five Buddhas, but the personified quintessence of the Truth Body of all Buddhas, visualized as present in the core of the soul, sealing your oneness with the universal ultimate reality of perfect freedom from the primordial beginninglessness of all time.

## OM AH HUM

In the deep space of the drop in the center of my spiritual heart, the changeless light body of the Truth Body, the primal savior All-good Samantabhadra, blue in color, in indivisible union with the white Truth Realm, All-good Samantabhadri, cross-legged in equipoise posture, sits on bright void lotus, sun, and moon cushions. To this great general ancestor of the three times Buddhas I bow, make offerings, take refuge, and pray. When I and others transit from life, just after leaving the body, when that pure, clear, reality light dawns, may Father Samantabhadra escort me from the front, and may Mother Samantabhadri support me from behind. Pray lead me to the state of All-good indivisible!

> When you pray for the sake of a deceased person, you substitute "the deceased So-and-so" for "I and others."

OM AH HUM

The clear white Vairochana and Dhatvishvari sport in union, holding wheel and bell, and sit cross-legged at the center, bright and void. To the Lord of the central Buddha-clan, I bow, offer, take refuge, and pray. When I and others transit from life, just after leaving the body, when those reality-between visions dawn, when I roam the life cycle through powerful delusions, on the light path of the bright Truth Realm wisdom, may Lord Vairochana guide my path! May supreme mother Dhatvishvari support me from behind! May they deliver me from the straits of terror of the between! May they carry me to perfect Buddhahood!

From here on you visualize the five Buddhas, grouped with their consorts and male and female Bodhisattva attendants in the center and four directions of your heart space. These should be visualized according to the descriptions of the mild deity groups in the Reality Between appearing on the "First" through the "Fifth" days on pp. 133–140 (see color insert, plates 5, 6, 7, and 8).

OM AH HUM

On the eastern petal of my spiritual heart, in the light space of the bright mirror wisdom, bright blue Vajrasattva sports with Lochana, holding vajra and bell. They sit cross-legged, bright and void. On his right stands white Kshitigarbha holding sprout and bell, on his left, white Maitreya, holding naga-tree flower and bell. Before him dances white Lasya holding mirror and bell, behind him, white Pushpa, holding a flower. To these six members of the Vajra clan, I bow, offer, take refuge, and pray. When I and others transit from life, just after leaving the body, when those reality-between visions dawn, when I roam the life cycle through powerful hate, on the light path of the bright mirror wisdom, may Lord Vajrasattva guide my path! May supreme mother Buddhalochana support me from behind! May they deliver me from the straits of terror of the between! May they carry me to perfect Buddhahood!

OM AH HUM

On the southern petal of my spiritual heart, in the light space of the bright equality wisdom, yellow Ratnasambhava sports in union with Mamaki. Holding jewel and bell, they sit cross-legged, bright and void. On his right stands yellow Samantabhadra holding garland and bell, on his left, yellow Akashagarbha, holding sword and bell. Before him dances yellow Mala holding a rosary, behind him, yellow Dhupa holding incense. To these six members of the Jewel clan, I bow, offer, take refuge, and pray. When I and others transit from life, just after leaving the body, when those reality-between visions dawn, when I roam the life cycle through powerful pride, on the light path of the bright equality wisdom, may Lord Ratnasambhava guide my path! May supreme mother Mamaki support me from behind! May they deliver me from the straits of terror of the between! May they carry me to perfect Buddhahood!

OM AH HUM

On the western petal of my spiritual heart, in the light space of the bright discriminating wisdom, red Amitabha sports in union with Pandaravasini. Holding red lotus and bell, they sit cross-legged, bright and void. On his right stands red Avalokiteshvara holding lotus and bell, on his left, red Manjushri, holding sword and bell. Before him dances red Gita holding a wheel, behind him, red Aloka holding a lamp. To these six members of the Lotus clan, I bow, offer, take refuge, and pray. When I and others transit from life, just after leaving the body, when those reality-between visions dawn, when I roam the life cycle through powerful lust, on the light path of the bright discriminating wisdom, may Lord Amitabha guide my path! May supreme mother Pandaravasini support me from behind! May they deliver me from the straits of terror of the between! May they carry me to perfect Buddhahood!

OM AH HUM

On the northern petal of my spiritual heart, in the light space of the bright, all-accomplishing wisdom, green Amoghasiddhi sports in union with Tara. Holding vajra-cross and bell, they sit cross-legged, bright and void. On his right stands green Sarvanivaranaviskambhin, holding book and bell, on his left, green Vajrapani, holding vajra and bell. Before him dances green Gandha, holding a skull bowl, behind him, green Nartya holding food. To these six members of the Action clan, I bow, offer, take refuge, and pray. When I and others transit from life, just after leaving the body, when those reality-between visions dawn, when I roam the life cycle through powerful envy, on the light path of the bright all-accomplishing wisdom, may Lord Amoghasiddhi guide my path! May supreme mother Tara support me from behind! May they deliver me from the straits of terror of the between! May they carry me to perfect Buddhahood!

OM AH HUM

On the eastern gate petal of my spiritual heart stand white Vijaya and Ankusha in union, in warrior posture. On the southern gate petal of my spiritual heart stand yellow Yama and Pasha in union, in warrior posture. On the western gate petal of my spiritual heart stand red Hayagriva and Sphota in union, in warrior posture. On the northern gate petal of my spiritual heart stand green Amrtakundali and Ghanta in union, in warrior posture. To the eight emanated Door-guards, Fathers and Mothers, I bow, offer, take refuge, and pray. When I and others transit from life, just after leaving the body, when those reality-between visions dawn, when I roam the life cycle through powerful instincts, on the light path of the bright four wisdoms in union, may these four fierce guardians guide my path! May the four great mother guardians support me from behind! May they deliver me from the straits of terror of the between! May they carry me to perfect Buddhahood!

OM AH HUM

In the light deep of the great bliss lotus at my crown, in the mandala of the clear brilliance of the bright white drop, the white divine Buddha Indra stands with his guitar; may he cut off pride, the door of rebirth among the gods. In the light deep of my nape, in the mandala of the clear brilliance of the bright green drop, the green titanic Buddha Vemachitra stands with his weapon; may he cut off envy, the titan birth door. In the light deep of the crystal hole of my life channel at my heart, in the mandala of the clear brilliance of the bright yellow drop, the yellow human Buddha Shakyamuni stands with his mendicant's staff; may he cut off lust, the human birth door. In the light deep of the coiling nerve wheel at my navel, in the mandala of the clear brilliance of the bright blue drop, the blue animal Buddha Simha stands with his book; may he cut off delusion, the animal birth door. In the light deep of the bliss source lotus at my secret place, in the mandala of the clear brilliance of the bright orange drop, the red pretan Buddha Jvalamukha stands with his box; may he cut off greed, the pretan birth door. In the light deep of the coiling nerve wheels on my foot soles, in the mandala of the clear brilliance of the bright black drop, the black hell Buddha Dharmaraja stands with his fire water; may he cut off hatred, the hell birth door.

To the six Buddhas, Emanation Bodies accomplishing beings' aims, I bow, offer, take refuge, and pray. When I and others transit from life, just after leaving the body, when those existence-between visions dawn, when I roam the life cycle through powerful instincts, on the light path of the bright four wisdoms in union, may the three upper

Buddhas guide my path! May the three lower Buddhas support me from behind! May they deliver me from the light path of the impure six realms! May they carry me to perfect Buddhahood!

OM AH HUM
The forty-two mild deities blaze with light rays of spontaneous energy of clear brilliance, their bodies mild and youthful, soft, supple, tenderly alluring, beautiful, adorned with the signs and marks. To that mild deity host of the vajra realm, I bow, offer, take refuge, and pray. When I and others transfer from life, just after leaving the body, when those reality-between visions dawn, when I wander in the cycle through powerful five poisons, on the light path of the bright five wisdoms, may the mild Fathers guide my path! May the Consort Mothers support me from behind! May the male and female Guardians support me from the boundaries! May they deliver me from the straits of terror of the between! May they carry me to perfect Buddhahood!

*THE SCIENTIST DEITY*
*INTERIOR MANDALA*

OM AH HUM
In this time of abiding in the life between, the forty-two mild deities, in the palace of my body's spiritual heart, sit vividly in bodies made of the five lights. When I transfer from life, just after leaving the body, may the mild deities emerge from within my heart. May they arise and fill the space before me. With ornaments and equipment, Lords and Consorts countless in number stand in the vastness of rainbow light, in their bright, void, rainbow light-ray bodies, with five-wisdom light-path penetrating brilliance and five-light drops, radiating sounds and rays. Naturally beautiful, clear, brilliant, lustrous, resonant—may they arise as if penetrating my heart. Along with those lights of the five wisdoms will come the impure six light paths of the six impure, erring ordinary life-realms. At the time when they arise for me, may the compassionate Lords of the mild deity host, sensitive, not weak in love, lead me on the path of the four wisdoms combined. May they bring me back from the path of the six impure realms!

In the next seven paragraphs, you conclude visualizing the mild deities, focusing on the Five Scientist Deities with their consorts in the center and four directions of your throat center space. Please refer to the descriptions in the Reality Between for the Seventh Day, pp. 145–148.

OM AH HUM
In the palace of the Beatific Body wheel in the center of my physical throat, in the vast sphere immersed in rainbows and lights, in the center of the beatific wheel lotus, there is the clear, red, Evolutionary Great Scientist, Padmanarteshvara, with five light-ray brilliance, bliss-void united with the red Wisdom Angel, manifesting in space, holding chopper and skull bowl. May the body Scientist host protect all beings!

OM AH HUM
In my throat beatific wheel's eastern petal, there is the clear, white, Earth-abiding Great Scientist, Padmanarteshvara, united with the white smiling Angel, manifesting in space holding chopper and skull bowl. May the mind Scientist host protect all beings!

OM AH HUM
In my throat beatific wheel's southern petal, there is the clear, yellow Life-lord Great Scientist, united with the yellow smiling Angel, manifesting in space, holding chopper and skull bowl. May the excellence Scientists protect all beings!

OM AH HUM
In my throat beatific wheel's western petal, there is the clear, red Great Seal Great Scientist, united with the red smiling Angel, manifesting in space, holding chopper and skull bowl. May the speech Scientists protect all beings!

OM AH HUM
In my throat beatific wheel's northern petal, there is the clear, green Effortless Great Scientist, united with the green, fierce, smiling Angel, manifesting in space, holding chopper and skull bowl. May the miracle Scientists protect all beings!

OM AH HUM
To the entire Scientist Hero and Angel host, I bow, offer, take refuge, and pray. When I and others transit from life, just after leaving the body, when those reality-between visions dawn, when I roam the life cycle through powerful instincts, on the light path of the clear orgasmic wisdom, may the hero Scientists guide my path! May the supreme

mother Angel host support me from behind! May they deliver me from the straits of terror of the between! May they carry me to the pure angelic worlds!

OM AH HUM
In this time of abiding in the life between, the Scientist Heros and Angels, in the palace of my body's throat beatific wheel, sit vividly in bodies made of the five lights. When I and others transit from life, just after leaving the body, may the Scientist Deity host emerge from within my throat. May they arise and fill the space before me. May they manifest music and dancing. May they shake and energize the whole universe. With their orgasmic wisdom light-path of brilliant, penetrating rays, when the animal delusion path arises, may the Scientist Deity host's compassion not be feeble. May they bring me back from the path of animal delusion! May they lead beings to the path of orgasmic wisdom! May they care for me compassionately, to recognize the reality of the between! May they consecrate me to become a Scientist Bodhisattva!

## THE FIERCE DEITY
## INTERIOR MANDALA

In the following, you visualize the fierce deities in the center and four directions of your brain center. You begin with the dark brown Chemchok Heruka and his consort Krodhishvari, who is a fierce form of the All-good Samantabhadra Buddha and consort and the personified essence of all fierce Buddha-deities. For further descriptions of these fierce deities, you should refer to the Fierce Deity Reality Between, Eighth through Twelfth Days, pp. 149–156, and color plates 6 and 8.

OM AH HUM
On my Vajrasattva crown, in the palace of my brain's skull mansion, in the radiant vastness of the rainbow flame-mass drop, sit the bodies of the Heruka Deity host.

OM AH HUM
In the central petal of my brain's skull mansion, in the radiant vastness of the rainbow flame-mass drop, stands the All-good Chemchok Heruka, with three faces, dark brown, white, and red, and six arms, the right three holding vajra, khatvanga, and small javelin, the left three

holding bell, bloody spear, and intestine-noose, united in indivisible bliss with Krodhishvari. May the Lord Father-Mother lead all beings!

OM AH HUM
Upon a throne in the central petal of my brain skull mansion, in the radiant vastness of the rainbow flame-mass drop, stands the Vairochana Buddha Heruka, with three faces, dark brown, white, and red, and six arms, the right three holding wheel, ax, and sword, the left three holding bell, mirror, and bloody spear, united in indivisible bliss with Buddha Krodhi. May the Blissful Heruka clan lead all beings!

OM AH HUM
Upon a throne in the eastern petal of my brain skull mansion, in the radiant vastness of the rainbow flame-mass drop, stands the Vajrasattva Vajra Heruka, with three faces, dark blue, white, and red, and six arms, the right three holding vajra, spear, and ax, the left three holding bell, bloody spear, and mirror, united in indivisible bliss with Vajra Krodhishvari. May the Vajra Heruka clan lead all beings!

OM AH HUM
Upon a throne in the southern petal of my brain's skull mansion, in the radiant vastness of the rainbow flame-mass drop, stands the Ratnasambhava Ratna Heruka, with three faces, dark yellow, white, and red, and six arms, the right three holding jewel, khatvanga, and club, the left three holding bell, bloody spear, and trident, united in indivisible bliss with Ratna Krodhishvari. May the Ratna Heruka clan lead all beings!

OM AH HUM
Upon a throne in the western petal of my brain's skull mansion, in the radiant vastness of the rainbow flame-mass drop, stands the Amitabha Padma Heruka, with three faces, dark red, white, and blue, and six arms, the right three holding lotus, khatvanga, and rod, the left three holding bell, bloody spear, and dart, united in indivisible bliss with Padma Krodhishvari. May the Padma Heruka clan lead all beings!

OM AH HUM
Upon a throne in the northern petal of my brain's skull mansion, in the radiant vastness of the rainbow flame-mass drop, stands the Amoghasiddhi Karma Heruka, with three faces, dark green, white, and red, and six arms, the right three holding sword, khatvanga, and rod, the left three holding bell, bloody spear, and mirror, united in indivisible

bliss with Karma Krodhishvari. May the Karma Heruka clan lead all beings!

OM AH HUM
To the twelve Heruka Lords and Ladies, I bow, offer, take refuge, and pray. When I and others transit from this life, just after leaving the body, when those reality-between visions dawn, when I roam the life cycle through powerful false perceptions, on the light path of the clear full five wisdoms, may the Heruka Fury Kings guide my path! May the Realm-goddess Fury host support me from behind! May they deliver me from the straits of terror of the between! May they carry me to perfect Buddhahood!

OM AH HUM
In the light vastness of the eastern petal of my skull mansion, stands a white Gauri, holding a skeleton club and a skull bowl. In the light vastness of the southern petal of my skull mansion, a yellow Chauri holds a bow and arrow and throws an impaling stick. In the light vastness of the western petal of my skull mansion, a red Pramoha holds a sea-monster victory standard. In the light vastness of the northern petal of my skull mansion, a black Vetali holds a vajra and a skull bowl. In the light vastness of the southeastern petal of my skull mansion, an orange Pukkasi devours fresh intestines. In the light vastness of the southwestern petal of my skull mansion, a dark green Ghasmari shakes a vajra and a skull bowl. In the light vastness of the northwestern petal of my skull mansion, a light yellow Chandali eats a heart and holds a headless body. In the light vastness of the northeastern petal of my skull mansion, a dark blue Shmashani holds and eats a headless body.

OM AH HUM
To the eight Gauri goddesses of the holy grounds, I bow, offer, take refuge, and pray. When I and others transit from this life, just after leaving the body, when those reality-between visions dawn, when I roam the life cycle through powerful false perceptions, on the light path of the clear sound, light, and rays, may the four Gauri goddesses guide my path! May the four Pukkasi goddesses support me from behind! May they deliver me from the straits of terror of the between! May they carry me to perfect Buddhahood!

OM AH HUM
On the outer eastern petal of my skull mansion, a dark brown, lion-faced Simhasya holds a corpse in her mouth. On the outer southern

petal of my skull mansion, a red, tiger-faced Vyaghrasya stands with her two arms folded. On the outer western petal of my skull mansion, a black, jackal-faced Shrgalasya eats intestines. On the outer northern petal of my skull mansion, a dark blue, wolf-faced Shvanasya rends a corpse. On the outer southeastern petal of my skull mansion, a pale yellow, vulture-faced Grdhrasya eats a corpse draped over her shoulder. On the outer southwestern petal of my skull mansion, a dark red, hawk-faced Kankhasya carries a flayed human skin. On the outer northwestern petal of my skull mansion, a black, crow-faced Kakasya holds a skull bowl and a knife. On the outer northeastern petal of my skull mansion, a light blue, owl-faced Ulukasya holds a vajra.

To these eight Simha ghouls of the holy places, I bow, offer, take refuge, and pray. When I and others transit from life, just after leaving the body, when those reality-between visions dawn, when I roam the life cycle through powerful false perceptions, on the light path of all visions being the eight holy places, may the four Simha ghouls guide my path! May the four Grdhra ghouls support me from behind! May they deliver me from the straits of terror of the between! May they carry me to perfect Buddhahood!

OM AH HUM
On the eastern gate petal of my skull mansion, a white, horse-faced Ankusha holds a goad and a skull bowl. On the southern gate petal of my brain skull mansion, a yellow, pig-faced Pasha holds a noose and a skull bowl. On the western gate petal of my brain skull mansion, a red, lion-faced Shernkhala holds a chain and a skull bowl. On the northern gate petal of my brain skull mansion, a green, serpent-faced Ghanta holds a bell and a skull bowl. To the four wisdom-emanated female Door Guardians, I bow, offer, take refuge, and pray. When I and others transit from this life, just after leaving the body, when those reality-between visions dawn, when I roam the life cycle through powerful false perceptions, to block the doors of the errors of the four types of rebirth may they open the doors of the four pure miraculous activities! May Ankusha and Pasha guide my path! May Shernkhala and Ghanta support me from behind! May they deliver me from the straits of terror of the between! May they carry me to perfect Buddhahood!

OM AH HUM
On the small channels outside the eastern gate of my skull mansion, the six powerful, peace-making Yoginis appear: the white, yak-faced Rakshasi holding a vajra; the pale yellow, snake-faced Brahmi holding a lotus; the pale green, leopard-faced Maheshvari holding a trident; the

pale blue, monkey-faced Lobha holding a wheel; the pink, mule-faced Kumari holding a pike; and the white, bear-headed Indrani holding an intestine-noose. May these six Yoginis arise from the east, make peace, and accomplish the activities of eradicating the terrors of the between!

OM AH HUM
On the small channels outside the southern gate of my skull mansion, the six powerful magnifying Yoginis appear: the yellow, bat-faced Vajra holding a razor; the orange, sea-monster-faced Shanti holding a vase; the orange, scorpion-faced Amrta holding a lotus; the pale yellow, hawk-faced Chandra holding a vajra; the yellow-green, fox-faced Gada holding a rod; and the yellow-black, tiger-faced Rakshasi drinking blood from a skull bowl. May these six magnifying Yoginis arise from the south, and accomplish the activities of expanding wisdom in the between!

OM AH HUM
On the small channels outside the western gate of my skull mansion, the six powerful dominating Yoginis appear: the red-green, vulture-faced Bhakshasi holding a club; the red, horse-faced Rati holding the trunk of a human corpse; the pink, eagle-faced Mahabali holding a rod; the red, dog-faced Rakshasi holding a vajra; the red, hoopoe-faced Kama shooting arrow from a bow; and the red-green, deer-headed Vasuraksha holding a vase. May these six dominating Yoginis arise from the west, and accomplish the activities of facilitating freedom in the between!

OM AH HUM
On the small channels outside the northern gate of my skull mansion, the six powerful destroying Yoginis appear: the blue-green, wolf-faced Vayavi waving a banner; the green-red, ibex-headed Narini holding an impaling stick; the dark green, pig-faced Varahi holding a noose made of tusks; the green-red, crow-faced Rati holding the flayed skin of a child; the dark green, elephant-faced Mahanasi holding a human corpse; and the blue-green, snake-faced Varuni holding a snake noose. May these six terrifying Yoginis arise from the north, and accomplish the activities of destroying misperceptions in the between!

OM AH HUM
In the eastern gate of my skull mansion, the white, cuckoo-faced Vajra holds a goad. In the skull mansion southern gate, the yellow, goat-faced Vajra holds a noose. In the western gate, a red, lion-faced Vajra holds a chain. In the northern gate, a green, snake-faced Vajra holds a bell;

may these four powerful female Guardians who do the work of emanation accomplish the activities of blocking the doors of birth!

OM AH HUM

To these twenty-eight powerful Yoginis, I bow, offer, take refuge, and pray. When I and others transit from this life, just after leaving the body, when those reality-between visions dawn, when I roam the life cycle through powerful false perceptions, on the light path of the brilliant sounds, lights, and rays, may the seven eastern goddesses guide my path! May the seven southern goddesses support me from behind! May the seven western goddesses sustain me from the borders! May the seven northern goddesses destroy and liberate! May they deliver me from the straits of terror of the between! May they carry me to perfect Buddhahood!

OM AH HUM

In this time of abiding in the life between, the sixty Heruka deities in the palace of the brain skull mansion on my crown stand vividly in their bodies formed of the five light-rays. When I and others transit from this life, just after leaving the body, may the Heruka deities emerge from within the brain and arise, filling entirely the world of the three billion universes; well adorned and equipped, Lords and Companions terrifying in demeanor, their fierce bodies in the vastness of sounds, lights and rays, with accoutrements of charm, bravery, and terror; sounding the roar of wildness, fatality, and ferocity, blazing with the wrath of oom passion, savagery, and fury; decorated with smears of bone ash, blood, and grease; wearing blood-dripping hides and tiger-skin skirts; adorned with skull garlands, snake sashes, and blazing with masses of flames; rumbling with the thousand thunders, "HA HA HUM PHAT! Strike! Kill!" They move about manifesting various heads and various implements. They shake the billion worlds in various ways. All their sounds, light rays, and energies are terrifying in appearance. When all these arise before me, may the compassionate fierce Heruka Deity host not stint of their compassion. When I roam the life cycle through powerful instincts, on the light path of abandoning visions of anguish, panic, and terror, may the fierce Heruka host guide my path! May the fierce goddess host support me from behind! May the Gauri and Simha Door Goddesses sustain me from the borders! May the eight great uplifting goddesses uplift me from the holy places! May the animal-faced goddess host eliminate obstacles! May the four great female Door guardians block the doors of rebirth! May they deliver me from the straits of terror of the between! May they carry me to perfect Buddhahood!

OM AH HUM

When I leave my loved ones and wander off alone, and empty forms arise in my perception, may the Buddhas exert the force of their compassion, and prevent the debilitating terrors of the between! When that brilliant wisdom light path dawns, may I recognize it as my own reality, free of fear and panic! When the mild and ferocious body forms arise, with fearless confidence, may I recognize the reality of the between! If I experience suffering under the influence of negative evolution, may the Archetype Deity clear all misery away! If the natural sound of Reality thunders like a thousand dragons, may it just become the sound of the Mahayana Dharma! When I follow evolution without refuge, may the Great Compassion Lord give refuge to me and others! When the instinct body suffers, may the samadhi of clear light bliss arise! May I not hate as enemies the realms of the five elements, but behold them as the pure realms of the five Buddha-clans! By the power of the blessings of the Mentors of the esoteric tradition, the compassion of the fabulous mild and fierce deity host, and my own pure high resolve—may everything I have prayed for be accomplished!

It would be ideal if, before using this text, you found a qualified lama as mentor, learned some basic preliminaries, and received permission or initiation to use these visualizations. In circumstances where that is not possible yet, but there is a basically respectful and positive attitude, it is all right to work on your own to become more familiar with the between-deities, to prepare yourself for the between-experience. The key to using this *Dharma Practice* successfully is continual repetition. When you first recite this and try to visualize it, you feel lost and uncomfortable. You find it difficult to visualize anything, you find the names and deities unfamiliar, your mind wanders away from your heart, throat, and brain centers, you feel worried, inadequate, confused, and perhaps irritated. Relax. Make color Xeroxes of the color plates and set them up in a pleasant space where you like to meditate. Resolve to read it quietly again and again. Think that the deities are there whether you notice them or not. After all, your rib cage is there, and how often do you think about it, rib by rib? As you read each paragraph, look at the corresponding picture and try to imagine your Vajrasattva light-body as containing that deity in that spot. Even a small flash of color, a rough outline of a form, is progress. As you continue, you will feel more and more at home with the practice, and, most important, more familiar with the various deities. Don't set yourself any strict goals. Don't hope for any peak experiences or fantastic visions—

and don't get attached or make claims about it if anything pleasant does happen. The big peak experience awaits us all after death in the between—the point is to be ready. Try to practice a little bit at a time. A secret is to always quit the practice when you're still enjoying it. Don't strain yourself to do as much as possible each time, or you will find yourself vaguely reluctant to start again the next session. If you work on this practice in this steady and persistent way, you will feel more prepared for anything bit by bit. Try also to memorize or familiarize yourself with the between-prayers and verses, study all parts of the *Natural Liberation,* and learn as much as possible about Buddhism and Tibetan civilization. It will be enjoyable and beneficial. May this bring happiness and good luck to all!

# THE NATURAL LIBERATION THROUGH NAKED VISION, IDENTIFYING THE INTELLIGENCE

The *Naked Vision* provides a summary of the philosophical and contemplative doctrines of the Great Perfection, considered the supreme and highest Tantra in the Nyingma Order, and foundational in the teachings of the *Book of Natural Liberation.* I include this, even though it has been translated before, because it is such a beautiful text, because its study will enhance the reader's understanding of the whole *Natural Liberation,* and because I happen to like it very much. Even though it expresses the highest and most advanced teaching, it has the special virtue for the general reader of making the metaphysical view of Buddhism accessible.

This text is philosophical, rather than experiential in the way of most of the *Book of Natural Liberation.* It concerns the profound reality underlying the Teaching, indeed, making possible liberation itself. It teaches radical nonduality, the immediate and liberating presence of ultimate reality in the here and now, and the actuality of peace, security, benevolence, and bliss. This is especially healing in our modern culture where some current interpretations of religions tend to devalue our immediate experience of life, and secularism reduces all to meaningless matter. Studying the *Naked Vision* will enhance the reader's understanding of all the other instructions of the *Book of Natural Liberation.* It conveys pure wisdom, that which finally is indispensable in the realization of true freedom.

Homage to the Three-bodied Deity, intelligence's natural clarity!

"Naked vision" is liberated intuition—unmediated experience. It can function when all conceptual direction, both conscious thought-orientation and unconscious ingrained prejudice, has been thoroughly suspended. The central notion is that all Deity is the natural clarity of intelligence itself. All positive awareness, love, confidence, stability, power, clarity, and goodness—the strong force of the universe—*is itself* our bare intelligence. Our task then is to strip away all confusions and distorted programmings and let our natural goodness be there, to find our own natural security in our actual deepest reality.

Here is taught the *Natural Liberation Through Naked Vision, Identifying the Intelligence,* from the *Profound Teaching of the Natural Liberation Through Contemplating the Mild and Fierce Buddha Deities.* Thus identifying your own intelligence, contemplate it well, O fortunate child!

## SAMAYA GYA GYA GYAH!

This expression reminds us that this teaching is esoteric, sealed by a vow and protected by angelic beings. The reason it has been traditionally kept a secret is not because of some elitism or stinginess on the part of enlightened teachers. It has been kept secret because it can easily be misunderstood by the uneducated, misunderstood as meaning that there are no efforts to be made toward freedom, that all ethical restraint, virtue, and mental development are really unnecessary, and that anything goes. When the raw egotist feels thus that his impulses should be allowed unchecked sway, that person tends to become harmful to himself and to others. However, after a person has cultivated detachment from blind passion, freedom from reactive hatred, and insight into the relativity of all attitudes and states of personality, this simple teaching no longer needs to be sealed away by angels. It becomes readily available. In modern society, particularly societies influenced by ideologies that teach that reality is either evil and threatening or neutral and ultimately meaningless, the literate public has the right to hear this radically positive teaching.

## THE QUINTESSENCE

## EMA HOH!

This expresses wonder and joy.

The one mind that pervades all life and liberation,
Though it is the primal nature, it is not recognized,
Though its bright intelligence is uninterrupted, it is not faced,
Though it ceaselessly arises everywhere, it is not recognized.
To make known just this objective nature,
The three times Victors proclaimed the inconceivable
Eighty-four thousand Dharma Teachings,
Teaching none other than this realization.
Though Scriptures are measureless as the sky,
Their import is three words identifying intelligence.
This direct introduction to the intention of the Victors—
Just this is the entry into freedom from progression.

> This simple teaching—the three words, "This is It!"—is the final
> point of all the other teachings of all the Buddhas. Their incon-
> ceivable compassion responds with every variety and complexity of
> therapy required by the variety and complexity of human self-
> entanglement. But the bottom line is that all goodness, wisdom,
> and peace is here and now in every atom and instant of being.

## THE NEED FOR THIS IDENTIFICATION

KYAI HO!

> This calls us to attention, to a joyful alertness.

Fortunate children! Listen here!
"Mind"—though this great word is so well known—
People do not know it, know it wrongly or only partially;
And by their not understanding its reality precisely,
They come up with inconceivable philosophical claims.
The common, alienated individual, not realizing this,
By not understanding her own nature on her own,
Suffers roaming through six life-forms in three realms.
Such is the fault of not realizing this reality of the mind.

We spend our lives trying to make ends meet, seeking to inform ourselves about what we need to know to succeed in the tasks we think essential to survival. But we have spent countless lifetimes suffering the loss of everything again and again, all because we have not realized what it is that we ourselves actually are. We have thought we were absolute life-centers, struggling against a hostile environment, trying to prolong our existence against all odds. We never recognized that our very intelligence itself is the same as the strong force that holds all things together, that we have always essentially been one with our highest fulfillment, our ultimate possible goal. So we always feared, fought, struggled, suffered, and put our effort into the exactly opposite direction.

Disciples and Hermit Buddhas claim realization
Of a partial selflessness, but do not know this exactly.
Bound up in claims from their treatises and theories,
They do not behold clear light transparency.

Disciples and Hermit Buddhas are the two kinds of Individual Vehicle saints. They have become genuinely liberated from a certain level of false self-addiction. They have developed true insight into reality. But their insight is not complete. Their instincts are still distorted, and they cannot melt down from all coarse and subtle structures into the transparency of ultimate reality.

Disciples and Hermits are shut out by clinging to subject and object,
Centrists are shut out by extremism about the two realities,
Ritual and Performance Tantrists, by extremism in service and practice,
And Great (Maha) and Pervasive (Anu) Tantrists,
By clinging to the duality of realm and intelligence.
They err by remaining dualistic in nonduality,
By not communing nondually, they do not awaken.
All life and liberation inseparable from their own minds,
They still roam the life cycle on vehicles of quitting and choosing.

Padma Sambhava critiques the Individualists for their perceptual dualism about subject and object. He critiques the Universalists (Mahayanists), who prefer the philosophy of centrism founded by Nagarjuna, for their overemphasis on either the relative or the ultimate reality, or even overfondness of the two-reality scheme itself. He critiques the ritualistic Tantric practitioners for their dualistic attitudes about the separation between themselves and the deities they invoke in their rituals and visualizations. He critiques the higher, more yogic Tantrists for remaining dualistic about the difference between their own minds and the diamond realm of perfection of the great mandalas, or pure environments.

Therefore, absorbing all created things in your free inaction,
Realize the great natural liberation of all things from this teaching
Of natural liberation through naked seeing of your own intelligence!
Thus, in the Great Perfection, everything is perfect!

Here he sets the Ultimate (Ati) Tantrists, the adepts of natural liberation, at the apex of all vehicles, engaged in the subtlest practice of nonpractice, of achievement of nonduality by radical immersion in immediacy without dualistic effort. This is the teaching of the Great Perfection.

SAMAYA GYA GYA GYA!

## THE DETAILED IDENTIFICATION

"Mind," this bright process of intelligence,
In one way exists and in another way does not.
It is the origin of the pleasure and pain of life and liberation.
It is accepted as essential to the eleven vehicles of liberation.

Again, the mind exists as the fundamental intelligence of reality, the essential void transparency that is the immovable strong force of the multiverse. But in another sense, it cannot be said to "exist" since there is ultimately nothing other than it, it "stands out" from no other nonexistent, it is the universal unity of the ultimate reality. The "eleven vehicles" is not the usual "nine vehicles" mentioned by Padma Sambhava, which include the three exoteric vehicles, the three lower Tantras, and the three highest Tantras. It rather refers as a general number to the many vehicles, non-Buddhist as well as Buddhist, that take one to liberation. Immediately following there are eleven names of mind, used in different Indian schools of thought. Each of these names is used by a different vehicle.

Its names are countless in various contexts.
Some call this mind "the mind-reality."
Some fundamentalists call it "self."
Some Disciples call it "selflessness."
Idealists call it by the name of "mind."
Some call it "transcendent wisdom."
Some call it "the Buddha nature."
Some call it "the Great Seal."
Some call it "the Soul Drop."
Some call it "the Truth Realm."
Some call it "the Foundation."
Some call it "the Ordinary."

It is hard to distinguish these eleven different types, though they seem to refer, respectively, to our author, Hindu philosophers, Buddhist Individualists, Idealists, Centrists, immanentists, three types of Tantric adepts, idealistic Tantrics, and our author again.

## THE THREE-POINT ENTRANCE

To introduce the three-point entrance to this itself—
Realize past awareness as trackless, clear, and void,
Future awareness as unproduced and new,
And present awareness as staying natural, uncontrived.

The "three points" here seems to refer to the threefold deconstruction of the three times (past, present, and future), freeing oneself from the reification of the passage of time in order to enter into timeless awareness.

Thus knowing time in its very ordinary way,
When you nakedly regard yourself,

Your looking is transparent, nothing to be seen.
This is naked, immediate, clear intelligence.

This is a quick resolution of the double-bind meditation of looking for the self looking for the self, which generates in insight meditation an internal spinning sensation that becomes the diamond drill of critical wisdom that cuts through all seeming substantialities of apparent intrinsically identifiable self, leading to the realization of voidness and the experience of freedom.

It is clear voidness with nothing established,
Purity of clarity-voidness nonduality;
Not permanent, free of any intrinsic status,
Not annihilated, bright and distinct,
Not a unity, multidiscerning clarity,
Without plurality, indivisible, one in taste,
Not derivative, self-aware, it is this very reality.

This passage recalls Nagarjuna's famous opening verse from his *Wisdom,* in which he sets forth the eight special qualifications of ultimate reality, not ceased, not produced, not permanent, not annihilated, and so on.

This objective identification of the actuality of things
Contains complete in one the indivisible Three Bodies.
The Truth Body, the voidness free of intrinsic status,
The Beatific Body, bright with freedom's natural energy,
The Emanation Body ceaselessly arising everywhere—
Its reality is these three complete in one.

Here, Padma indicates how the Three Bodies of perfect Buddhahood are present in everything, and cannot be excluded from transparency, from the infinite nonduality of universal perfection. Thus the entrance herein is not just a mental leap into a subtle realm of blissful aloofness, but into a pure immediacy, a total presence that expands infinitely into contact with all reality, beyond the duality of simplicity and complexity.

## THE FORCEFUL METHOD

To introduce the forceful method to enter this very reality,
Your own awareness right now is just this!
It being just this uncontrived natural clarity,
Why do you say, "I don't understand the nature of the mind"?
As here there is nothing to meditate upon,
In just this uninterrupted clarity intelligence,
Why do you say, "I don't see the actuality of the mind"?
Since the thinker in the mind is just it,
Why do you say, "Even searching I can't find it"?
Since here there is nothing to be done,
Why do you say, "Whatever I do, it doesn't succeed"?
As it is sufficient to stay put uncontrived,
Why do you say, "I can't stay still"?
As it is all right to be content with inaction,
Why do you say, "I am not able to do it"?
Since clear, aware, and void are automatically indivisible,
Why do you say, "Practice is not effective"?
Since it is natural, spontaneous, free of cause and condition,
Why do you say, "Seeking, it cannot be found"?
Since thought and natural liberation are simultaneous,
Why do you say, "Remedies are impotent"?
Since your very intelligence is just this,
Why do you say, "I do not know this"?


> These expressions are quite simple, though their impact is profound.
> Padma challenges the ordinary thought-habits through which we
> separate ourselves from the experience and responsibility of simply
> understanding our actuality and so being invited to live according
> to that understanding in freedom.


Be sure mind's nature is groundless voidness;
Your mind is insubstantial like empty space—
Like it or not, look at your own mind!
Not fastening to the view of annihilative voidness,
Be sure spontaneous wisdom has always been clear,
Spontaneous in itself like the essence of the sun—
Like it or not, look at your own mind!
Be sure that intelligent wisdom is uninterrupted,

Like a continuous current of a river—
Like it or not, look at your own mind!
Be sure it will not be known by thinking various reasons,
Its movement insubstantial like breezes in the sky—
Like it or not, look at your own mind!
Be sure that what appears is your own perception.
Appearance is natural perception, like a reflection in a mirror—
Like it or not, look at your own mind.
Be sure that all signs are liberated on the spot,
Self-originated, self-delivered, like clouds in sky—
Like it or not, look at your own mind!

There is no thing not included in the mind,
Where is meditation other than from the mind?
There is no thing not included in the mind,
There is no teaching to practice other than mind-practice.
There is no thing not included in the mind,
There is no commitment to maintain outside the mind.
There is no thing not included in the mind,
There is no goal to be achieved outside the mind.
Look again! Look again! Look at your own mind!
Looking out there into the realm of space,
The mind will not emanate its reflections;
Looking here within your own mind,
There is no emanator of mind's emanations.
Your mind is clarity without hallucinations.
It is the Truth Body, self-aware, clear light voidness,
Cloudless and translucent like sunrise in the sky,
Unrestricted by forms, it is clearly known everywhere.
Whether you realize this point or not makes a great difference.

This primally unproduced, spontaneous clear light,
A wonder that this awareness-child lacks parents!
This spontaneous wisdom, a wonder no one made it!
Having never known a birth, a wonder it can never die!
Obviously clear, a wonder it lacks a seer!
Wandering in the cycle, a wonder it is not real evil!
Beholding Buddhahood, a wonder it is not real good!
Being everywhere, a wonder it does not know reality!
Beyond this, a wonder it hopes for other fruits!
It being yourself, a wonder you seek it elsewhere!
Ema! This brilliant, thingless, now-awareness,

Just this is the pinnacle of all views!
This nonperceiving, universal, total freedom,
Just this is the pinnacle of all meditation!
This uncontrived, relaxed approach to life,
Just this is the pinnacle of all conduct!
This unsought, primal, effortless achievement,
Just this is the pinnacle of accomplishments!


## THE FOUR INERRANCIES
## AND FOUR NAILS

The teaching of the Universal Vehicle's four inerrancies:
This great vehicle is unerring in view,
As it is this brilliant now-awareness,
Called "vehicle" since clear and unerring.
This great vehicle is unerring in meditation,
As it is this brilliant now-awareness,
Called "vehicle" since clear and unerring.
This great vehicle is unerring in conduct,
As it is this brilliant now-wisdom,
Called "vehicle" since clear and unerring.
This great vehicle is unerring in fruition,
As it is this brilliant now-awareness,
Called "vehicle" since clear and unerring.

Teaching the four great nails of changelessness:
This great nail of changeless view
Is just this brilliant conscious now-awareness,
Called "nail" since firm in the three times.
This great nail of changeless meditation
Is just this brilliant conscious now-awareness,
Called "nail" since firm in the three times.
This great nail of changeless conduct
Is just this brilliant conscious now-awareness,
Called "nail" since firm in the three times.
This great nail of changeless fruition
Is just this brilliant conscious now-awareness,
Called "nail" since firm in the three times.

## THE ONENESS OF TIMES

The instruction teaching oneness of three times:
Abandon the notion "past," not following former traces;
Sever mental connections, not following future plans;
Hold not the now, stay in the experience of space.
Free of meditation, do not meditate on anything,
Rely on mindfulness, undistracted without distraction,
Free of concentration and distraction, nakedly behold.
Self-aware, self-knowing, self-clear brilliance,
Just that arising is "enlightened spirit,"
Unmeditatable, beyond being object of knowledge,
Undistractible, natural bright clarity.
Vision-voidness natural liberation
Is brilliant void Body of Truth.
Realizing Buddhahood is not achieved by paths—
Vajrasattva is beheld right now.

## VIEWS, MEDITATIONS, ETHICS, FRUITIONS

The instruction to terminate the six extremes:
Though there is a huge number of discordant views,
In this self-aware mind, this self-original wisdom,
There is no duality of view and viewed.
Seek the viewer in viewing and not viewing.
When the viewer is sought it is not found,
So then the end of views is reached.
The impact of the view comes down just to that!
In the total absence of any view to view,
Don't sink to the false void of utter nothing,
The clear brilliance of self-aware now-consciousness—
Just that is the view of Great Perfection!
Here, there is no realizing-not-realizing duality.

Though there is a huge number of discordant meditations,
On the straight-up path of self-aware common consciousness,
There is no duality of meditation and meditated.
Seeking the agent of meditating and not meditating,
When you seek the meditator and do not find it,
Then the end of meditations has been reached.

The impact of meditation comes down just to that.
In the utter absence of meditation and meditated,
Don't succumb to the wild darkness of delusion.
In the clear brilliance of uncontrived now-consciousness,
That is the uncontrived and balanced contemplation.
Here, there is no abiding-nonabiding dualism.

Though there is a huge number of discordant ethics,
In the exclusive drop of self-aware wisdom
There is no duality of actor and acted.
Seek the agent of acting and not acting;
Seeking that actor itself, it is not found,
Then you reach the end of ethical actions.
The essence of ethics comes down just to that.
In that utter absence of action and acted,
Don't succumb to the errors of impulsive instinct.
In the uncontrived clear brilliance of now-consciousness,
Without choosing or being deceived by contrivance,
Just that is the perfect ethical action,
Free of the dualism of perfect and imperfect.

Though there is a huge number of discordant fruitions,
In the self-aware mind, itself the effortless Three Bodies,
There is no duality of attained and attaining.
Seek the attainer itself of the fruition!
Seeking that attainer itself, it is not found,
Thus the end of projected fruitions is reached.
The essence of fruition comes down just to that.
In that utter absence of attainment of fruition,
Don't succumb to worry about abandoning and undertaking.
This effortless clear brilliance of self-aware now-consciousness,
Is itself the realization of the manifest Three Bodies.
It is itself the fruition of the primal Buddhahood.


*THIS KNOWING*

This knowing, free of eight extremes like being and nothing,
Is called the center, not collapsed in any extreme;
It is called uninterrupted mindful, aware intelligence.
As it has the essence of voidness and awareness,
It is named the "essence of the Blissful Lords."

If you know this import, you transcend everything,
So it is called Transcendent Wisdom.
Since it surpasses mind, free of limit and origin,
It is called the Great Seal!
Thus, realizing it or not realizing it is the foundation
Of liberation and bound life, happiness and suffering—
So it is called the universal foundation.
Since it abides in nothing special, the inner space of the normal,
That very distinct, brilliant consciousness itself
Is given the name normal consciousness.
Whatever well-conceived poetic name it may be given,
In fact, other than just this self-aware now-consciousness,
Who would want anything more?
Like looking for its tracks when you have the elephant,
Scanning the whole universe, it's impossible to find.
Except through mind, it's impossible to reach Buddhahood.
Not recognizing this, if you seek mind outside,
Looking for something else, how can it find itself?
It is like a fool gawking at a crowd,
Forgetting himself among them,
Not recognizing himself, looking for himself,
Mistaking others for himself.
If you do not see the basic reality of things, not knowing
Your perceptions as your mind, you deliver yourself to the life cycle.
Not seeing your mind as Buddha, you obscure Nirvana.
Life and liberation, by knowing and not knowing,
In an instant there is no distinction between them.

Seeing one's mind as elsewhere is an error;
But erring and not erring are actually the same.
A being has no second continuum of mind;
When mind is left in itself unmade, it's free.
If you don't know error itself as mind,
You'll never realize the impact of reality,
Self-arisen, self-created, self looks into self,
These visions first arise from where?
Where do they stay in the meanwhile?
Finally, where do they go?
It's like a crow's reflection in a pond;
It flies up from the pond, but the reflection doesn't leave.
So perceptions arise from the mind;
Rising from the mind, they are freed in the mind.

*MIND IS ALL*

Mind itself, this clear void all-knowing, all aware,
It is like sky, primal clarity-voidness indivisible.
In the clarity of original intuitive wisdom,
Just that determination is reality.
The reason is that all appearance and existence
Is known as your own mind; and this mind itself
Is realized, spacelike, in its intelligence and clarity.

Though the example of space refers to reality,
It is just a symbol that rather partially does so;
Mind itself is universally clear, void, and intelligent.
And space is unintelligent void, free of solid objects.
Thus space cannot fully illustrate the import of mind—
Do not vacillate, but focus on mind's actual reality.

All this superficial appearance
Is exclusively truth-status-free, like fear.
For example, all appearance and existence, life and liberation,
Is beheld uniquely as your natural mind.
Then, just by transforming the process of your mind,
You can perceive your transformation of the outer world.
Therefore everything is the perception of the mind,
The six migrations each have their specific perceptions,
The outsider fundamentalists have their absolutisms and nihilisms.
The nine vehicles each have their individual views.
Seeing variety, distinguishing variety,
They err by holding dichotomies and clinging to distinctions.
All appearances understood as mind,
Seeing all without any grasping, one awakens.

One does not err by perceiving, one errs by clinging;
But knowing clinging itself as mind, it frees itself.
All you perceive is the perception of mind,
Apparent inanimate objects of environment are mind.
Apparent animate six kinds of beings are mind.
Apparent happiness of higher humans and gods are mind.
Apparent horrid-state sufferings are mind.
Apparent misknowing five addictive poisons are mind.
Apparent original wisdom intelligence is mind.
Apparent realization of goodness and liberation are mind.

Apparent obstructions of devils and ghosts are mind.
Apparent good of deities and accomplishments are mind.
Apparent various purities are mind.
Apparent nonconceptual, one-pointed focus is mind.
Apparent things' signs and colors are mind.
Apparent signless nonelaboration is mind,
Apparent nonduality of one and many is mind
Apparent lack of being- and nothing-status is mind.

Nothing is apparent outside of the mind.
Mind-reality ceaselessly dawns as all appearance.
Dawning, nondual like water and waves of oceans,
It is liberated in the experiential reality of mind.
Though names are ceaselessly designated to referents,
Objectively nothing exists outside the unity of mind.
That unity is groundless and rootlessly free.
It cannot be seen in one vision in any direction;
It is not seen as something, as it is free of any status,
It is not seen as void, for it shines as intelligent clarity,
And it is not seen separately, void and clarity being nondual.

Now your own awareness is clear and distinct;
Though it acts so, an agent is not known.
Though free of intrinsic reality, experiences are perceived.
If you practice this, you will be fully liberated.
You will realize regardless of the sharpness of your faculties.
Though both sesame and milk produce oil or butter,
They will not without pressing or churning.
Though all beings are the actual essence of Buddhahood,
They won't awaken without practice.
With practice, even a cowherd will awaken;
Though he can't explain, he can directly determine.
Tasting the sugar in your mouth,
You don't need others to explain it.
If they don't understand this reality, even pandits will err.
Though they're expert in explaining the nine vehicles,
It's like giving directions from hearsay to where they've never been—
They haven't been even close to Buddhahood for an instant.

If you realize this reality, you're naturally free from virtue and vice.
If you don't, all your virtues and vices bring lives in heavens or hell
Just realizing your mind as void intuitive wisdom,

Virtue and vice cannot enforce their effects.
Just as a fountain cannot spring forth from empty sky,
So virtue and vice are de-objectified in voidness.

Therefore, to see intuitively your own naked intelligence,
This *Natural Liberation Through Naked Vision* is extremely deep.
So investigate this reality of your own intelligence.

Profound! Sealed!

EMA! O Wonder, *Identifying Intelligence,*
*The Natural Liberation Through Naked Vision,*
Is for the benefit of later generations of beings in the decadent era,
As I composed all my Tantras, Scriptures, and Instructions,
However few and brief, with them in mind.
Though I teach them now, I conceal them as treasures—
May those with good evolution come to discover them!


SAMAYA GYA GYA GYA

This treatise clearly identifying intelligence, called *The Natural Liberation Through Naked Vision,* composed by the Abbot from Udyana, Padma Sambhava, may it never be lost until the end of the life cycle!

# GLOSSARY

**adamantine.** The Sanskrit *vajra* means "thunderbolt," "diamond," "adamantine," and so forth, various objects connoting immutability and unbreakability. In Vedic India it was the weapon of the tribal father-god, Indra, a kind of thunderbolt grenade that he threw down from the heavens to break the citadels of the enemy. The Buddhists took this primal symbol of the supreme power of the universe and made it a symbol of universal love and compassion, in order to affirm their vision that love is the strong force in the universe. Thus vajra is used in names of Buddha-deities to indicate that they are in touch through wisdom with the realm of ultimate reality and that they express the natural universal compassion.

**adept, great.** "Adept" is used to translate the Sanskrit *siddha*, referring to a practitioner of Tantra who has attained Buddhahood in his or her ordinary body, having gone beyond life, death, and the between, yet remaining in association with his or her previous gross body in order to relate liberatively with contemporary beings.

**aggregates.** From the Sanskrit *skandha*, literally meaning "heap." There are five of these aggregates, constituting the normal sentient being's body-mind complex: those of form, sensation, conception, volition, and consciousness. They are called "aggregates" to indicate their lack of fixed structure, that they are rather loosely coherent masses of items in their respective categories, which themselves are merely heuristic. Thus the scheme of the aggregates is used contemplatively to allow the self-investigator to discover his reality of freedom from rigid self.

**AH.** A mantra, or mantric seed-syllable, which symbolizes the speech of all Buddhas, called the "speech-vajra of all Buddhas." It is associated with the Beatific Body, the color ruby, and the throat complex of the Tantric practitioner.

**Akshobhya.** One of the five Archetypal Mild Buddhas, Lord of the Vajra Buddha-clan, associated with the eastern direction and the Buddha-land Abhirati. In the *Natural Liberation,* he represents the mirror wisdom, the transmutation of the poison of delusion, the color blue, and the aggregate of form. His Buddha-consort is Buddhalochana, his male bodhisattva attendants are Kshitigarbha and Maitreya, his female bodhisattvas are Lasya and Pushpa. In the *Natural Liberation,* he is sometimes referred to as Vajrasattva, perhaps due to the fact that he is the Buddha of the Vajra clan.

**all-accomplishing wisdom.** This is one of the five wisdoms. Resulting from the transmutation of envy, it is associated with the emerald and the color green, and with the Archetype Buddha Amoghasiddhi. It is called "all-accomplishing" or "wonder-working" because it is the wisdom that can coordinate the efforts of many beings; its opposite, envy, is what keeps beings in a state of conflict. The idea is that, once beings' energies work together instead of against each other, there is nothing they cannot accomplish, including miracles.

**All-around Goodness.** In the *Natural Liberation* and in the teachings of the Nyingma Order in general, the Buddha Samantabhadra, in male and female forms, is a kind of Ur-Buddha or primal Buddha, a Buddha-form very close to the absolute reality of the universe. His/her name means "All-around Goodness" to indicate that the deepest reality of everything is freedom itself, that which allows the happiness of beings and therefore that which they consider utter goodness. Samantabhadra is a famous Bodhisattva in the Universal Vehicle literature, who is already associated with omnipresence, having the special tendency to manifest himself simultaneously and infinitely in all subatomic particles of all universes while maintaining his presence in his ground dimension.

**Amitabha.** One of the five Archetypal Mild Buddhas, Lord of the Lotus Buddha-clan, associated with the western direction and the Buddha-land Sukhavati. In the *Natural Liberation,* he represents the individuating wisdom, the transmutation of the poison of lust, the color red, and the aggregate of conception. His Buddha-consort is Pandaravasini.

Amitabha is especially famous in Asia because of the *Pure Land Sutra* (the *Sukhavativyuha*), in which a method is taught for the ordinary person to rely on the compassion of Amitabha in order to attain rebirth in his Buddha-land. This formed the basis of the Pure Land School of popular Buddhism that attracted numerous adherents throughout the Universalist Buddhist world.

**Amoghasiddhi.** One of the five Archetypal Mild Buddhas, Lord of the Karma Buddha-clan, associated with the northern direction and the Buddha-land Prakuta, also called Karmasampat, "Evolutionary Success." In the *Natural Liberation,* he represents the all-accomplishing wisdom, the transmutation of the poison of envy, the color green, and the aggregate of volition. His Buddha consort is Tara, sometimes called Samayatara.

**angel.** I use "angel" to translate the Sanskrit *dakini,* a fierce and also erotic female deity that appears to practitioners of the Tantra to teach, inspire, assist, and admonish. The Vajradakini, "Diamond Angel," is a female form of perfect Buddhahood, the female equivalent of a Heruka, a male, Herculean, Buddha-deity manifestation.

**Archetype Buddha, or Deity.** This translates the Tibetan *yi dam* (Skt. *ishthadevata*), a deity-form of enlightenment chosen by a Tantric practitioner as a model of her ideal goal of embodied enlightenment. The archetype Buddha or archetype deity can be approached as an independent being in some ritual, contemplative, and narrative contexts, while it can also be adopted as a contemplative role-model, in practices in which the yogini or yogi identifies with the deity and seeks to become the deity itself. Thus the deity's form becomes an ideal or archetypal structure of the enlightenment desired by the practitioner.

**Avalokiteshvara.** The "Lord who does not look away from suffering," Avalokiteshvara is a celestial Bodhisattva (a dedicated seeker of enlightenment) who is the archetype of universal compassion throughout the Buddhist world. Actually, he already became a Buddha millions of eons ago, but vowed that he would emanate as millions of Bodhisattvas *after* attaining the perfect enlightenment of Buddhahood, in order to stay close to suffering beings and to help them find their freedom and happiness. In his celestial forms, he is associated with the Buddha Amitabha being a member of the Lotus Buddha clan. In his male forms he associated with benevolent kingship throughout Buddhist Asia (His Holiness the Dalai Lama is believed to be an emanation of Avalokiteshv as well as with the fierce deity forms who protect beings from evil, such as the horse-head-crowned Hayagriva (Padma Sambhava himself is believed to be a terrific emanation of Avalokiteshvara). In his female forms he is associated with nurturing mother-figures such as White Tara and Kuanyin, and with fierce savioress-figures such as Green Tara, Shri Devi, and others. In the *Natural Liberation,* Avalokiteshvara is often invoked as the "Lord of Compassion."

**awareness.** Synonym of consciousness, intelligence, and mind. Buddhist languages have a rich vocabulary for aspects of mind and subtle mental states, due to the Buddhist sense of the power and importance of mind in the universe. On the subtlest levels, awareness in the form of wisdom can be associated with colors, forms, and even energies and substances, such as the subtle neurotransmitter red and white drops in the subtle body. More usually, awareness is differentiated from the material realm, and a complex mind-matter dualism is sustained as a way of keeping mindful of the elusive nature of reality, ever resisting the naive reductionism of dogmatic theorists.

**Beatific.** The adjective from "beatitude," used to translate the Sanskrit *sambhoga,* the term for the Bliss Body of Buddhahood. The evolutionary perfection of Buddhahood is said to be experienced in the form of Three Bodies, of which this Body represents the ultimate, subtle subjective enjoyment of being a Buddha as a being who has realized perfect union with the infinite freedom of ultimate reality (see **Body**).

**between, the.** "Between" is used in at least three senses: its basic colloquial sense of the whole period between death and rebirth; its technical sense in the set of the six betweens, the life, dream, meditation, death-point, reality, and existence betweens; and in the sense of "phase of a between," where the experience of a particular period in one of the six betweens is itself called a between.

**between-being.** A being who has passed through death and whose mind, soul, or life-continuum has emerged from the gross body of the lost life, has embodied itself in a subtle energy, "mind-imaged" body, similar to the simulated embodiment of consciousness in a dream, and xperiences the processes in the between of wandering in search of either eration or an ordinary rebirth.

**bliss (bliss-void indivisible).** Sanskrit *sukha* means "happiness" as the opposite of *duhkha,* "suffering," in a range from modest relief and comfort up to physical orgasmic bliss and supreme spiritual bliss. In the tantric context, the Universalist emphasis on compassion—the will to relieve the suffering of others—transmutes into the implementation of love, the will to provide happiness to others, and so the conscious cultivation of bliss becomes a technical concern. To transmit happiness to others, one must develop one's own happiness to overflowing. Thus, the highest tantric expression of the nonduality of relative and absolute realities is the term "bliss-void indivisible," where bliss is the relative, wisdom-generated forms of the Buddhaverse and void is the ultimate freedom reality that makes such creativity possible.

**bodhisattva.** The Sanskrit *bodhisattva* is composed of *bodhi,* meaning "enlightenment" (wisdom of selflessness, selfless compassion), and *sattva,* meaning "being" or "hero/heroine." Most simply, it means someone who has dedicated himself or herself to do whatever it takes over countless lifetimes in order to attain perfect enlightenment in order to save all beings from suffering. A being becomes a bodhisattva by conceiving the spirit of enlightenment, through 1) imagining the possibility of enlightened consciousness, 2) seeing how it alone gives the ability effectively to help others find their happiness, 3) seeing how dedicating all one's lives of efforts toward that goal is the only sensible way to live, and 4) resolving to undertake that universal responsibility oneself. This transformation from ordinary being to "enlightenment hero/heroine" is formally sealed by the solemn taking of the vow of the bodhisattva. Thus a beginner bodhisattva need not be very advanced in enlightenment, merely firmly dedicated to universal love and compassion. In the modern context, it is important to mention that the messianic bodhisattva vow only makes sense for those who feel convinced that they are going to be around in the life-process for an infinite future in any case, so they might as well undertake the saving of all beings. Such a messianic complex would be insane for those who consider their existence to last only one lifetime; there would never be time for such a universal saving of beings, and so such pressure would be pointless.

**Bodhisattva.** When capitalized, it refers to those bodhisattvas who have long cultivated their spirit of enlightenment and have become nearly Buddhas, or else have already become Buddhas and are still manifesting as Bodhisattvas in order to let beings feel more close to them.

**body isolation.** This refers to the first of the five perfection stages, a stage wherein the body becomes isolated from ordinariness of experience, and concretely reenvisioned as a wisdom-perfected body expressing the compassion of all Buddhas.

**body, speech, and mind.** This triad is very basic in Buddhist thought, being the three levels of evolutionary existence. Buddhist ethics divides its ten basic laws into three of the body, not to kill, steal, or commit sexual misconduct; four of speech, not to lie, slander, chatter, or revile; and three of mind, not to covet, hate, or hold misguided views. A person must therefore be responsible for herself on all three levels. At Buddhahood, the triad becomes the Three Buddha Bodies, ordinary body becoming the Emanation Body, speech the Beatific Body, and mind the Truth Body.

**Body (the Three Buddha Bodies).** A Buddha is no longer an ordinary being, a self-habit-ridden individual caught inside his skin. So Buddhists developed a number of ways of expressing the extraordinary qualities of the experience of enlightenment. The Three Bodies is one of the most important of these. At enlightenment the ordinary mind expands in an experience of oneness with the infinity of beings and things, which becomes a permanent awareness, called the Body of Truth, or Body of Reality. This is the highest fruit of wisdom, a state of virtual omniscience, Nirvana—a perfect, ultimate freedom, and the uttermost fulfillment of all selfish concerns. At the same time, the ordinary speech and body do not lose their continua of life. Body and speech are anyway seen by Buddhists as being interactive, the body reaching out from self-centeredness to touch other persons and things, and speech communicating the content of mind to others, linking mind to mind. Therefore the continuum of speech expands as a celebration of the mind's attainment of infinite oneness, becoming a consummate and infinite joy experienced as a Body of Beatitude, which is a sort of subtle or ethereal body made of the sheer joy at being free of suffering, at having realized the absolute nature of reality. It is as infinite as reality, a subtle radiant omnipresence of a Buddha's joy throughout all things. Finally, the continuum of ordinary body expands with enlightenment into an Emanation Body, a limitless number of individuated manifestations which arise out of the background energy of the Beatific Body, when a Buddha wishes to interact with ordinary beings, who cannot perceive their oneness with the Beatific presence in and around them, who persist in the misknowing individual theater of suffering and alienation. For them, infinite mind and speech magically create whatever gross embodiments are appropriate to relate to them, to liberate them from their suffering, and ultimately to inspire them to discover their own enlightenment and their own beatitude. These Three Buddha Bodies are aligned with the ordinary processes of death, between, and life, with sleep, dream, and waking, as well as with mind, speech, and body. (See p. 33 and following pages.)

**body-mind complex.** This is schematized in various ways in Buddhist contemplative sciences. The five aggregates mentioned above are one of the schemes. In the tantric context, the scheme of gross, subtle, and extremely subtle is important in the analysis of the death, between, and rebirth processes. The gross is the ordinary body-mind, the elemental body as nexus of the five sense organs coordinated with the six sense consciousnesses. The subtle is the "diamond body" of neural channels, winds, and drops coordinated with the three subtle intuitions, luminance, radiance, and imminence. And the extremely subtle is the indestructible drop made of the subtlest wind-energies coordinated with the clear light transparency intuition, the subtlest mind and the seed of enlightenment. (See p. 35.)

**Buddha.** An Awakened or Enlightened Being, defined as one who has reached the peak of evolution, by developing his or her wisdom and compassion over countless lifetimes until both have become perfect. Wisdom is perfect when all things are understood by it, and compassion is perfect when all beings are liberated by it; a Buddha is thus said to have completely fulfilled both his or her own self-interest as well as all altruistic concern for the needs of others. A Buddha is said to possess Three Bodies, the Bodies of Truth, Beatitude, and Emanation (see **Body**). Shakyamuni, who lived in India about 2500 years ago, is the historical Buddha of our era on this planet. He is sometimes called "the Buddha," or "Buddha," but it is not his personal name. In the absolute sense, there is only one Buddha, as the Truth Bodies of different Buddhas cannot be distinguished from each other. But in the relative sense, there are countless Buddhas, as each being who perfects evolution enjoys his or her own Beatitude and extends his or her Emanations for the sake of other beings. A Buddha can manifest as either male or female, or as both male and female in union.

**Buddha-clan.** See **clan**.

**Buddha-couple.** See **couple**.

**Buddha-deity.** See **Archetype Buddha.**

**Buddha-land.** Sanskrit *buddhakshetra* refers to the environment of a Buddha, indicating that the evolutionary transmutation of the finite individual into an infinite body of awareness takes the environment with it, so to speak. As beings are relational nexi of relative self and environment, the enlightened transformation of one implies the transformation of the other. Usually, in popular Buddhism, this is most recognizably expressed in the descriptions of the heavenly Buddha-lands of the archetype Buddhas, such as Amitabha of the western Buddha-land, Sukhavati; these environments are as otherworldly and unearthly as they are radiant and exquisite. My personal popular term for Buddha-land is "Buddhaverse," which I oppose to "universe," the latter being a world turning around the single, self-centered individual, and the former being a world turning around enlightened wisdom where self and other are ultimately indistinguishable.

**Buddhaverse.** See **Buddha-land.**

**channels.** Sanskrit *nadi* (Tib. *rtsa*) refers to pathways of neural energies within the subtle nervous system of the Tantric yogi or yogini. These are considered physical, and are clearly somewhat analogous to the central nervous system of modern physiology, including the brain, spine, and various nerve ganglia. However, just as clearly they constitute the structure of the subtle body, and they are closed, and so in a sense not present, in ordinary beings who have not opened them by means of a systematic contemplative experimental program of visualization and exercise. I prefer to think of them as a holographic patterning that can be imposed upon the central nervous system by the stabilized and cultivated imagination, something like a software channeling of electrical impulses in certain magnetic patterns around a hard disc of a computer. The channels worked with by yogis of the *Natural Liberation* consist of the main central (mid-brow to crown, down the spine to the coccyx, and to the genital tip) channel, the *avadhuti,* with its right and left *rasana* and *lalana* channels, passing through the center of the five wheels or lotuses at brain, throat, heart, navel, and genital levels, each wheel having its own specific structure.

**Chemchok, Chemchok Heruka.** This is the central archetype Buddha-ty of the *Secret Essence (Guhyagarbha) Tantra,* highly popular in the gma Order of Tibetan Buddhism, and of salient importance in the *al Liberation,* figuring as the main Lord among the fierce deities, as Samantabhadra does among the mild deities. As a "Heruka," he is a Herculean, "blood-drinking" male deity, symbolizing the adamantine power of enlightenment to overwhelm all evil and negativity of the world. The critical fire of wisdom transmutes the "blood"—the essential constitutive energy of the suffering-permeated life cycle—into the elixir-fuel of the dynamism of liberation, the power of compassion. He has many forms, ranging from one with one face and two arms and two legs up to a thousand-headed and thousand-armed figure.

**chopper.** This is the *kartari,* the vajra-scepter-handled curved knife held in the right hand of many of the fierce deities, especially the female ones, symbolizing critical, analytic, dissective wisdom, which cuts through and chops up all delusive appearances of intrinsic substantiality, reducing all things to voidness and hence to suitability for transformation into wisdom manifestations of liberating beauty.

**clan (the five Buddha-clans).** Sanskrit *kula* is often translated as "family," which has the modern connotation of nuclear family, of parents and children. "Clan" conveys the ancient extended family that includes cousins, uncles, aunts, and so forth, which is more appropriate for the Buddha *kula,* which include a larger number of members. In the *Natural Liberation,* the five clans are the Buddha, Vajra, Jewel, Lotus, and Evolution clans, respectively fathered by the five Buddhas: Vairochana, Akshobhya, Ratnasambhava, Amitabha, and Amoghasiddhi. They are mothered by the female Buddhas Vajra Dhatvishvari, Lochana, Mamaki, Pandaravasini, and Tara, and each includes a number of male and female Bodhisattvas, fierce deities, and adept heroes and heroines.

**clear light (transparency).** Sanskrit *prabhasvara* indicates the subtlest light that illuminates the profoundest reality of the universe. It is a light like glass, like diamond, like the predawn twilight, different from the lights of sun, moon, and Rahu, the planet of the darkness. It is an inconceivable light, beyond the duality of bright and dark, a light of the self-luminosity of all things. Hence "transparency" is a good rendering, as is "clear light," as long as "clear" is understood as "transparent" and not as "bright."

**Clear Science Collection.** One of the three collections of the texts of the Tibetan Buddhist sciences, the collection of the analytic and systematic teachings of the higher education in wisdom.

**compassion.** Sanskrit *karuna* means the will to free others from suffering, based on an empathetic sensitivity to that suffering. Its opposite is hatred, which wills others to suffer. Its counterpart is love, which wills others to have happiness along with freedom from suffering. Universal compassion is considered the automatic reflex of perfect wisdom, since the realization of essential selflessness is an experience of the ultimate unity of self and other, which causes the suffering of others to become one's own, making the will to eliminate it spontaneous and immediate.

**consort.** This refers to the partner, either male or female, but more usually female, in a Buddha-couple, such as Vajra Dhatvishvari, Vairochana's consort. Sometimes the Father and Mother in a Buddha Father-Mother couple are considered different divine beings, sometimes only the double manifestation of a single being. The Buddhist belief is that all beings, whatever their superficial sexual identity, are potentially both male and female—each has male and female aspects and energies in his or her being. The empathetic ability to transcend sexual identity-habits is cultivated by Tantric archetype meditation, wherein a male will meditate on himself as a female archetype Buddha, a female will meditate on herself as a male archetype Buddha, and both will meditate on themselves as a male and female Buddha-couple in union. See **couple.**

**continuum, life-continuum.** Sanskrit *samtana* refers to the energy-continuity of a living being that proceeds from moment to moment in a life and from life to life in an individual's evolutionary progression. It is an important concept because the Buddhist critique of fixed self makes language of "soul" and "essence" relatively rare—though not totally absent—in most contexts.

**couple, Buddha-couple.** Tibetan *sangs rgyas yab yum,* literally "Buddha Father-Mother," refers to a single enlightened individual as two beings, male and female in union. This is not as puzzling as it might seem, if we remember that the enlightenment transmutation is a passage from being a bounded, singular, self-centered individual, usually with one sexual identity or another in a given life, into being an infinite, multi-bodied, omnipresent, universalized individual capable of manifesting whatever embodiment interacts most beneficially with whomsoever. The manifestation as a pair in sexual union intends to demonstrate the union of wisdom (Mother) and compassion (Father), showing the capacity to adopt all beings, helping them out of the life cycle of suffering and giving them a new life of happiness in the Buddhaverse.

**creation stage.** The first stage of the practice of the Unexcelled Yoga Tantras, the stage involving the visualizational creation out of emptiness of the pure realm of enlightenment, the mandala palace and its environment and ornament, and the pure embodiment of enlightenment, the Archetype Deity with its blissful body, speech, and mind.

**Dakini.** See **angel.**

**darkness, dark-light.** The subjective experiential sign of attaining the deepest level of the subtle mind, the level of "imminence," where one is in a state of being about to enter the clear light of the ultimate. It is likened to a cloudless darkened sky, thus a bright blackness, not a mere absence of light. In the first part of this state one is consciously endarkened, and in the final moment of it one loses consciousness as well, passing immediately into the transparent state beyond consciousness and unconsciousness, as it is sometimes described.

**death.** This is the point of freedom when the subtle mind, indestructible clear light drop, or soul of a particular life loses connection with the embodiment of that life. It is perhaps beyond consciousness and unconsciousness, though ordinary people transit it unconsciously, never noticing the all-too-rapid (for them) transition from the unconscious segment of imminence into clear light and back into imminence. Death is understood as a pure negation, a perfect zero, a timeless moment, a widthless boundary, and it is aligned with absolute reality, with the Body of Truth, with the ultimate clear light. A Buddha, an enlightened being, is thus one whose death is her infinite body of ultimate reality, her concrete permanent resting place, which nevertheless not only never obstructs her relative experience of the interconnected realm of beings, but makes it indivisible from freedom and openness and therefore perfectly blissful. Needless to say, such a being is no longer afraid of death.

**death-point between.** The same as **death** (see above) in the technical terminology of the *Natural Liberation,* referring to the scheme of the six betweens (see **between**). The death-point between is the boundary between the life between and the reality between. The death-point between is the inconceivable moment when all beings are as close as possible to their own highest enlightenment. It is the point of ultimate freedom, where the reality of freedom becomes most manifest. So if a being is prepared, ready, and focused, it is the moment when the bond of evolutionary karma can be broken and liberation and enlightenm can be attained. Therefore, it marks the very center of the *Natural Liberation.*

**deity.** Sanskrit *devata* is an Indo-European cognate with Latin *deus,* so the translation choice is rather obvious. Buddhism was mistaken by early European scholars as "atheistic," projecting back into Buddhist Asia a kind of nineteenth-century secularistic naturalism. In fact, Buddhists do not accept the idea of an omnipotent, world Creator, but many believe in a pantheon of deities in an elaborate range of heavens—a total of around twenty-seven layers of heavens in the desire, pure form, and formless realms. These heavens contain untold billions of deities, ranging from what we might think of as jewel-bodied angels, seraphs, and cherubs, to vast energy-field deities as big and as long-lived as universes, to subtle, virtually disembodied, formless realm deities. In the context of Universalist and Tantric teachings and practices, the enlightened Buddhas and Bodhisattvas can be envisioned and encountered in such deity forms, usually the more angelic, jewel forms of the desire realm deities. They aim to open the imaginations of suffering beings to the expanded power of enlightened beings, either to reach out to us, or to provide us with role-models for reaching out to others as we become enlightened. So the deities in the *Natural Liberation* are called Buddhas or Archetype Deities in such a context.

**Dharma.** One of the Three Jewels, the Jewel of the Buddha's teaching. It can also mean the ultimate reality itself that is taught in the teachings, the path that leads to its realization, the qualities that derive from it, and so forth. In Indian usage prior to the Buddha's time, it tended to mean "religion," "law," "duty," and "custom," patterns that hold human behavior and thought under control. These "pattern-maintaining" meanings still coexist in Sanskrit and other Buddhist languages with the Buddha's more liberating or "pattern-transcending" meanings, causing considerable confusion for translators in some contexts.

**Dhatvishvari.** Literally meaning "Queen Goddess of the Realm (of Truth)," this title suits the female Buddha who is either the female form of the Buddha Vairochana or his Buddha-consort.

**dream between.** Another of the six betweens (see **between**), within the subdivision of the life between into deep sleep, dream, and waking betweens. Of these three, only the dream between is singled out as one he six betweens, because of its important similarities to the reality existence betweens. In certain practices, falling asleep is used as a rehearsal of the death-dissolution process; arising in the subtle body-mind of the dream is used as a rehearsal of the between-experience; and awakening is used as a rehearsal of a voluntary rebirth process. The coarse body of the five senses is absent in the dream between, and the mind fabricates a subtle body for itself out of its own imagery; it sees with simulated eye-senses, it hears with simulated ear-senses, and, more rarely, it smells, tastes, and touches with simulated nose-sense, tongue-sense, and skin. This is considered similar to the way the between-being fabricates a between-state, mind-made body out of its own image-bank.

**drops.** Sanskrit *bindu* refers to chemical essences (something like the modern neurotransmitters) that focus awareness within the subtle nervous system. In the subtle body, the channels form the structure, the winds serve as the energies that move things and cause transformations of experience, and the drops serve as the nodes of subjectivity that focus awareness within the realm that opens up when consciousness has been withdrawn from its functions in receiving and coordinating sense-data from the gross senses. These drops are also associated with the genetic material that is the essence of the male and female sexual fluids. The yogic mastery of their subtle potentials represents the sublimation of the creative energies that ordinarily form the suffering life cycle into the reconstruction of the divine realm of the enlightened mandala. Thus, red drops refer to the female genetic essence, carried within the blood, and the white drops refer to the male genetic essence, carried within the semen. This is a difficult and abstruse subject, but this note can orient you to what is meant by this expression.

**education, higher.** Sanskrit *adhishiksha* refers to the three avenues of the experiential Dharma, the ethical, meditational, and intellectual, the higher educations in justice, mental concentration, and wisdom, that correspond to the Three Collections of the Vinaya, Sutra, and Abhidharma texts. This word is often translated as "training," which is in the same area, but which implies a military or animal-training type of discipline, where behavioral conditioning is the operating principle. The Buddhist task is to bring out the deep moral sensitivity, the most powerful mental intensity, and the most acute, comprehensive, and transformative intellectual insight. For these high goals, education, as the bringing forth of inner potential, seems more appropriate than training, the imposition of preconceived patterns of conformity.

**Emanation Body.** See **Body.**

**energy.** This term—sometimes "neural energy"—is used for the subtle inner winds that fuel the subtle body's activity, moving the drops around the channels. They also create the extremely subtle body of the indestructible drop that is the ground of the clear-light enlightened awareness of the subtlest soul. There are five main energies and five branch energies. The five main energies are the life, evacuative, articulative, digestive, and pervasive energies, each associated with a particular channel-wheel, with a particular archetype Buddha, a particular wisdom, and so forth. The branch energies are associated with the Buddha-consorts, and with the five elements and so forth. These energies are also important in Buddhist medicine, underlying the technology of acupuncture and the understanding of most mental as well as many physical disorders.

**equalizing wisdom.** One of the five wisdoms, this one is associated with the Buddha Ratnasambhava, the color yellow, the transmutation of pride and miserliness, and the apotheosis of the sensation aggregate.

**esoteric.** The Buddha often critiqued teachers for holding back their best teachings, out of stinginess or lack of compassion for their disciples. However, Buddhism does consider some teachings better kept secret, or esoteric, until students are advanced enough to understand them properly. Such was (and still is, in some respects) the tradition surrounding the Tantras. On the surface, the erotic and terrific imagery of those texts and arts that are needed for the exploration of the unconscious constitute one good reason for a modicum of secrecy, as such imagery leads to all sorts of misunderstanding. But more importantly, secrecy is required to keep ambitious practitioners from getting ahead of their appropriate stage and hurting themselves by a premature attempt to plumb the depths of the psyche. Before exploring passions and transmuting them into the path, one must have achieved a secure capacity for detachment and restraint. Before encountering the ferocious and terrific forces of the psyche, one must have cultivated a determined commitment to universal love and compassion that can withstand confrontation with the demonic. And most importantly, before cultivating Buddha pride and divine confidence in rehearsing the sense of enlightened identity, one must have a rigorous insight into identitylessness, to avoid becoming stuck in a delusive enlightenment megalomania. Thus, while the *Natural Liberation* consciously opens up the treasury of depth psychology of the Tantric tradition for the sake of ordinary people to help them face their deepest crises, some aspects of the path are still kept esoteric.

*Esoteric Communion.* The *Guhyasamaja* Tantric tradition, in which the subtleties and intricacies of Unexcelled Yoga are particularly well explained and systematically arranged for study and practice, from which many of the ideas in the introduction are drawn.

evolution, evolutionary. Sanskrit *karma* and *karmika,* which I translate in this way because I consider "action" too general, and hence vague. Karma specifically means mental, verbal, and physical actions that lead to life-affecting and life-constituting consequences. The modern materialistic worldview considers the structures of our present lifetimes to have been caused by the genetic reembodiment of the subtly encoded experiences of millions of previous representatives of our species, through the processes of biological evolution. The Buddhist worldview considers the structures of our present lifetimes to be caused by the spiritually genetic reembodiment of our own experiences from millions of previous lifetimes, subtly encoded in a spiritual gene we bring with us, combined with the physical genes we receive from our parents, in a complex process of spiritual and biological evolution.

existence between. Sometimes called the "procreation between," this is one of the six betweens, located in the cycle between the reality between and the life between. It is fully described in the *Natural Liberation* itself, in the chapter of the translation by that name.

exoteric. The opposite of esoteric, the kind of teaching and practice that is safe to make fully public.

extremely subtle body-mind. This nondual combination of the indestructible drop composed of the subtlest wind-energies and the clear-light enlightened awareness is the Buddhist soul, that entity or continuum that can be said to progress from life to life, and to mutate out of the suffering life cycle into enlightenment. See body-mind complex.

Father-Mother, Buddha Father and Mother. See couple.

fierce deity. These are of several kinds: 1) the terrific Buddha forms that manifest wisdom and compassion in ways needed to overwhelm the habitual fierceness of egotistical drives and egotistically driven beings; 2) the terrific Bodhisattva forms that serve as protectors of spiritual persons, defending them against those who would consume or obstruct them; 3) the wrathful, bloodthirsty worldly deities and spirits who have given themselves over to anger and hatred, and have thereby become demonic and harmful. The fierce deities of the *Natural Liberation* are mostly of the first type, though a few Bodhisattva protectors are mentioned, such as Mahakala. As fierce as these deities can appear, they have no hatred in them whatsoever, not even righteous hatred against evildoers. Their fierceness is "tough love," tough compassion, like the fierceness of a mother who scolds her child not to stick its finger in the electric socket. Thus the previous translation "wrathful deities" was misleading by suggesting they were to some degree filled with wrath. "Fierce" refers to their manifestation, not a judgment about their accompanying mental state.

**five aggregates.** See **aggregates.**

**five Buddhas.** Archetype Deities representing the five wisdoms: Vairochana, the ultimate reality wisdom; Akshobhya, the mirror wisdom; Ratnasambhava, the equalizing wisdom; Amitabha, the individuating wisdom; and Amoghasiddhi, the all-accomplishing wisdom. They also represent the transmutation of the five aggregates, consciousness, form, sensation, conceptions, and volitions, respectively, and the transmutation of the five poisons, delusion, hate, pride, lust, and envy, respectively. See **clan** and individual Buddhas' names.

**five poisons.** Delusion, hate, pride, lust, and envy.

**five wisdoms.** The five poisons mentioned above are transmuted into ultimate reality, mirror, equalizing, individuating, and all-accomplishing wisdoms.

**Form Body.** The altruistic aspect of enlightenment, developed from the individual's continua of body and speech, subdivided into the Beatific and Emanation Bodies. See **Body.**

**Four Noble Truths.** The basic formula the Buddha used to teach his breakthrough insight into the nature of suffering and the way to freedom from it. The truths are called "noble," since they are true for a noble person (defined not in class terms but as one who has become gentle by realizing selflessness and overcoming egotism), and not for an alienated, egocentric, deluded individual. The truths are 1) that all delusion-driven life is suffering; 2) the causes of that suffering are mis-knowledge and evolution; 3) there is freedom from such suffering; 4) the path to that freedom consists of a spiritual education in morality, meditation, and scientific wisdom. The first of these truths has attracted the most notice, but the third is the most important, being the Buddha's key achievement and his "good news." Quite a few people noticed that life is suffering; very few first achieved, and then taught to others, a practical and effective way to freedom from suffering.

**Geluk Order.** This is the most recent of Tibet's major monastic orders, founded around 1400 by the Lama Tsong Khapa (1357–1419), based on the older Kadam Order founded by Atisha (982–1054). Famed for its widespread expansion of monasticism in Tibet, its scholarship, and its numerous great incarnations, it produced the Dalai Lamas and Tibet's unique monastic government.

**gene, spiritual.** Sanskrit *gotra* means the seed of one's propensities, structures, affinities, and fortune developed from the evolutionary action of previous lives. It is a gene that constitutes the mind and attitudes of a being, just as the genes of father and mother structure that being's body.

**great adept.** See adept, great.

**Great Perfection.** Tibetan *rdzogs chen* means the teaching and practice of the supreme form of Unexcelled Yoga Tantra, called Atiyoga, in the Nyingma Order of Tibetan Buddhism. It is expressed very clearly in the *Natural Liberation Through Naked Vision* (chapter 8), and is foundational to all the between teachings of the *Natural Liberation,* which can be effective only if it is indeed true that the natural reality of everything is itself liberation, freedom, bliss, and enlightenment. The Great Perfection stresses a sudden method of forceful entry into the awareness of this reality, the kind of radical shift of habitual awareness required of a being during the death-point between, when they must turn back their habitual progressive orientation to the next experience and confront from the subtlest subjectivity the immediacy of freedom. The Great Perfection is said to be the step beyond the perfection stage of Unexcelled Yoga Tantra, according to the way the Nyingma scholars define the perfection stage. The way Tsong Khapa defines the perfection stage, the Great Perfection corresponds with its fourth and fifth stages, enlightenment and integration, which correspond to the fourth initiation, the Great Word Initiation (which is just like Great Perfection teaching in its radical affirmation of the immediacy of complete enlightenment).

**Great Seal.** Sanskrit *mahamudra* indicates the same radical and direct approach to ultimate realization as the Great Perfection teaching (see above). It is a terminology based on the notion of reality as a seal of experience, ultimate reality being the supreme seal of wisdom's insight, favored in the Kagyu Order of Tibetan Buddhism.

**gross body-mind.** See **body-mind complex.**

*Guhyasamaja Tantra.* See *Esoteric Communion.*

**guru.** The Sanskrit word for teacher, it literally means "heavy," and connotes the sense of authority possessed by the teacher in the conservative brahminical culture. The Tibetans translated it as *lama,* meaning "unexcelled," allowing the figure to have great authority, but diminishing the sense of hierarchical superiority.

**Hayagriva.** The fierce deity form of Avalokiteshvara, very closely associated with Padma Sambhava himself, the author of the *Natural Liberation.*

**Hero (Scientist), Heroine.** Heroes and heroines (Skt. *virayogini*) are male and female adepts who have attained perfect Buddhahood through the path of Unexcelled Yoga Tantra and manifest themselves as deities in order to assist practitioners.

**Heruka (Vajra Heruka).** A Heruka is a Herculean, "blood-drinking" male Buddha-deity, symbolizing the adamantine power of enlightenment to overwhelm all evil and negativity of the world. See **Chemchok.**

**Higher education.** The three higher educations are ethical, meditational, and intellectual, leading to the perfection of justice, samadhi, and wisdom; they constitute the practice of the eightfold path, which is the fourth Noble Truth.

**HUM.** This mantra syllable is known as the quintessential "mind-vajra" of all Buddhas, symbolizing the integration of the universal, absolute, and divine within the particular individual. Thus it often occurs at the end of mantras, signifying that the spiritual attainment, deity, or positive energy invoked has been integrated within the individual. It may correspond in some respects to the Christian *Amen* that concludes prayers.

**imminence.** This is the deepest state of the subtle mind, just next to the extremely subtle mind of clear light wisdom. It is divided into two halves, an initial moment when there is a consciousness of intense darkness, and a second moment of total unconsciousness. It is called "imminence" (Skt. *upalabdhi,* Tib. *nyer thob*) because it is the state where ultimate reality clear light is about to occur in consciousness. See **darkness.**

**implements.** The various deities hold implements in their hands, vajra-scepters, vajra bells, choppers, skull bowls, and so forth, which symbolize the special insights, states, and skills they wield for the benefit of beings.

**indestructible drop.** This is a name for the extremely subtle body, which at that extremely subtle level is actually indivisible from the mind of clear light wisdom. It is the embodiment of the Buddhist soul, the vehicle of the subtle continuum of mind that migrates through death to successive lives, and that evolves into the inconceivable, omnipresent, relative Beatific Body and ultimate Truth Body body-mind of all Buddhas. See **body-mind complex.**

**Individual Vehicle.** This is my translation for the term developed by Universal Vehicle (Skt. *Mahayana*) Buddhism for the foundation form of Buddhism, which I also call Individualist, or monastic Buddhism. The term was originally derogatory, referring to the narrow-minded refusal of early monastic Buddhists to accept the possibility of the Buddha also having taught a Universal, Messianic form of Buddhism. In recent eras of Universalist civilizations, it is a descriptive term and not derogatory, as the foundational aspect of monastic Buddhism is respectfully accepted. Thus, when it is used in Tibetan Buddhism nowadays, it means a vehicle suitable for transporting the individual to freedom and enlightenment.

**Individualist Buddhism.** See **Individual Vehicle.**

**individuating wisdom.** One of the five wisdoms, the transformation of conceptions and the transmutation of lust, associated with the Buddha Amitabha, the Lotus Buddha-clan, the color red, and the awareness of the distinctions between things, their particularity and individuality.

**indivisible.** This frequently used term indicates the nondual nature of reality, in terms of relative and ultimate perspectives. The basic indiv ibility is that of relative and absolute, but in Tantric terminology there is frequent reference to the indivisibilities of compassion and wisdom, bliss and void, clarity and void, and awareness and voidness.

**initiation.** Sanskrit *abhishekha* (Tib. *dbang bskur ba*) means literally "an anointment," as in the coronation of a king or queen, the ritual acknowledgment of a being's assumption of a special transformation, blessing, authority, and responsibility. In Unexcelled Yoga Tantra there are four main initiations, the vase, secret, wisdom intuition, and word initiations, which empower body, speech, mind, and the integration of all three to learn, practice, and realize all levels of the Tantric path.

**Inner (Mind) Science.** Sanskrit *adhyatmavidya* is the scientific tradition cultivated first within the Buddhist institutions of higher learning over the last millennia and then within all Indian spiritual institutions, based on the Buddha's original insight that the most powerful, subtle but controlling, aspect of nature is mind, accessed through the being's interior, not through the coarser level of material energies. For example, from the Inner Science perspective, the key, most creative and triggering, ingredient in a nuclear bomb is human hatred; thus hatred must be scientifically investigated, understood, and technologically controlled, if the world is to be made safe against nuclear holocaust.

**integration.** Sanskrit *yuganaddha* is the Unexcelled Yoga Tantra name for Buddhahood, the fifth and highest of the perfection stages, indicating that relative and ultimate, individual and universal, body and mind, bliss and wisdom, male and female—all dualities—are integrated in this experience of fulfillment.

**Ishvari goddesses.** Sanskrit *ishvari* means "goddess," in the sense of a powerful, superhuman female form in which enlightened beings manifest for the benefit of suffering beings, especially beings traversing the subtle realms of the between.

**isolation (body, speech, mind).** These are states on the perfection stage of Unexcelled Yoga Tantra. See **body isolation.**

**Jewels, Three.** The Buddha, Dharma, and Sangha: the teacher; the teaching, and the reality of freedom it teaches; and the community that realizes the teachings and reality. These are the three most precious ·ings for a Buddhist, in which he or she "takes refuge"—finds a haven from the extreme dangers of the suffering life cycle, and finds assurance of the positive evolutionary direction of his or her succession of lives.

**Kadam Order.** An important monastic order in Tibetan Buddhism, founded by Atisha (982–1054) and his main disciple, Dromtonpa, and based on the synthesis of the monastic, messianic, and apocalyptic Buddhisms of India. It is organized around the central messianic teaching of the spirit of enlightenment of love and compassion for all beings, with renunciative, wisdom, and esoteric teachings organized into a systematic path. Tsong Khapa later revived this order, and it became known as the Geluk Order after the early 1400s.

**Kagyu Order.** An important monastic order in Tibet, descended from Vajradhara Buddha through the great Indian adepts Tilopa and Naropa, to Marpa, Milarepa, and Gampopa, the Tibetan founders. Marpa, a layman, was the key translator who brought the esoteric Indian teachings into Tibetan practice. Milarepa was the key practitioner, who spent a lifetime integrating the teachings into his being; he is sometimes considered the first ordinary Tibetan (*i.e.,* not already a Buddha or Bodhisattva reincarnation) to become a perfect Buddha in a single lifetime. Gampopa was the main organizer, since he was a monastic, a scholar learned in the Kadam Order's curriculum; he synthesized the yogic and tantric teachings of Marpa and Milarepa with ethical and intellectual disciplines needed by an enduring institution. The Karmapa Lamas were important representatives of a branch of this order, benefiting Tibetan Buddhism a great deal, especially during the fifteenth and sixteenth centuries, and on into the present.

**Kalachakra Tantra.** The "Time Machine Tantra," this is one of the most important and elaborate of the Unexcelled Yoga Tantras, with a number of distinctive features. It is one of the favorites of the Dalai Lamas, and the Namgyal Monastery of the Potala Palace in Lhasa is the monastery most renowned for its expertise in the arts associated with this Tantra. Its vision of Buddhahood is of an evolutionary time machine, an omnipresent force of wisdom and compassion in close contact with planetary beings throughout all the intricacies of their history.

**karma.** See **evolution.**

**khatvanga staff.** A Buddha deity implement commonly held by adepts and angels, symbolizing their mastery of the subtle nervous system with its inner channels, winds, and drops, for the sake of manifesting enlightenment to practitioners in the subtle realms of dream, between, and samadhi.

**Krodhishvari.** The fierce female deities. See **fierce**.

**lama.** This means "spiritual teacher" in Tibetan, and represents a highly honored profession, since the lama is the indispensable doorway to the practice and performance of Tantra. I have translated it as "mentor" when it seems best to use an English equivalent.

**life.** This translates three Tibetan words, *tse,* which means "lifespan" or "life time"; *skye ba,* which literally means "birth"; and *'khor ba,* which means *samsara,* or "endless cycle of suffering." In the expression "life between," it is the meaning of the second of these Tibetan words that is conveyed by "life"; in the expression "life cycle," it is the third.

**life between.** See **life**.

**life cycle.** See **life**.

**Lotus clan.** See **clan**.

**luminance.** The most surface state of the subtle mind (Skt. *aloka*), it corresponds to the desire-oriented instinctual natures, and the inner sign of the moonlit autumn sky during death dissolutions and birth arisals. The other two states of the subtle mind, the sun-lit radiance and the dark-lit imminence, are also sometimes called "luminances," and sometimes "luminance wisdoms."

**magic body.** The subtle body generated by the mind and imagery that is created on the third of the perfection stages, the stage of self-consecration. It is the highest, esoteric, consciously created form of the kind of subtle body normally experienced by the dreamer in ordinary life, or by the between-being in the subtle between-states. It is therefore essential to the technology of accelerating the evolutionary progress normally achieved through heroic deeds during many death-, between-, and life-sequences.

**Mahakala.** A fierce deity who protects practitioners during their journey toward enlightenment. His myth is that he was once a powerful demon who conquered even the most powerful gods, due to the possession of a special boon from the supreme god Brahma. He was then subdued by the Bodhisattvas Manjushri and Avalokiteshvara, working in concert, and subsequently put his powers into the service of the Dharma.

**Mahayana.** See **Universal Vehicle.**

**Maitreya, Dharma Lord.** A great Bodhisattva whose name means "Loving One," he presently resides in his main embodiment in the Tushita heaven, whence he descends to earth to benefit beings in many guises. In Buddhist mythology, he is due to manifest the supreme Buddha deeds, similar to those of Shakyamuni, on this earth sometime in the next thousands (or tens of thousands) of years.

**mandala.** This literally means "an essence-protecting environment." Mandalas are most well known as geometrical paintings or drawings that look like the floor plan of a building or the orbit of a planet. They are three-dimensional perfected environments, Buddhaverses or Buddha-lands, created by the enlightenment of an individual as a place that expresses his or her enlightenment. They are realms through which other beings can be incorporated into that enlightenment perspective. A Tantric practitioner learns the mandalic architecture of a particular type of enlightenment when she is initiated into a Tantric yoga practice, and the creation stage consists largely of developing the ability to visualize every detail of the total mandalic environment, to the degree where the yogini can feel completely secure in the divine surrounding. Often mandalas have a central space for the meditator's divine Buddha-embodiment, a palace or mansion with a highly complex and beautiful architecture.

**mandala palace.** See **mandala.**

**MANI.** A Sanskrit word meaning "jewel," it is used in the famous mantra of Avalokiteshvara, the Lord of Compassion, OM MANI PADME HUM (OM—the jewel in the lotus—HUM). The jewel symbolizes compassion, as the lotus symbolizes wisdom, though there are many other layers of symbolism as well. See **OM MANI PADME HUM.**

**mantra.** Literally meaning "saving the mind," a mantra is a creative sound considered expressive of the deepest essence of things and understandings, so its repetition can evoke in a formulaic or even magical way a state of enlightenment or positive energy. Some mantras resemble sentences, and express some wish, vision, or affirmation, while others are just a single syllable or two, containing the germ of a deity, realm, or state of concentration. See **AH, OM,** and so forth.

**meditation, meditational higher education.** See **education, higher.**

**mentor, mentor-Buddha, mentor yoga.** I use this to translate the Tibetan word *lama,* itself the Tibetan translation of Sanskrit *guru,* which in esoteric Buddhism refers to a special type of spiritual teacher, the relationship with whom is based on the deepest aspirations of the practitioner, as he represents the Three Jewels of Buddha, Dharma, and Community through mind, speech, and body.

**Meru, Mount.** The axial mountain of the archaic Buddhist and general Indian cosmology, wherein the earth is flat, floating on a cosmic ocean, with four continents radiating out from the cosmic mountain. The sun and moon are said to circle around it and to go behind it when they disappear from view. When we encounter Meru in a Buddhist text, we can think of it as corresponding to our sense of the planetary axis in our modern cosmology.

**mild deity.** "Mild" is my translation for previous translations' "peaceful," the opposite of "fierce," my translation for previous translations' "wrathful." The term emphasizes demeanor, avoiding prejudice as to the inner state of these Buddha-deities, all of whom are unmoving from a state of absolute inner tranquillity and joy, whether showing mild or fierce forms.

**Mind Science.** See **Inner (Mind) Science.**

**mirror wisdom.** One of the five wisdoms, the transformation of the form aggregate and the transmutation of delusion, associated with the Buddha Akshobhya (in the *Natural Liberation* system), the Vajra Buddha-clan, the color white, and the awareness that all things reflect ultimate reality, as in a perfect mirror.

**neural channels, drops, energies, or winds.** I add the adjective "neural" to these three elements of the subtle body, to indicate their subtle physiological nature. See **body-mind complex.**

**nirvana.** The state of supreme freedom from suffering that is the goal of all Buddhist practice, it is attainable by all beings because it is the final truth of their condition. In some forms of Buddhism it is pictured as a state beyond the world, but in the Universalist Buddhism of Tibet and East Asia, it is considered nondual from the ordinary world of relativity. In fact, realization of nirvana transforms the ordinary relative world into an extraordinary perfect environment or Buddhaverse.

**Nyingma Order.** One of the four orders of Tibetan Buddhism, the one that gives us the original *Natural Liberation* literature. It began during the era of the Tibetan empire with the founding of Samyey Monastery in the eighth century, due to the efforts of the abbot Shantarakshita, the adept Padma Sambhava, and the emperor Trisong Detsen. At the time it was not an order, it was just the first full Buddhist institution in Tibet. Later, in the eleventh century, when the other Tibetan orders were founded, the Nyingma set up its own distinct foundation, basing itself on the older translations and teachings. Thus its name, Nyingma, means "older." Its general teaching is the same as all Tibetan Buddhist school's. Its special teaching is the Great Perfection teaching of immanent enlightenment. In modern Tibet before the destruction, the Nyingma Order had the second highest number of monastic communities, around 1500, in which it conducted a sophisticated curriculum of study and practice, as well as ministering to the surrounding society in numerous ways.

**OM.** This mantric syllable is called "the body-vajra of all Buddhas." It invokes the power of the divine and universal, resonating with its omnipresence, and therefore occurs at the beginning of most other mantras.

**OM AH HUM.** These three invoke the body, speech, and mind of all Buddhas, resonating with the Emanation, Beatific, and Truth bodies of the Buddhas, and containing the totality of enlightened presence.

**OM MANI PADME HUM.** This mantra is the sacred heart of the Bodhisattva of universal compassion, Avalokiteshvara. Its meaning is "OM—the jewel in the lotus—HUM," the jewel being loving compassion and the lotus being the wisdom of ultimate reality. The mantra is especially popular in Tibet, where it used to be carved everywhere on mountainsides, on all wheels—their turning articulated the blessing of the mantra—on the lips of everyone as they went about their daily business. Tibetans believe that the Bodhisattva is omnipresently concerned with their welfare, and they repeat the mantra constantly to reaffirm their own devotion and solidarity with the Bodhisattva of Compassion. They also believe that he is incarnate in their leader, His Holiness the Dalai Lama, which explains the depth of their devotion to him.

**ordinary.** "Ordinariness" (Tib. *thun mong nyid*) is a Tantric concept, where the world as perceived by the unenlightened is considered ordinary, maintained by delusion and filled with suffering, and the real world, revealed through wisdom and perceived through enlightened senses, is considered "extraordinary" (Tib. *thun mong ma yin pa*), a purified, enlightened, mandalic, Buddhaverse realm of happiness and abundance. "Ordinary" is frequently used with "between," "reality," "perception," and other terms. Sometimes "ordinary" is used nondually as the ultimate.

**Padma Sambhava.** The "Lotus-born One," he was one of the greatest adepts, and is the author of the *Natural Liberation.* In his mythic biography, he issued from the mouth of the cosmic Buddha Amitabha in the form of a rainbow-trailing meteor, shooting down to earth into the Dhanakosha lake in northwest India of ancient times. Later a jeweled lotus sprang up in those waters, and a radiant child appeared there, to be adopted by the king of that country, Udyana. After living for centuries and attaining inconceivable wisdom and abilities, he journeyed to Tibet to tame the savage tribal deities of that mountain land, writing many profound texts and hiding them in sealed treasuries for future generations. After taming, or civilizing, Tibet, he departed for his own pure land, the Copper Mountain Paradise, somewhere in the jungles of Madagascar, Africa, or South America, where some Tibetans believe he still resides today.

**PADME.** Part of the mantra **OM MANI PADME HUM.**

**perfection, great.** See **Great Perfection.**

**perfection stage.** This is the second stage of the Unexcelled Yoga Tantras, which follows on the successful completion of the **creation stage.** After the practitioner has developed the ability to totally transform his perception and conception, so that he stably perceives his environment as the pure mandala, his body as a deity body, his speech as Buddha-mantra, and his mind as Buddha-wisdom, all three isolated from ordinariness, imperfection, and impurity, he is ready and secure enough to enter the practice of the rehearsal of death, the between, and the rebirth processes with a view to accelerating his evolutionary accumulation of the stores of merit and wisdom to gain Buddhahood within a single lifetime or at most a few lifetimes. These processes are usually numbered five or six, including the stages of body isolation, speech isolation, mind isolation/self-consecration/magic body, clear light/enlightenment, and integration. The *Natural Liberation* gives teachings in this advanced area, but skillfully puts them into a more accessible context, so that the general public can avail themselves of this sophisticated science and technology in the crisis of death and the between.

**poisons.** There is a famous set of three poisons, ignorance or delusion, lust, and hatred, which are considered the driving force of the world of suffering. In Tantric texts, these three are expanded by the addition of pride and envy to make a group of five poisons, or root addictions, that drive the life cycle.

**pretan.** Sanskrit *preta* refers to that life-form located on the wheel of life-forms (the Buddhist "great chain of being") between hell-beings and animals. It has often been translated as "hungry ghost," following the literal meaning of the Chinese characters chosen for the Chinese translation of the term. They are not ghosts since they have a real-life embodiment and are not stuck in the between-state hanging around their former life realm (the Buddhist description of a ghost). They are definitely hungry and thirsty, the nature of their lives being forms of extreme dissatisfaction and frustrated craving. There simply is no good word to describe these poor creatures, so I use *pretan.*

**psychonaut.** A "voyager into the soul," an apt term for the Buddhist adept, who voluntarily abandons the pseudo-security of this planet of delusion, with its solid ground of ordinary, individuated suffering, to launch herself through the death-dissolutions into the subtle between-states to deepen her wisdom by exploring the unconscious and to expand her compassionate heroism by serving universes of beings on the subtle level, and then returns to the ordinary embodiment of the adept to assist her contemporaries.

**pure land.** See **Buddha-land.**

**radiance.** The middle, sun-lit state of the subtle mind of radiance-luminance-wisdom. Corresponding to the anger-related instinctual natures, it is between the states of luminance and imminence.

**Ratnasambhava.** One of the five archetypal Mild Buddhas, Lord of the Jewel Buddha-clan, associated with the southern direction and the Buddha-land Shrimat. In the *Natural Liberation,* he represents the equalizing wisdom, the transformation of the aggregate of sensations, the transmutation of the poison of pride, and the color yellow. His Buddha-consort is Mamaki.

**reality.** Used to translate the Sanskrit *dharmata, satya,* and even *Dharma.* It is an important word in Buddhism since enlightenment purports to be the perfect knowledge and awareness of the actual condition of things, and the possibility of liberation from suffering is based on the truth of that condition and the untruth of the ordinary condition of suffering.

**reality between.** One of the six betweens, named in that way due to the fact that the individual experiencing it is as close as he can get to the realization of the liberating reality of freedom, either in its first section, the death-point between (sometimes made into a separate between), or in its main sections, the mild and fierce deity betweens.

**Sakya Order.** One of the four orders of Tibetan Buddhism. It was founded in the eleventh century with the establishment of the Sakya Monastery in 1073. It shares the same general Buddhist teaching as the other orders, its special teachings being the *Hevajra Tantra* and a special version of the path combined with that, called "Path and Fruition."

**samadhi.** An important Sanskrit word for meditational practice and meditational achievement. Usually defined as "one-pointedness of mind," it can also refer to creative mind states after enlightenment, mental concentrations that produce special light rays, liberating environments for disciples, and so forth. It has now entered the English language.

**Samantabhadra, Buddha and Bodhisattva.** See **All-around Goodness.**

**samaya.** A Sanskrit word usually meaning "vow" or "commitment," it is used in the *Natural Liberation* as a concluding mantra in several contexts, where it signifies that the teaching is sealed by vows, and people should not use such teachings for other than spiritual purposes.

**Sangha.** See **Jewels, Three.**

**secret initiation.** See **initiation.**

**seed mantra, syllable.** A particular single-syllable mantra considered to contain the essence of a deity or samadhi, such as TAM, for Tara.

**self.** Sanskrit *atma* is the reflexive pronoun made into an entity, the ego or coordinator of individual experience. The Buddha's deepest, most unique insight is expressed as "selflessness," his understanding that the habitual exaggeration of the status of the self into an absolute, fixed, unchanging, intrinsically identifiable identity—what he called mis-knowledge—is the source of all suffering, the fundamental distortion at the core of the individual being's programming that puts the individual into the impossible situation of being against the universe. But the Buddha often refers to the self, and never rejects the existence of a relative, practical, changing, flexible self. He calls upon it to assume responsibility for the individual's fate, and critiques as a serious error the nihilistic idea that there is no such thing and that one does not exist at all. Of the falsely absolutized selves, there are said to be two kinds, the personal, interior, or subjective self and the objective self of things and processes in the world. These are the falsely reified objects of the conscious and unconscious self-habits or self-addictions, which cause all the suffering in the world.

**selflessness.** There are two kinds in the Buddhist technical literature on identity, the subjective selflessness and the objective selflessness. Subjective selflessness is the reality of our not having fixed, substantial selves; it is the absence of a solid, unchanging core self. A synonym of objective selflessness is emptiness or voidness, which is not a realm of blackness, but the fact that things are empty of intrinsic reality, void of intrinsic identity. See **self.**

**Shakyamuni Buddha.** The supreme Emanation Body of our historical era, the historical figure (ca. 563–481 B.C.E.) whose life story provides the paradigm of the attainment of enlightenment.

**skull bowl.** A symbolic implement of fierce deities that demonstrates their insight into their own death and their turning of it into a vessel for liberating activity.

**soul.** That which is the deepest personal essence of a living being, which journeys from life to life and takes rebirth, and which becomes enlightened finally. The Buddha's famous teaching of selflessness has often been translated in the past as "soullessness," and was used to confirm the Western sense that Buddhism is nihilistic and atheistic. The Buddha rejected any absolute, unchanging, fixed, intrinsically substantial, intrinsically identifiable soul, just as he rejected the same kind of self or ego. But relative, changing, relational, living, conventional entities that can usefully be termed ego, self, and soul are never prohibited in Buddhist psychology. In the *Natural Liberation* in particular, the extremely subtle body-mind very much qualifies as the soul of the being who is undergoing death, the between, and liberation or rebirth.

**spiritual gene.** Sanskrit *gotra* refers to the subtle encodement within the life-continuum of an individual of the instinctual residue of her past lives' evolutionary experiences and actions, which is carried as a subtle "drop" into the next life, wherein it interacts with the physical genes from father and mother to determine the character of the being in that life. The Tibetan Buddhist vision of conception is rather beautiful, a moment where the father's white drop meets the mother's red drop, and the individual's blue drop enters within their union.

**subtle body-mind.** See **body-mind complex.**

**Tantra.** A type of Buddhist (and Hindu and Jain) teaching that emphasizes spiritual technology and contemplative arts rather than philosophical contents. Sanskrit *tantra* refers to "continuum," and relates to the verb "to weave." In Buddhism, the Tantra concerns itself with the rebuilding of the extraordinary realm of enlightenment by the energies of wisdom, after the demolition of the ordinary world of suffering, which is upheld by the energy of ignorance. It tends to be considered esoteric, as it could be misunderstood as denying the existence of the world of suffering, when taken out of context. The *Natural Liberation* emerges from the Tantric science and literature, but it is formulated to be accessible to a wider public.

**Tara.** The Bodhisattva or Buddha of compassionate activity, she is widely loved throughout Tibet and all of Universalist Buddhist Asia. As a Bodhisattva, she is considered indivisible from the Bodhisattva Avalokiteshvara, being his female counterpart, while he is her male counterpart. While Avalokiteshvara is considered the manifestation of the concentrated compassion of all Buddhas, Tara is the manifestation of the concentrated compassionate dynamism of all Buddhas. She is much more dynamic than he is. As a Buddha, she is the consort of Amoghasiddhi, the contemplative green Buddha of the north, who symbolizes the all-accomplishing, or miracle-working, wisdom. There are innumerable manifestations of Tara, as many as beings require, but her most famous are the peaceful white Tara, who brings protection, long life, and peace, and the dynamic green Tara, who overcomes obstacles and saves beings in dangerous circumstances.

**treasure-text.** The great masters of ancient times sometimes wrote teachings that they deemed too advanced for their contemporaries, so they concealed these teachings in caves, temples, lakes, even in the subconscious minds of beings, to be discovered in the future by "treasure-discoverers" (Tib. *gter-gton*) and then made available to people of those future eras.

**Truth.** For the most part a synonym of reality, though sometimes a statement that corresponds to or indicates that reality. See **reality.**

**Truth Body.** See **Body.**

**tulku.** The Tibetan word for the Emanation Body of the Buddha. Those Tibetan lamas called tulku are believed to be the conscious reincarnations of lamas who became adepts and attained enlightenment and the power of conscious reincarnation in previous lives. They are considered "Incarnational Emanation Bodies" (Skt. *janmanirmanakaya*) of Buddhas, lesser in stature than Shakyamuni, who is seen as a Supreme Emanation Body, due to the lesser fortune of the beings of later eras, though no less wise or compassionate.

**Udyana.** Tibetan *U rgyan,* the Buddhist country in northwestern India (perhaps present-day Pakistan or Afghanistan) where Padma Sambhava was first born, sometimes still thought of in the present as a paradise of Dakini-angels invisible to the ordinary inhabitants there.

**Unexcelled Yoga (Tantra).** The most advanced of the four kinds of Buddhist Tantras.

**Universal Vehicle.** The Mahayana, or messianic form of Buddhism that emphasizes the teaching of love and compassion, the inevitable implication of selfless wisdom. Providing a social teaching and a vehicle to carry all beings to enlightenment, it is built upon the foundation of the Individual or monastic Vehicle that is designed to carry beings one by one.

**Universalist Buddhism.** See **Universal Vehicle.**

**Vairochana.** One of the five archetypal Mild Buddhas, lord of the Realized Lord Buddha-clan, associated with the central region and the Buddha-land Ghanavyuha. In the *Natural Liberation,* he represents the ultimate reality wisdom, the transmutation of the poison of hate, the color white, and the aggregate of consciousness. His Buddha-consort is Vajra Dhatvishvari.

**vajra.** See **adamantine.**

**Vajra Heruka.** See **Heruka.**

**Vajrasattva.** One of the archetypal Mild Buddha-deities, he is sometimes considered the lord of a sixth Buddha-clan, and sometimes is associated with Akshobhya, the lord of the Vajra clan. In the broadest Tantric terms, he is considered the archetypal male form adopted by the Buddha when he teaches the esoteric Tantric teachings. Therefore, any of the Tantric Buddha-deities can be called Vajrasattva.

**vase initiation.** See **initiation.**

**warrior's posture.** A heroic, dancing stance, related to the pose adopted by an archer for shooting.

**winds, neural.** See **body-mind complex.**

**wisdoms, five wisdoms.** The ultimate reality, mirror, equalizing, individuating, and all-accomplishing wisdoms, associated with the five aggregates, five poisons, five Buddhas, five colors, and five directions.

**womb door.** The metaphorical door that blocks the between-being's entrance into a womb and involvement in the process of rebirth. The being is instructed in "blocking" this portal during the existence between in order to try to avoid delusion-driven rebirth and to attain liberation.

**wonder-working wisdom.** See **all-accomplishing wisdom.**

**Yama.** The Vedic and Hindu Lord of Death, he is popularly depicted as the judge of the dead at the gates of hell, who weighs their good and evil evolutionary deeds and decides their fate. His minions come to take the soul away at death, leading it down to the court of Yama. They are called Yama deities.

**yogi, yogini.** A yogi is a male practitioner of Buddhist yoga, the "yoking" of one's life energies to their knowledge and understanding. A female yogi is called a yogini.

# ESSENTIAL
# BIBLIOGRAPHY

Avedon, John F. *In Exile from the Land of Snows.* New York: Knopf, 1984.

Cranston, Sylvia, and Carey Williams. *Reincarnation: A New Horizon in Science, Religion, and Society.* New York: Julian Press, 1984.

Gyatso, Geshe Kelsang. *The Clear Light of Bliss.* London: Tharpa, 1985.

Gyatso, Tenzin, H.H. the Dalai Lama. *Kindness, Clarity, and Insight.* Ithaca, N.Y.: Snow Lion, 1984

————, et al. *MindScience: An East-West Dialogue.* Boston: Wisdom Publications, 1991.

Lati Rinpochay and Jeffrey Hopkins. *Death, Intermediate State and Rebirth.* Ithaca, N.Y.: Snow Lion, 1985.

Lodo, Lama. *Bardo Teachings.* Ithaca, N.Y.: Snow Lion, 1987.

Mullin, Glenn H. *Death and Dying: The Tibetan Tradition.* Ithaca, N.Y.: Snow Lion, 1986.

Nyima Rinpoche, Chokyi. *The Bardo Guidebook.* Kathmandu: Rangjung Yeshe, 1991.

Rangdrol, Tsele Natsok. *The Mirror of Mindfulness*. Boston: Shambhala, 1989.

Rhie, Marylin, and Robert A. F. Thurman. *Wisdom and Compassion: The Sacred Art of Tibet*. New York: Abrams, 1991.

Sogyal Rinpoche. *The Tibetan Book of Living and Dying*. San Francisco: HarperCollins, 1992.